Scandalous Son

The Elusive Search for Dolley Madison's Son, John Payne Todd

by

Philip Bigler

APPLERIDGE
PUBLISHERS

APPLERIDGE
P U B L I S H E R S

First Edition, June 28 2015

Copyright © 2015 by APPLE RIDGE PUBLISHERS

Scandalous Son: The Elusive Search for Dolley Madison's Son,
John Payne Todd

Apple Ridge Publishers
217 Bob White Lane
Quicksburg, Virginia 22847

http://www.appleridgepublishers.com
http://www.scandalous-son.com

ISBN: 978-0-578-14413-9

PRINTED IN THE UNITED STATES OF AMERICA

Dedicated to my loving wife

Linda Mimms Bigler

Also by Philip Bigler

TEACHING HISTORY IN AN UNCIVILIZED WORLD

TEACHING IS TOUGH! *A Practical Guide to Classroom Success*

REMEMBERING JOHN F. KENNEDY: *The New Frontier and the Nation's Capital*

LIBERTY & LEARNING: *The Essential James Madison*

IN HONORED GLORY: *Arlington National Cemetery, the Final Post*

HOSTILE FIRE: *The Life and Death of Lt. Sharon A. Lane*

BE A TEACHER: *You Can Make a Difference*

WASHINGTON IN FOCUS: *A Photographic History of the Nation's Capital*

FAILING GRADES: *A Teacher's Report Card on Education in America*

Cover Images

Dolley (Payne) Madison
Portrait by Joseph Wood ca.1817
Virginia Historical Society

John Payne Todd
Portrait by Joseph Wood ca. 1817
Image copyright © The Metropolitan Museum of Art:
Art Resource, NY
Watercolor on Ivory, 2 5/8 x 2 1/16 inches

Table of Contents

Timeline

1729   The Mount Pleasant plantation is established in the Virginia piedmont by Ambrose Madison.

1732   Ambrose Madison dies, allegedly poisoned by three slaves; Frances Taylor Madison assumes ownership of the property.

1749   James Madison Sr. marries Nelly Conway.

1750   James Madison Sr. assumes ownership of the Mount Pleasant estate.

1751   James Madison Jr. is born at Port Conway, Virginia on March 16.

1764   The Montpelier great house is finished.

1768   Dolley Payne is born in Guilford County, North Carolina on May 20.

1778   The artist Joseph Wood is born in New York.

1783   The Todd Family relocates to Philadelphia after freeing their slaves.

1790   Dolley Payne marries Quaker lawyer, John Todd on January 7; Benjamin Franklin dies in Philadelphia at age 84.

1791   Mary Todd opens a boarding house to help support her family; the first United States census is conducted; Rhode Island ratifies the Constitution by a 34 to 32 vote; the Bill of Rights is ratified.

1792   John Payne Todd is born in Philadelphia on leap day, February 29; Dolley Payne Todd's father dies on October 24.

1793	James Madison departs on March 17 from Philadelphia after Congress adjourns; Dolley Payne Todd gives birth to her second child, William Temple; the first of James Madison's Helvidius essays are published in the Philadelphia newspapers; John Todd dies on October 24, the same day as his youngest son William succumbs to the yellow fever epidemic; George Washington seeks James Madison's advice about the possibility of relocating the government due to the ongoing epidemic in Philadelphia; James Madison returns to Congress in Philadelphia circa December 1.
1794	Eli Whitney receives a patent for the cotton gin, revolutionizing the cultivation of cotton in the south; James Madison meets the widow Dolley Payne Todd, circa June 1; James Madison and Dolley marry at Harewood, the home of Dolley's sister, Lucy Washington on September 15; the Society of Friends expels Dolley Madison on December 26 for having married outside of the faith.
1795	Dolley Madison and Payne Todd visit Monticello for the first time.
1796	John Adams is elected president; Thomas Jefferson becomes Vice President.
1797	James Madison retires from Congress and returns to Montpelier with Dolley, Payne Todd, and Anna Payne (Dolley's sister); Jefferson visits Madison at Montpelier; construction begins to transform Montpelier into a duplex.
1798	The Alien and Sedition Acts become law; the Virginia Resolution is passed in Richmond.
1799	James Madison is elected as a delegate to the Virginia General Assembly; George Washington dies at Mount Vernon.
1800	Charles Adams, the son of John and Abigail dies from alcoholism; Madison's younger brother, Francis, dies.
1801	James Madison, Sr. dies at Montpelier; Thomas Jefferson is inaugurated as the nation's third president; Madison becomes Secretary of State and moves with Dolley and Payne Todd to Washington, DC.

1803	Louisiana Purchase; the "Merry Affair" disrupts Anglo-American relations; Elizabeth "Betsy" Patterson of Baltimore marries Jerome Bonaparte.
1803-1805	John Payne Todd attends school at the Alexandria Academy in the District of Columbia.
1804	Anna Payne, Dolley's younger sister, marries Richard Cutts; Alexander Hamilton is shot and killed in a duel with Vice President, Aaron Burr; Payne Todd is extremely ill in July while staying with his parents in Washington, D.C.
1805	Dolley Madison suffers a serious knee injury and is taken to Philadelphia for treatment; James Madison Cutts is born; Payne Todd, age 13, is enrolled at St. Mary's College in Baltimore on December 1.
1806	James Madison sends Dolley's brother, John C. Payne, to Tripoli to serve as a secretary to the America diplomatic representative, George Davis.
1807	Mary Coles Payne, Dolley Madison's mother, dies.
1809	Payne Todd accompanies the newly elected President, James Madison, to Washington, D.C.; extensive alterations and construction of a new wing begin at Montpelier.
1811	John C. Payne returns to the United States from his posting in Tripoli.
1811-1812	Phoebe Morris stays with the Madison's at the White House; Payne Todd is in Washington, D.C. living with his family while on hiatus from school.
1812	Justice Thomas Todd marries Lucy Washington on March 29 at the White House, with Payne Todd and Phoebe Morris as members of the wedding party.
1813-1815	Payne Todd serves as a member of the American Peace delegation to Europe with Henry Clay, Albert Gallatin and John Quincy Adams.
1814	The British burn the United States Capitol and the President's Mansion during the War of 1812.

1816	John Payne Todd presents Thomas Jefferson with a gift of a travel thermometer; Jefferson reciprocates giving Todd two Turkish pistols with 20-inch barrels.
1817	Joseph Wood paints portraits of President and Mrs. Madison in Washington, D.C.; Wood also creates a miniature of John Payne Todd; James Madison retires to Montpelier after two terms as president.
1818	Payne Todd purchases Toddsberth in Orange County for $540.
1820	Todd visits Phoebe Morris for four days at Bolton Farm; the Missouri Compromise is passed.
1825	Phoebe Morris dies at her home at Bolton Farm.
1826	Both Thomas Jefferson and John Adams die on July 4, the 50th anniversary of the signing of the Declaration of Independence.
1829	Andrew Jackson is inaugurated as president; Nelly Conway Madison, James Madison's mother, dies at Montpelier on February 11 at age 98; Payne Todd is imprisoned for the first time due to outstanding debt.
1830	Payne Todd is imprisoned a second time at the Prune Street prison in Philadelphia; Todd is released on July 4 and returns to Montpelier.
1831	William Lloyd Garrison begins publication of the abolitionist newspaper, the Liberator; President James Monroe dies on July 4; Nat Turner leads a slave rebellion in Southampton, Virginia, killing over 50 whites.
1832	Anna Payne Cutts, Dolley's beloved younger sister, dies.
1835	Alexis de Tocqueville publishes *Democracy in America*.
1836	James Madison dies on June 28 at his Montpelier home.
1837	Dolley Madison moves temporarily to Washington, DC.
1840	Payne Todd charters the Montpelier Marble Company.

1841	A spring fire destroys the main house at Toddsberth; former Governor James Barbour dies at his home in Orange County.
1844	Dolley Madison is forced to sell the Montpelier estate; the House of Representatives honors the former first lady with a seat in Congress.
1848	The United States Congress finally agrees to purchase the papers of James Madison for $25,000; Photographer Mathew Brady successfully convinces Dolley Madison to sits for a daguerreotype portrait.
1849	Dolley Madison dies in Washington, D.C. on July 12 at the age of 81.
1850	Annie Payne marries Dr. James H. Causten on April 9; President Zachary Taylor dies in office, his remains are placed temporarily in the Public Vault at Congressional Cemetery; the Compromise of 1850 is passed by Congress and signed by the new president, Millard Fillmore.
1852	At the age of 59, John Payne Todd dies at his residence on Pennsylvania Avenue and is buried at the Congressional Cemetery in Washington, D.C.; Dolley Madison's remains are transferred to the Causten vault; Annie Payne Causten dies on November 9 at age 33 and is interred alongside her aunt.
1854	Toddsberth is sold to William C. Scott.
1858	Dolley Madison's body is returned to Montpelier on January 12 for burial beside her husband's remains.
1862	Lt. John Hampden Chamberlayne visits Toddsberth and records his impressions.
1901	The duPont family purchases Montpelier.
1928	Montpelier is inherited by Marian duPont Scott.
1937	A photo of the ballroom at Toddsberth appears in a Fredericksburg newspaper.

1956	The Dolley Madison daguerreotypes are discovered in Pennsylvania.
1987	The old Toddsberth property is purchased by William Crum at a foreclosure sale.
2003	The Montpelier Foundation begins the process of deconstruction of the manor house to return it to its Madison era appearance.
2009	The restored Montpelier opens to the public; the Causten Vault at Congressional Cemetery undergoes a major renovation.
2014	Work on the Causten Vault is completed; the remains of sixteen individuals are reinterred to the site, including those of Annie Payne and James H. Causten.

Notes & Acknowledgments

The genesis for *Scandalous Son* began in 2009 while I was serving as the Director of the James Madison Center at James Madison University. I had just completed the publication of *Liberty & Learning: the Essential James Madison* in conjunction with the 200th anniversary commemorations of Madison's presidency. During the course of the research for that book, my friend and collaborator, Annie Lorsbach Mintkin, and I attempted to find the location of Toddsberth, the home of Dolley Madison's son, John Payne Todd. We were sorely disappointed to discover that none of the original structures remained although, despite decades of overgrowth, there was ample evidence of Todd's failed marble quarry. It was amazing to both of us that there had been very little of substance written about Dolley's only surviving child. Instead, Payne Todd was easily dismissed by historians and biographers as a reprobate, thus conveniently disposed of as a mere footnote to the otherwise remarkable history of the Madison family. Yet this seemed far too simplistic and unjust. No one should have their entire life reduced to a few terse sentences. It was this epiphany that made me determined to write a biography of John Payne Todd.

Over the course of the next five years of research, I was frustrated to discover that there were huge gaps in Payne's written legacy. What did remain was scattered and incomplete. His chronic alcoholism likewise resulted in Payne literally vanishing for weeks or months at a time. During these dark times, his whereabouts and do-ings were unknown to the dismay of his distraught parents and to subsequent historians. So *Scandalous Son* quickly became an "elusive search" and it evolved from a biography into a parable about the dark side of the "American Dream." It is the all too common story of rags-to-riches-to-rags in just three generations. Payne Todd's saga is actually emblematic of the problems and difficulties children of great people face. His life story is one of failed expectations and disappointments, as well as public failure and the evils of unearned wealth and inherited status.

The Madison Papers became one of the most valuable sources of information for me in conducting research on the period. The University of Virginia is continuing its scholarly efforts to compile all of James Madison's papers during the time he served as secretary of state and later as president. In recent years, the university has also undertaken the Herculean task of compiling a complete documentary history from Madison's 29-year retirement. To date, just two volumes of the "Retirement Series" have been published and these books span only the years from 1817 through 1823. The books are a wealth of information and offer valuable insights into both James and Dolley Madison's thoughts and life at Montpelier. Undoubtedly, subsequent volumes will discover additional material that will add to our historical understanding of their relationship, as well as that with John Payne Todd.

At the Library of Congress, the microfilm from the Cutts Family Collection of James and Dolly Madison (microfilm 14,326-IP) is an excellent primary source. Likewise, the memorandum book (from the Papers and Collection of Peter Force, microfilm mm 82043026) kept by John Payne Todd from 1844 to 1848 is available, although the poor quality of the medium makes reading it tedious and challenging. Unfortunately, access to the original documents was denied by the administrators at the Library of Congress. It is certainly understandable that government repositories are protective of their collections, but their cavalier attitude poses serious obstacles to writers and researchers who are at the mercy of such bureaucrats.

Denying access to important documents, manuscripts, and other primary source materials is Orwellian and historical truth remains undiscovered—forgotten, sequestered and buried deep within the bowels of isolated stacks. The current research situation at the Library is intolerable and it means that historical discoveries will be a product of chance rather than a result of serious academic research. This may be emblematic of the current digital age, but the pervasive indifference is not only embarrassing in the American republic but unacceptable. Government overseers are the curators of the nation's documentary legacy, but the American people are its proprietors.

In marked contrast to the manuscript division, the Library of Congress's still pictures and photographic division was extraordinarily helpful. They have made monumental steps in digitizing much of their enormous collections and these items are well-cataloged, accessible, and downloadable.

One of the most remarkable resources for material on Dolley Madison is the Greensboro Historical Museum in North Carolina. Their collection of Madison-era artifacts includes several original Dolley Madison letters, as well as correspondence and documents written by Dr. James Causten and his wife, Annie. I was granted unrestricted access to these invaluable resources and I am particularly grateful to archivist, Elise Allison, for her help and gracious assistance. The museum generously allowed me to photograph and reproduce many of these items for publication, including a rare calling card from John Payne Todd circa 1819.

I am also indebted to the White House Historical Association for the use of the Gilbert Stuart portrait of Dolley Madison. They also provided me with a high quality image of the famous George Washington portrait that Dolley Madison rescued during the War of 1812. The staff at Artres (Art Resources) has also been exceedingly helpful, and I am particularly indebted to Kay Menick for her help and timely assistance in obtaining various museum permissions and rights. Artres manages an impressive collection of the nation's most cherished artworks and is an amazing resource for scholars, researchers, teachers, and students.

During the course of my research, I was privileged to get to know Anne Riordan who currently resides in Orange County. She kindly introduced me to her mother, Mary Agnes Gipson Harlow, who shared her marvelous memories of playing on John Payne Todd's old Toddsberth estate during the Great Depression. I also had the opportunity to meet Dana and Mark Amos, who currently own much of the land that once constituted the old Payne Todd's plantation. They allowed me to explore, walk, and photograph the grounds.

I discovered that there is only one known photograph of Toddsberth. It appeared almost 80 years ago in an edition of the *Fredericksburg Star.* It shows the "round house" in ruins, but the actual picture has long since disappeared and the existing microfilm version is of such poor quality as to be unreproducible. I was fortunate to meet Bernadette Fitzgerald, a talented art student at James Madison University, and commissioned her to do a pen and ink drawing based upon the old newspaper image. Her drawing of Payne Todd's round house is astonishing and is a vital addition to this book.

The staff at James Madison's Montpelier has done a remarkable job in preserving the legacy of James and Dolley Madison. I would particularly like to thank Matt Reeves, the Director of Archaeology and Landscape Restoration, and Meg Kennedy, the Director of Museum Services, for their assistance and encouragement in this project. I am also indebted to the staff at Congressional Cemetery. They kindly provided me access to their burial records including the ledgers containing the interment information for Dolley Madison and John Payne Todd. In 2009, a major renovation was begun at the cemetery of the Causten Vault. Upon opening the mausoleum, Smithsonian anthropologist Doug Owsley discovered that: "The interior of the vault was quite disheveled due to collapse of the wooden coffins and heavy shelving that originally supported the higher level interments." Eventually, 16 of the 22 interred remains were recovered, including those of Dolley Madison's beloved niece, Annie, and her husband, James H. Causten. As Dr. Owsley explained: "Because of the way that we removed (archaeologically excavated) the vault, and with our forensic background, we were able to successfully separate out commingled remains. Both Annie Payne Causten and James were identified, and later returned with included information that gave the name and burial number of each individual. For our records, we assigned each person a burial number, which was later associated with a name." The work on the vault was finished in the summer 2014.

As always, I have depended upon my wife, Linda, for her sound editorial advice and assistance. Likewise, my friend and colleague, Lee Congdon, Professor Emeritus at James Madison University, has been encouraging and supportive during this endeavor. Over the years, we have enjoyed many afternoons in conversation at Harrisonburg's Boston Beanery, where we are always welcomed by our friends, Cheryl Harpine and Kim Williams. To all of these remarkable people and the others who have helped bring *Scandalous Son* to fruition, I give my thanks.

"Errors like straws upon the surface flow,
Those who would seek for pearls must dive below."

One of James Madison's favorite quotations

In his diary entry for June 13, 1839, John Quincy Adams relates that the quote came from "a small album [owned my Miss Mary Cutts] with engraved devices at the top of some of the pages...signed J.M." See Allan Nevins, Ed. (1969). *The Diary of John Quincy Adams 1794-1845: American Diplomacy, and Political, Social, and Intellectual Life from Washington to Polk.* New York, Frederick Ungar Publishing Co., p. 498.

Scandalous Son

*The Elusive Search
for Dolley Madison's Son,
John Payne Todd*

(Library of Congress)

Preface
Historic Congressional Cemetery

Congressional Cemetery is a long forgotten landmark in the nation's capital of Washington, D.C. ironically in a city that prides itself for its sense of history and tradition as well as for its numerous monuments and memorials.[1] The 35 acres of grounds at Congressional are located in the southeast quadrant of D.C. enclosed by 17th Street, Potomac Avenue, E Street, and the Anacostia River. But despite its convenient access by the Potomac Avenue Metro stop and its proximity to the United States Capitol, few tourists dare to venture out to this historic graveyard, preferring instead to visit the better known, well-manicured surroundings of Arlington National Cemetery.[2] Just a few blocks away from Congressional is Robert F. Kennedy Memorial Stadium. The aging sports arena was once the celebrated home to baseball's Washington Senators and to the Washington Redskins. It was the site of many of the legendary tape measure homeruns hit by the great Frank Howard as well as for the heroic football feats of quarterback Billy Kilmer and Coach George Allen's "Over the Hill Gang." But the Senators abandoned the nation's capital for Texas in 1971 while the Redskins moved to the larger and more lucrative confines of FedEx Field in Landover, Maryland in 1997.[3] Since then, RFK Stadium has been virtually abandoned and is now used only for an occasional soccer game or rock concert. Without its fans or football, the stadium is a decaying artifact of an earlier era,

The eastern acreage of the cemetery is immediately adjacent to the D.C. Jail. The massive prison complex consists of several imposing, ugly brick buildings containing cells and dormitories. It incarcerates on average over 2,000 of the District's most hardened, notorious and dangerous criminals. The correctional facility itself is encircled by an impenetrable fence which is topped with razor-sharp barbed wire and protected by well-armed guards stationed in strategically placed watch towers. The surrounding residential neighborhoods seem curiously out of place within this context. The homes are mostly modest duplex and single family dwellings built before World War II. They are now much coveted by a new generation of young, urban professionals who are enticed to the area by appealing housing prices which are only available in older urban neighborhoods in the midst of demographic transition.

Gravestones at Congressional Cemetery in southeast Washington, DC. The District's massive jail complex dominates the cemetery's eastern vista. (Philip Bigler)

The past has not been kind to Congressional Cemetery. In the 19th century, grave robbers sometimes exhumed and stole recent burials. In more recent times, much of the cemetery's magnificent (if sometimes eclectic) funeral architecture was thoughtlessly broken and vandalized. In 1957, two teenage boys were arrested by the police after having desecrated over 130 grave stones during a Halloween drinking binge. In 1991, members of a bizarre religious cult broke into one of the cemetery's above ground mausoleums and stole several skeletal remains from its interior vaults.[4] Adding to the ongoing humiliation of Congressional was the lack of adequate funds needed for routine maintenance and landscaping. The grounds quickly became overgrown with grass and weeds, making Congressional an ideal haven for drug addicts, vagrants, and derelicts. It subsequently became a potentially dangerous place, especially after dark.

In 1972, Congressman Tom Railsback of Illinois was the first to sound the public alarm. He claimed that "Congressional Cemetery is in dire need of our help. Family vaults have been stripped of their doors. Trees and other foliage are overgrown. There are piles of beer cans and whiskey bottles."[5] Adding to the growing public awareness of the historic cemetery's plight was the high profile funeral for FBI Director, J. Edgar Hoover at Congressional. Several dozens of unpaid volunteers valiantly attempted to make the grounds more presentable for the anticipated national television coverage. They cut the grass, raked up

FBI Director J. Edgar Hoover. Hoover was buried in his family's plot in 1972 and the burial led to renewed public attention to Congressional's plight. (Library of Congress)

dead leaves and cleaned headstones but it proved to be a futile effort. As one individual lamented, she was "…shocked and heartbroken at the disgraceful condition of the cemetery. Grass was knee high, some tombstones overturned and it looked like a forgotten place."[6] In 1997, Congressional Cemetery earned the dubious distinction of being listed as one of "America's Most Endangered Historic Places" by the National Trust for Historic Preservation.[7]

The harsh glare of the public spotlight proved fortuitous since it led to an increase in private and government efforts to save the cemetery from further deterioration. The Association for the Preservation of Historic Congressional Cemetery (APHCC) was formed in part to "conserve the physical artifacts, buildings, and infrastructure of the cemetery [and] to celebrate the American heritage represented by those interred here."[8] This organization quickly became a powerful advocate for the cemetery's ongoing conservation efforts and helped manage much needed repairs and renovation of the grounds. It also began an effective lobbying campaign to secure additional sources of funding.

Paradoxically, the cemetery's economic salvation came from an unorthodox and unexpected source. Cemetery officials decided to permit residents of the surrounding neighborhoods to exercise and unleash their dogs within the property's fenced grounds for a $250 tax-deductible fee. In addition to the annual dues, the owners were assessed a $50 additional levy for each pet (up to three animals). The so-called "cemetery dogs" were required to be neutered and their owners were expected to clean up after them.[9] The continual presence of a large number of dogs on the premises had the additional benefit of serving as a deterrent to loiterers and derelicts. As one article explained, the dogs became the "eyes and ears on duty [so that] Congressional is mostly free and clear of riff raff and vandals."[10]

Congressional Cemetery represents a vital and irreplaceable part of American history. When the District of Columbia was originally created in the late 18th century, there were no provisions made in the initial designs for the establishment of a public cemetery.[11] Government planners wrongly assumed that the district would have few permanent residents since the federal legislature would be in session for just a few months each year. Thus, any burial needs that arose could easily be accommodated by local area churches. But few realized that the new capital's geographical location along the Potomac River's marshlands was deadly. Indeed, the region's ungodly summer heat coupled with its fetid water supply spawned swarms of malaria-laden mosquitos which made the city virtually uninhabitable. All who could wisely abandoned Washington city for more hospitable regions, but still disease and pestilence took their toll and death became a common place occurrence.

The Andrew Ellicott map for the new capital, 1792. Although the planning for Washington was meticulous, no provisions were initially made for a public cemetery. The city's location along the Potomac's disease-infested swamp and mash lands proved deadly for federal officials. (Library of Congress)

In 1807, several prominent members of the Christ Church Episcopal congregation created the Washington Parish Burial Grounds on a 4.5 acres tract in southeast Washington.[12] The first burial took place that year when stonecutter, William Swinton, was interred on April 11 in Section 1115.[13] A few months later, Connecticut Congressman Uriah Tracy died while in residence in the District of Columbia and he was likewise buried in the new cemetery.[14] At this time, the transportation of human remains was impractical due to poor transportation and primitive embalming techniques. As such, many of the country's early legislators who died while in office had little choice but to be buried within the convenient confines of the Christ Church cemetery. The growing number of burials of deceased Congressmen and Senators ultimately led to the renaming the cemetery "Congressional" to more accurately represent it new mission as the primary burial ground for the federal government.

To honor and recognize those legislators who died while in office, the Architect of the Capitol, Benjamin Latrobe, was commissioned to design an appropriate, uniform marker which would be placed at cemetery.[15] Latrobe's insipid cubical design for the sandstone monuments was unimaginative and many vocal critics considered them highly unattractive. One detractor wrote, "They are built of free or sandstone, painted white, have each four panels, on one of which are engraved, in black letters, the name, age, period of death, &c., of the deceased, and topped with a small pyramid…[the monuments are] plain and rather tasteless…Some more beautiful design might be substituted without adding much to the expense."[16] In her book, *Historic Congressional Cemetery*, Rebecca Boggs Roberts explains further that "…the monuments were considered ugly. Sen. George Frisbie Hoar, of Massachusetts, stated that the idea of being buried under one 'brings a new horror to death.'"[17]

In the 1830s with the advent of railroad transportation as well as with improved coffins and the development of arterial embalming, the ability to return deceased members of Congress and other dignitaries to their native state for burial became much more practical.[18]

The grave of Vice President Elbridge Gerry. Gerry is the only signer of the Declaration of Independence buried in Washington, DC. Many early government officials who died while in office were buried at Congressional. (Philip Bigler)

As such, the need for permanent government grave space diminished so the cemetery decided to adapt to the changing demands by constructing a new "Public Vault." This austere, utilitarian mausoleum was designed to serve as a temporary place of repose for the deceased while transportation could be arranged to return the body

The Public Vault at Congressional Cemetery. Completed in 1835, the above ground mausoleum served as the temporary resting place for over 3,000 people including Presidents William Henry Harrison, John Quincy Adams, and Zachary Taylor. (Philip Bigler)

to their home state for proper burial. The Public Vault became operational in 1835 and cost over $5,000 to construct. Over the years it would be used to store the remains of numerous prominent individuals including Presidents William Henry Harrison, John Quincy Adams, and Zachary Taylor; Vice President John C. Calhoun; and, notably, First Lady Dolley Madison.[19]

Dolley Madison died on July 12, 1849 at the age of 81. After a grand funeral service was conducted at St. John's Church, her body was transported to Congressional and placed inside the Public Vault in temporary repose while arrangements could be made to return her home to Orange County, Virginia. Unfortunately, there were no funds available to complete the transfer since the Madison family fortune had long since been squandered by Dolley's alcoholic son, John Payne Todd. Todd continued his unruly ways, oblivious to the lamentable fate of his mother. Just three years later, he died from complications caused by typhoid fever. He was buried at Congressional Cemetery on January 18, 1852, a cold and bitter day. There were no eulogies given in his honor and no one mourned his passing. One newspaper did note laconically that John Payne Todd was the "late eccentric son of Mrs. Madison" and that he had a "strange and absorbing influence over his mother."[20]

Eventually, the grave was marked with a modest granite stone which bears the simple inscription: "Beloved Son of Dolley Madison." Over the years, the stone has been damaged and chipped but few people notice or care to visit this lonely site. Rather than acknowledge Payne Todd as the sole heir to the Madison legacy, he has become a mere footnote in the lives of James and Dolley Madison remembered simply as their *scandalous son*.

The grave of Dolley Madison's son, John Payne Todd. (Philip Bigler)

ENDNOTES

1 The two best resources on the history of Congressional Cemetery are Abby Arthur Johnson's *In the Shadow of the United States Capitol: Congressional Cemetery and the Memory of the Nation* and Rebecca Boggs Roberts and Sandra K. Schmidts *Historic Congressional Cemetery* from the Images of America series.

2 The Potomac Avenue Metro is accessible by both the Blue and Orange lines.

3 FedEx Field is the largest venue in the National Football League with a seating capacity in excess of 91,000. The irony is that the Washington Redskins play in Maryland, not the District of Columbia.

4 See the Congressional Cemetery website at http://www.congressionalcemetery.org for historic news articles.

5 Congressman Tom Railsback quoted in Abby Johnson and Ronald Maberry Johnson (2012). *In the Shadow of the United States Capitol: Congressional Cemetery and the Memory of the Nation.* Washington, DC, New Academia Publishing, p. 265.

6 Helen Anthony quoted in Johnson, p. 289.

7 Johnson, p. 335.

8 See the Association for the Preservation of Historic Congressional Cemetery's mission statement at http://www.congressionalcemetery.org/mission-statement.

9 Information on the Congressional Cemetery "dog walking" program is available at: http://www.congressionalcemetery.org/dogwalking-program.

10 See Cemetery Dogs: Serving Historic Congressional Cemetery at http://www.cemeterydogs.org/.

11 Johnson, p. 11.

12 Rebecca Boggs Roberts and Sandra K. Schmidt (2012). *Historic Congressional Cemetery: Images of America.* Charleston, SC, Arcadia Publishing, p. 10.

13 William Swinton was a stonecutter working on the construction of the US Capitol when he died. See Roberts, p. 11.

14 Tracy was buried on July 19, 1807 in R24/1. See Johnson, p. 23 and the Congressional Cemetery online list of interments.

15 Many of the current 171 markers at Congressional Cemetery are actually cenotaphs.

16 George Waterston quoted in Johnson, p. 47.

17 George Frisbie Hoar quoted in Roberts, p. 31.

18 Johnson, pp. 71-73.

19 Roberts, p. 32.

20 *The Fredericksburg News* quoted in Philip Bigler and Annie Lorsbach (2009). *Liberty & Learning: The Essential James Madison.* Harrisonburg, VA., The James Madison Center, p. 136

Chapter One

1790 - 1799

"[M]y little Payne will have a generous
& tender protector."

Dolley Payne Todd

U nder the provisions of the recently ratified United States
Constitution, the new federal government was mandated to
conduct an immediate census of the country's inhabitants
and to repeat the procedure every ten years.¹ In accordance with
this requirement, President George Washington signed into law on
March 1, 1790 a Congressional authorization for America's first ever
national census. ² Over the ensuing months, some 650 enumerators
(census takers) attempted to provide a true tally of the number of
people living within the geographical confines of the United States.
The infant nation's expansive boundaries stretched from the Atlantic
seaboard to the distant frontiers and sparse settlements along the
eastern banks of the Mississippi River. The count was to include the
vast numbers of enslaved people who were to be tabulated by prior
agreement as 3/5ths of a person for the purpose of both representa-
tion in Congress and taxation.³

The arduous task of interviewing all of the country's residents was
indeed formidable and it was made even more difficult by a perva-
sive suspicion that the entire process was a government conspiracy
or "...some scheme for increasing taxation." This meant that many

of the nation's citizens "were inclined to be cautious lest they should reveal too much of their own affairs. There was also opposition...on religious grounds, a count of inhabitants being regarded by many as a cause for divine displeasure."[4]

Adding to the general confusion was the reality that small, stubborn Rhode Island had continually refused to ratify the Constitution, objecting to the original document on the grounds that it lacked an explicit, written bill of rights. Nevertheless, it was strategically decided that the semi-autonomous state should be included in the overall count and this decision would prove to be fortuitous. Rhode Island, isolated and surrounded, finally accepted its inexorable destiny by agreeing to accept the new federal government albeit reluctantly by a narrow 34 to 32 favorable vote.[5] The Vermont territory was likewise included in the 1790 census even though that region would not achieve actual statehood until the following year. Over the next several months, both Kentucky (1792) and Tennessee (1796) would be admitted to the union after reaching the required minimum population bringing to 16 the total number of states in the republic by the turn of the century.

The first census revealed that there were over 3,893,000 inhabitants in the United States, and that number included some 694,280 slaves. In Orange County, Virginia, the home of Congressman James Madison, slaves constituted virtually half of the area's overall population.[6] America, though, was still a sparsely settled country with just 4.5 inhabitants per square mile. Most of the people were engaged in small, subsistence farming and lived clustered along the Atlantic seaboard or near navigable rivers. There were few roads or turnpikes and those that did exist were primitive and dangerous, frequently made impassable by rainfall or snow storms. Bridges were virtually unknown, so streams had to be either forded on horseback or traversed by ferry.[7] For the new president, George Washington, it required a minimum of eight days of arduous travel to make the journey from his Mount Vernon home to New York City, a distance of less than two hundred miles.

There were very few cities or towns of any size in the United States in 1790. Philadelphia was, by far, the nation's largest port and urban center but its resident population of 28,522 was miniscule when compared to the great European capitals such as Paris or London.[8] The only other noteworthy cities in the country were Baltimore (13,503), Charleston (16,359), Boston (18,320), and New York (49,401). New York had been the site of the Confederation Congress for four years (1785-1789) and served briefly as the new federal capital under the Constitution. But after vigorous debate and the ultimate approval of the "Residence Act" in 1790, Congress agreed to relocate the government to a newly created federal district situated along the banks of the Potomac River. The 10-mile square site was undeveloped, swampy, and malarial, and it was expected to take at least decade before the required federal buildings could be constructed and made inhabitable. These included the building of a new "President's Palace" as well as a suitable capitol for the national legislature. In the interim, it was decided to relocate temporarily the entire federal government to Philadelphia, the most cosmopolitan and urbane city in the country. Despite its brief occupation by British forces during the war, Philadelphia had recovered its prosperity and was renowned as the home of the great Benjamin Franklin.[9] It was also the center for American scientific thought as well as the historic and spiritual site of American independence. The city certainly had ample public facilities to accommodate the needs of the national government as well as to house the president, the cabinet, and members of Congress. It seemed to be the perfect location to begin to put into practice the ideals of the American republic.

JUST 17 YEARS AFTER declaring its independence, the infant American republic was again in peril. This time, however, the nation was beset upon by an unseen but equally deadly enemy. Indeed, two hundred of the good citizens of Philadelphia were dying every week from a rampant yellow fever epidemic that had begun in late July, 1793 after a thirty-three year hiatus.[10] The misery of

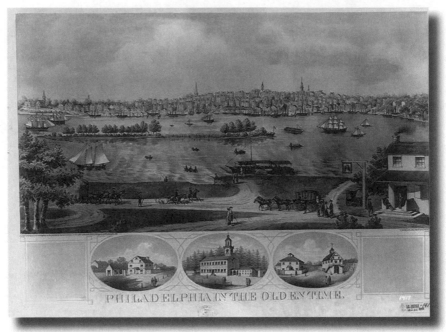

A view of Philadelphia during the 18th Century. Philadelphia served as the temporary home to the federal government while the new capital was being contructed in the newly formed District of Columbia. The yellow fever epidemic of 1793 devestated the city and caused a constitutional crisis. (Library of Congress)

the city's citizens was exacerbated by the oppressive summer heat and the lack of meaningful rainfall. Swarms of flies and mosquitoes spawned by the city's poor sanitation and general filth infested the city reminding many residents of the great Biblical plagues during the time of Moses. Fully half of Philadelphia's population of 30,000 had wisely chosen to evacuate the close confines of the city for the countryside, but they left behind the poor, the ill, the destitute and the dying. There were, though, a few heroic, civic-minded humanitarians who valiantly remained to minister to the needs of the sick.

The American Secretary of State, Thomas Jefferson, reported on the dire situation in a personal letter to his close friend, Virginia Congressman James Madison: "The fever spreads faster," Jefferson wrote. "Deaths are now about 30 a day. It is in every square of the city. All fleeing who can. Most of the offices are shut or shutting. The banks shut up this day. All my clerks have left me but one…"[11]

In fact, virtually all of the federal government's employees had abruptly left the temporary capital of the republic and its members were now widely scattered throughout the country. Many vowed that they would never to return to the ill-fated city. President George Washington pondered the fate of the infant American republic but he did so from the safety of his plantation home at Mount Vernon.

During this critical time, a promising, young Quaker lawyer, John Todd, was living in a handsome yet subdued brick house prominently located at the corner of Fourth and Walnut Streets (51 South Fourth Street), just one block away from Congress Hall. Despite the constant danger posed by the yellow fever epidemic, Todd felt compelled to remain within the city limits in order to tend to the pressing legal needs of many of his ailing clients. Likewise, he felt a strong familial obligation to care for his parents who were already infected by the deadly disease.

The home of John and Dolley Todd in Philadelphia. The young couple had been married only three years and had two children when the yellow fever epidemic struck. (Library of Congress)

John Todd was hardly a reckless or foolish man by nature. He had taken the precaution of removing his young family to the relative safety of Gray's Ferry. Situated along the soothing banks of the Schuylkill River, it was located in the rural outskirts of the city and safely removed from any imminent danger. But Todd's bride of three years, Dolley Payne, was in frail health, still recuperating from the difficult birth of the couple's second child, William Temple. She had been forced to make the exodus to Gray's Ferry while lying prostrate on a stretcher. She was accompanied on this journey by her sister, Anna, as well as by her new born child and his sibling, the two year old Payne.[12]

It was a traumatic time for the Todd family. Dolley continued to agonize over her husband's fate and well-being and on October 4, she wrote a plaintive letter to her brother-in-law: "…[my] Love'd Husband in perpetual danger…I am almost d[i]stracted with distress & apprehension… I have repeatedly Entreated John to leave home from which we are now unavoidably Banished—but alas he cannot leave."[13] Just three weeks later, John Todd would be dead from the fever and Dolley would be facing an uncertain fate as a 25-year old widow.

DOLLEY PAYNE WAS BORN in Guilford County, North Carolina on May 20th, 1768 during a time of increased tensions between Great Britain and the American colonies. The passage of the hated Townshend Duties the previous year had further exacerbated the precarious political situation as the American colonies became increasingly radicalized by oppressive British taxation policies. Her parents, John and Mary Payne, were devout members of the Society of Friends (Quakers) and they had only recently relocated their family from Virginia to the region.[14] Their motivation for undertaking such a dramatic, domestic upheaval remains uncertain, but in the staunchly Anglican Virginia colony there was open hostility towards so-called dissenter religions and many sects, including the Quakers, found themselves subjected to persecution, discrimination and even imprisonment. The more remote North Carolina countryside certainly offered a more hospitable and peaceful haven for the Payne clan to practice their faith free from any unwanted government interference. It also promised the opportunity to pursue a more insular, contemplative life free from the incursions of politics and the temptations of modern life.

The Payne family's time in North Carolina, however, was mysteriously brief and after several months they returned to their home state in 1769. John Payne had arranged to purchase some property in Hanover County which was well-known as the ancestral home of the great orator and Virginia patriot, Patrick Henry. The Payne's modest plantation was geographically situated near both the James and York Rivers in the eastern tidewater region of Virginia just several miles to the north of the small but growing hamlet of Richmond. Like many of his neighbors, John Payne owned a few slaves and they were put to work in the plantation's tobacco fields. For a pious Quaker, though, the sordid practice of owning human chattels posed a serious spiritual and ethical quandary. Indeed, the Society of Friends explicitly denounced slavery but at the same time, Virginia's statutory law discouraged any voluntary owner manumission. By 1782, the state legislature modified and liberalized this policy and John Payne now felt morally compelled to emancipate all of his slaves despite the considerable financial hardship and economic burden it would pose for his large family. [15] It was an admirable act of courage and conscience, but once again Payne felt the need to relocate his family and this time he decided to move to the far more enlightened capital of the Confederation, Philadelphia.

Dolley Payne as a young Quaker woman in Philadelphia. (Library of Congress)

By now, the Payne's third child and eldest daughter, Dolley, had matured into an attractive, vivacious teenager. For her, the prospect of living in the nation's largest and most cosmopolitan city was exhilarating. As one of her contemporaries would later recall: "She came upon our comparatively cold hearts in Philadelphia, suddenly and unexpectedly with all the delightful influences of a summer sun, from the Sweet South, in the season of May and at the age of sixteen, bringing with her all the warm feelings and glowing fancies of her native State."[16] Yet many within the city's large Quaker community took a dim view of any explicit signs of vanity or personal ostentation. Some disparaged Dolley's stylish clothing while others criticized her fashionable shoes. The young girl's adolescent exuberance and "dashing tendency of her character" led to censure and further approbation.[17] Dolley would later remember this youthful period of her life with some bitterness, writing to her sister, Anna, about "…the time when *our Society* used to controle me entirely, and debar me from so many advantages and pleasures."[18]

Still, despite the dissonance, Dolley remained spiritually attached to her church and continued her Quaker education while in Philadelphia "…in all the strictness of the sect to which the family belonged."[19] Her early letters made regular written use of the archaic "thy" and "thee," a stylistic characteristic of the more pious religious sects in the early United States.

For Dolley's father, though, the move to Philadelphia proved to be personally disillusioning as well as an economic disaster. His efforts to establish himself as a starch merchant proved to be a dismal failure and his debts correspondingly accumulated. This, in turn, led to the condemnation of his fellow church goers who viewed such financial difficulties as solid evidence of a character flaw and of divine approbation. In fiscal desperation, Payne's wife began to take-in boarders in an effort to help alleviate the family's growing monetary difficulties.[20]

In 1790 at age 22, Dolley Payne greatly improved her family's social and financial circumstances by marrying a well-respected Quaker lawyer, John Todd. The couple exchanged their simple vows before their congregation on January 7, 1790 and a few days later, an official announcement of the nuptials appeared in print in the *Pennsylvania Mercury*:

> *Thursday last was married at Friends' meeting*
> *In Market-street,* John Todd, *jun. Esq. Attorney*
> *At Law, to Miss* Dolly (sic) Payne, *of this city.*[21]

John and Dolley Payne's initial marital bliss was amplified by the birth of their first child, John Payne Todd. The boy was a leap year baby, born on the feast of Saint Oswald—February 29, 1792.[22] It was also a day that had been traditionally steeped in superstition and accompanied by many bad omens. With the advantage of historical hindsight, Payne's uncommon birthday seemed to foreshadow what would be an ignoble life for the boy. Just six months later, Dolley Payne Todd's father died a broken, sad, and embittered man.[23]

DR. BENJAMIN RUSH HAD had earned widespread acclaim as one of America's foremost physicians. His wisdom, medical scholarship, and intellectual integrity were well-renowned as were his impeccable credentials as a devout patriot as one of Pennsylvania's nine signers of the Declaration of Independence. Still, Dr. Rush was very much a product of the 18th century and had little understanding about the actual causes and transmission of infectious diseases. Like his fellow physicians, he was reduced to using his own personal observations to formulate his medical hypotheses and he relied heavily upon past experience and precedence rather than actual science in his efforts to cure ailing patients.[24]

Virtually every year during the late summer months, there was an onset of the so-called "fall ague" or the "autumnal disease."[25] These predictable outbreaks were usually benign and believed to be caused by the polluted, stagnant, foul air that was typical of cities during the Federalist era. Indeed, dead animals frequently littered the streets; there were no real sanitary facilities; and horse manure was omnipresent. This noxious mixture attracted a variety of ver-

Dr. Benjamin Rush. Rush was one of the nation's leading physicians and treated many patients during the Philadelphia yellow fever epidemic. (Library of Congress)

min and insects while producing an incredible stench and unhealthful conditions.[26] When a typical outbreak of the fever struck, the inflicted residents simply took to their beds, suffered and sweated for a few days in the miserable heat, and then usually recovered without any medical intervention. There were, of course, always a few fatalities and those were publically announced with the solemn tolling of church bells.

In July 1793, however, Dr. Rush was one of the first physicians to realize that the most recent onset of the fever in Philadelphia was atypical. He noted that his patients exhibited symptoms that were unusually severe and frequently lethal. In a pamphlet that he would publish later chronicling the epidemic, Rush noted: "I remarked to Dr. Foulke and Dr. Hodge, that I had seen an unusual number of bilious fevers, accompanied with symptoms of uncommon malignity, and that I suspected all was not right in our city. Dr. Hodge immediately replied, that a fever of a most malignant kind had carried off four or five persons…and that one of them had died in twelve hours after the attack of the disorder. This information satisfied me that my apprehensions were well founded."[27]

The sick complained of violent headaches and were beset with frequent bouts of nausea and vomiting. Their eyes soon turned yellow and, as Rush clinically observed: "in some, the skin became purple, and in others black. I heard of one case in which the body was yellow above, and black below its middle."[28] The Secretary of State, Thomas Jefferson likewise noted the symptoms in a letter to

James Madison: "[The illness] comes on with a pain in the head, sick stomach, then a little chill, fever, black vomiting and stools, and death from the 2d. to the 8th Day."[29]

The lack of accurate and timely information about the epidemic only added to the growing panic within the city.[30] Jefferson again wrote: "The yellow fever increases... [The sick] are much scattered through the town. And it is the opinion of the physicians that there is no possibility of stopping it. They agree it is a non-descript disease, and no two agree in any one part of their process of cure."[31] Some residents tried lighting bonfires in an effort to purge the air of impurities while other citizens futilely drenched themselves in vinegar or enveloped themselves in clouds of tobacco smoke to ward off the disease.[32] Several of the Philadelphia newspapers began to print formulas for homespun tonics and other remedies, most of dubious effectiveness.[33] One resident lauded the curative power of drinking tar water, writing: "I have a great Opinion of Tar Water and have followed drinking it this great while and [have convinced] as many of our Family as I can persuade to drink it..."[34] This dreadful concoction, developed by an Irish cleric, consisted of combining one part tar to four parts water. After settling, it would create a disgusting potion that would allegedly cure virtually all diseases including the yellow fever.[35]

Without a viable or effective cure available, everyone was terrified and the streets remained virtually disserted. Philadelphia's physicians soon realized that the most effective method of reducing the growing sense of panic was to issue an edict ordering the churches to stop the tolling of their bells announcing the dead. This measure effectively concealed the true and increasing death toll from public knowledge.[36]

No one was sure how or even when the yellow fever epidemic had actually begun but speculation was rampant. Dr. Rush was convinced that the outbreak had its origins with a cargo of tainted coffee that had been imported to Pennsylvania from the West Indies aboard the schooner, *Amelia*.[37] The shipment had been spoiled in transit and was carelessly dumped at Ball's Wharf where it continued to rot and "putref[y] there to the great annoyance of the whole neighbourhood."[38] Still others reasoned that the disease had come via the large influx of French-speaking refugees who had fled the brutal slave rebellion that was then ravaging the island on Saint Domingue.[39] Indeed, an estimated 2,000 immigrants had flooded into Philadelphia that summer, desperate and destitute, having lost virtually everything during the political unrest.[40] This theory garnished further support when several of the sailors who had been involved in transporting the exiles from the island had died at "Richard Denny's boarding house on North Water Street."[41]

Apocalyptic reports in the city's many newspapers were commonplace. These fabricated and frequently outlandish stories only further alarmed an already terrified population. One newspaper, for instance, alleged: "…that dogs, geese, and other poultry, also that wild pigeons were sickly in many parts of the country, and that fish on the Susquehanna, and oysters in the Delaware bay, were so unpleasant that the inhabitants declined eating them. At the same time, flies were found dead in great numbers, in the unhealthy parts of the city. The weather was dry in August and September. There was no second crop of grass. The gardens yielded a scanty supply of vegetables, and of an inferior size and quality. Cherries were smaller than usual, and pear and apple-trees dropped their fruits prematurely, in large quantities. The peaches, which arrived at maturity, were small and ill tasted."[42]

As the plague continued to rage, Dr. Rush administered to the sick by using the customary methods of blood-letting and purging. He recorded that the "remedies for this fever were bleeding, vomits, purges, sweats, and a salivation and blisters."[43] In reality, these primitive medical treatments did little to alter the natural progression of the disease—some patients recovered naturally while others died, often from the contributing factors of loss of blood and dehydration.

The most effective antidote was to prevent infection in the first place and this was partially achieved through the spontaneous evacuation of the city. Thomas Jefferson observed: "Every body, who can, is flying from the city, and the panic of the country people is likely to add famine to disease. Tho becoming less mortal, it is still spreading, and the heat of the weather is very unpropitious. I have withdrawn my daughter from the city, but am obliged to go to it every day myself. "[44] Another city resident recorded: "It looks as if the City of Philadelphia must become almost a Desolation; the latest, most moderate and most credible Accounts say that the greater half of the Houses in the City are shut up & without Inhabitants occasion'd by the Deaths and Removals..."[45]

The federal and state governments were hardly heroic during this time of crisis and did little to inspire confidence or reassure its citizens. Pennsylvania Governor Thomas Mifflin abandoned the city in early September. President Washington did likewise, retreating to the sanctuary of his distant Virginia home.[46] Secretary of State Jefferson was one of the few cabinet members who voluntarily chose to remain in the capital in an effort to give an appearance of normality but he confided to James Madison in a letter his true motivation: "I would really go away, because I think there is rational danger, but that I had before announced that I should not go till the beginning of October, & I do not like to exhibit the appearance of panic. Besides that I think there might serious ills proceed from there being not a single member of the administration in place."[47] Just four days later, though, the well-intentioned Jefferson abruptly changed his plans since his staff refused to stay in plague-ridden Philadelphia. He again wrote to Madison: "All my clerks have left me but one: so that I cannot go on with business. I shall therefore set out in 3. or 4. Days..."[48]

The Secretary of the Treasury, Alexander Hamilton, had no option but to stay in Philadelphia. He had already contracted the fever and was far too sick to risk travel. His avowed political opponent

Gray's Ferry outside of Philadelphia. Located on the Schuylkill River, John Todd sent his wife, Dolley, and their two children to the area in an effort to excape the yellow fever epidemic. Dolley was still weak from having recently given birth to her son, William. (Library of Congress)

in the cabinet, Thomas Jefferson, privately denigrated Hamilton's illness and callously challenged the Secretary's personal integrity. "Hamilton is ill of the fever," Jefferson wrote, "...He had two physicians out at his house the night before last. His family think him in danger, & he puts himself so by his excessive alarm. He had been miserable several days before from a firm persuasion he should catch it. A man as timid as he is on the water, as timid on horseback, as timid in sickness, would be a phenomenon if the courage of which he has the reputation in military occasions were genuine. His friends, who have not seen him, suspect it is only an autumnal fever he has."[49] These petty and malicious allegations were unworthy of Thomas Jefferson and were soon proved false. Jefferson was forced to recant but did so reluctantly and without apology allowing only that: "H[amilton] had truly the fever, and is on the recovery, & pronounced out of danger."[50]

The lawyer, John Todd, had tried to persuade his parents to join the growing exodus from the city but to no avail. Before long, both were critically ill with the dreaded fever and ever the dutiful son, Todd chose to remain with his parents and attempt to nurse them back to health. On October 2, his father was the first to die while his mother succumbed to the plague just ten days later.[51]

Having been in such close, direct contact with the disease, John Todd was reluctant to join Dolley and his two children in their self-imposed exile. He feared that he, too, may have become infected from his stint in the city. When he finally chose to leave Philadelphia, Todd found it exceeding difficult to find suitable lodgings since all of the nearby tavern-keepers and farmers were suspicious of anyone who had recently come from the city, fearing potential contagion.

After a prolonged separation, Todd was lonely and desperately yearned to see his beloved wife and infant sons. He decided to continue on to Gray's Ferry despite the risks but according to his brother, Todd was "fearful of himself and unwilling to endanger the health of his family…he slept by himself in a lower apartment of the house."[52] Not long thereafter, Todd began to experience the ominous symptoms of the plague and "apprehensive of the prevailing fever coming on, Johnny went fourteen miles back to the city."[53] Finding shelter at his brother's home but no cure, the disease rapidly progressed and on October 24, John Todd became yet another victim of the yellow fever epidemic. Perhaps mercifully, he was spared the knowledge that his seven week old son, William, had also contracted the disease and had died that very same day.[54]

In an instant, Dolley Payne Todd had been transformed from a young, energetic 25-year old wife into a grieving widow. She was facing a difficult and uncertain future. The following month, Dolley's mother wrote poignantly: "How shall I express my feelings? O it seems to me as if my heart would brake my Poor Dear Dolley what dose she and will she suffer, how distressing is her situation the same day consined her Dear husband and her little babe to the silent grave she has no friend in town… to depend on she is here among strangers and friendless she is in debt for the burial of her babe and nearly moneyless having only nineteen Dollars Left and a number of other Debts to pay."[55]

Dolley Payne Todd was resolute in her determination to persevere despite her current circumstances. She would do everything to protect her beloved Payne from harm and the two of them would brave their uncertain future together, united in a familial bond that could never be broken no matter what the world had in store.

AS THE FALL WEATHER gradually began to cool, President George Washington was facing yet another serious governmental dilemma. It had been just four years since the Constitution had been ratified and the overall health of the American republic was still fragile and its ultimate fate was undetermined. The legislative branch was required to convene in December but there were growing doubts that a quorum could be achieved due to "...the calamitous situation in Philadelphia."[56] Pennsylvania's Governor Mifflin had informed Washington that over 3,500 people had died in the city and there was no sign that the epidemic was abating. "If cool weather accompanied with rain does not put a stop to the Malady," Washington mused, "distressing indeed must be the condition of that City."[57]

During the American Revolution, the Confederation capital had often been relocated as necessitated by military and political expediency. At various times, Congress had met in York, Princeton, Annapolis, Trenton, and New York. Given the dire circumstances in 1793, Washington requested that Attorney General, Edmund Randolph, render an opinion on whether or not the president had the authority under the new Constitution to unilaterally move the capital and temporarily convene Congress at a different, safe location. Randolph, though, was incommunicado and Washington wrote to James Madison in frustration, "I have received no answer nor is it probable I shall do it soon, as I believe [Randolph] has no communication with the Post Office."[58] The President then asked Madison, widely acknowledged to be the leading authority on the Constitution, to review the document and provide his expert opinion on the matter. "Time presses," Washington wrote, "and the Malady at the usual place of meeting is becoming more & more alarming. What then, do you think is the most advisable course for me to pursue in the present exigency?"[59]

Madison received Washington's letter while safely ensconced at Montpelier. He carefully began a review of his copious notes and other materials related to the Constitution to determine if it would be possible for the president to expand his authority during such an emergency. Remarkably, Madison did not rely upon his memory or his personal understanding of the Constitution but treated the issue as a dispassionate, honest scholar. He was ultimately forced to conclude: "From the best investigation I have been able to make in so short a time, the first expedient, tho' most adequate to the exigency, seems to require an authority that does not exist under the Constitution and laws of the U. States."[60] Even a president's benign intentions did not grant him power to relocate the capital under the United States Constitution.

Fortunately, by late October, the weather had turned dramatically colder and a series of hard frosts had destroyed the deadly mosquito population. The epidemic had been broken and things slowly began to return to normal. John Beckley, a Republican political partisan, wrote to Madison: "...that there is now as perfect safety from contagion of any kind as was ever known here; there is not known a single case of the yellow fever in the City or its suburbs; the Citizens have returned almost universally, the public Offices are all opened, as well as ill the public & private seminaries, business of every kind is resumed, the Markets as fully attended & supplied as ever, and in short no vestige of the late calamity remaining, except in the mournful remembrances of those whose friends & relatives have fallen victims to it."[61] The unofficial death toll was placed at around 5,000 people, roughly 10% of Philadelphia's population. The nation had fortuitously averted a serious Constitutional crisis when Congress was able to reconvene that December in the city.

IT WAS ALSO NOW safe for Dolley Payne Todd to return to her old home on 8th and Market Streets. She was accompanied by her 18-month old son, Payne, as well as her younger sister, Anna. Dolley's mother, after a series of personal and financial setbacks, had finally chosen to abandon Philadelphia for Virginia and was living temporarily with her daughter, Lucy, and her new husband, George Steptoe Washington.

John Todd, despite his youth, had wisely prepared for the eventuality of his own demise and had left behind a detailed last will and testament. In it, he bequeathed his entire fortune "…to the dear wife of my bosom and first and only woman whom all and only affections were placed…Trusting that as she has proved an amiable and affectionate wife."[62] He also instructed his widow to take care of their only surviving child and to "…prove and Affectionate Mother to my little Payne…My last Prayer is may she Educate him in the Ways of Honesty tho' he may be obliged to beg his Bread remembering that will be better to him than a name and Riches."[63]

Todd's foresight in putting his estate in good order did not immediately solve Dolley's difficulties and she soon found herself in dire financial straits. The Philadelphia court system was backlogged with the large number of probate cases stemming from the high numbers of fatalities that had occurred during the previous year's yellow fever epidemic. The judges, despite their best efforts, could do little to expedite their massive caseloads in a timely manner. Compounding Dolley's difficulties was the fact that her brother-in-law, James Todd, was withholding important documents from her.[64] In exasperation, Dolley wrote to him in February 1794: "As I have already suffered the most serious Inconvenience from the unnecessary Detention of my part of my mother in law's property and of the Receipt Books and papers of my late Husband—I am constrained once more to request—and if a request is not sufficient—to *demand* that they be delivered this day—as I cannot wait thy return from this proposed Excusion without material injury to my affairs. The bearer waits for thy answer."[65] James Todd did further damage to his delicate relationship with Dolley when he urged her to sell her husband's extensive library in order to raise money quickly. She steadfastly refused and responded in exasperation, "I was hurt My dear Jamy that the Idea of his Lib[r]ary should occur as a proper source for raising money. Book's from which he wished his Child improved, shall remain sacred, I would feel the pinching hand of Poverty before I disposed of them."[66]

Dolley was finally forced to hire a Quaker lawyer, William Wilkins, to assist her in settling these many disputes and in obtaining her much needed inheritance. At the same time that she was dealing with these painful financial matters, she was trying to cope with her profound sorrow, mourning the unimaginable loss of both her husband and infant son. Quaker tradition and practice expected a widow to grieve privately and to dress soberly while withdrawing from society for an extended period of time. The practical reality, though, was that Dolley was still just 25-years old and an extremely attractive woman. According to Anthony Morris, every time she entered a room, "…[Dolley] raised the mercury…in the thermometers of the Heart to fever heat."[67] She could simply not afford to live alone for long since she needed to find a suitable protector for her beloved son, Payne.

It was during this interlude that Dolley Todd chose to prepare her own will as a precaution against an untimely death. In the document signed in May 1794, she designated a family friend, Aaron Burr, to serve as little Payne's sole guardian. In her will, she instructed the New York Senator to make sure that adequate provisions were made to ensure her son's future education. Dolley wrote: "And as the education of my son is to him and to me the most interesting of all earthly concerns, and far more important to his happiness and eminence in Life than the increase of his estate, I direct that no expense be spared to give him every advantage and improvement of which his Talents may be susceptible."[68]

With the return of spring, Dolley decided to enjoy the warm weather and to emerge from her self-imposed hibernation. She began to take long, leisurely walks through the crowded streets of Philadelphia and she quickly attracted the attention of numerous young men who saw her not only as a vivacious and beautiful woman as well as an eligible and potentially wealthy widow. Her friend, Eliza Collins, recalled that potential suitors would "station themselves where they might see her pass." Still Collins and other Quakers were shocked by the daily spectacle of gawping strangers stalking Dolley and scolded her to "Hide thy face—there are so many staring at thee."[69] One of her many admirers, although less conspicuous and far more restrained, was the famous congressman from Virginia, James Madison.

JAMES MADISON WAS 43-YEARS old in 1794 and most of his friends and acquaintances assumed that he was destined to live the remainder of his life alone, a life-long bachelor. His few known attempts at earlier romance had ended in abject failure. The most notable episode had been his ill-fated relationship with Catherine "Kitty" Floyd a decade earlier while still serving in the Confederation Congress. In 1783, Madison had fallen deeply in love with the 15-year old daughter of a fellow delegate, William Floyd of New York.[70] In April, Madison informed his friend, Thomas Jefferson, about the couple's plans to marry. "Since your departure the affair has been pursued," he wrote to Jefferson. "Most preliminary arrangements although definitive will be postponed until the end of the year in congress. At some period of the intervail I shall probably make a visite to Virginia. The interest which your friendship takes on this occasion in my happiness is a pleasing proof that the disposetions which I feel are reciprocal."[71]

Madison and Kitty exchanged miniature water-color portraits as tokens of their affection. Painted on ivory by one of the nation's premier portrait artist and naturalists, Charles Willson Peale, Madison affectionately presented his image as a gift to Kitty in a velvet-lined container and had it mounted so that it could be worn as a pin.

During the summer, while Madison was preoccupied with his duties with the federal government, Kitty returned to New York

James Madison and Catherine "Kitty" Floyd. These two miniatures were painted by the renowned artist, Charles Willson Peale, and were exchanged as engagement gifts by the couple. After a few weeks, Kitty broke off their engagement and instead married a New York medical student.
(Library of Congress)

State with her father. There, she impulsively became enamored with a promising young medical student and callously, even cruelly, broke off her engagement to Madison.[72]

Thomas Jefferson was shocked when he heard the terrible news and tried to console Madison. He wrote: "I sincerely lament the misadventure which has happened, from whatever cause it may have happened." He then offered the following sagacious advice: "Should it be final however, the world still presents the same & many other resources of happiness, and you possess many within yourself, firmness of mind & intermitting occupations will not long leave you in pain."[73]

Madison immersed himself in his work, taking solace in his duties in Congress as well as in his efforts to reform the deeply flawed Articles of Confederation. His books likewise offered additional sanctuary and Madison occupied his time by reading and studying. He began to formulate an ambitious plan for an entirely new federal

government and with the subsequent success of the 1787 convention as well as his critical role in the ratification of the Constitution
and the Bill of Rights, Madison's reputation as a scholar and as a
renowned government thinker soared. He was revered by many and
respected even by those who might have disagreed with him politically.

With Congress back in session in 1794 and Philadelphia ruturn-
ing to normalcy, Madison took notice of the beautiful widow Todd.
He asked his former Princeton classmate, Aaron Burr, to intercede
on his behalf and to arrange for a personal introduction. Dolley was
flattered and overjoyed at the prospect of meeting the famous Madison despite their significant difference in age (17 years). She wrote
to a friend: "Thou must come to me,—Aaron Burr says that the great
little Madison has asked to be brought to see me this evening."[74]
Madison was already enthralled with Dolley Todd and, as historian
Irving Brandt observed, seemed to be "…ready to fall in love with
extraordinary rapidity."[75]

It was by all accounts, a whirlwind romance. Dolley was most
anxious to find a suitable stepfather to take care of her beloved
little Payne, and James Madison seemed to be the perfect candidate. Rumors about the burgeoning relationship began to circulate
throughout the city and the news even reached President Washington. His wife, Martha, delicately questioned Dolley about her alleged romance and assured her of their approval: "Well, if you are,
don't be ashamed, be proud. He'll make a husband all the better for
those seventeen extra years. Between him and the General there's
great esteem and friendship."[76] Jefferson was likewise excited about
the prospect of James and Dolley's marriage. He could envision the
couple returning to Virginia where they would live in close proximity to Monticello so that they could enjoy their friendship free from
the travails of politics and public life.[77]

In August, Dolley's Quaker attorney, William Wilkins, also af-
firmed the relationship writing that "Mr. M[adison] is a Man whom
I admire. I knew his Attachment to you...His p(ersonal) Character

therefore I have every reason to believe is good and amiable. He unites to the great Talents which have secured him public Approbation those engaging qualities that contribute so highly to domestic Felicity. To such a Man therefore I do most freely consent that my beloved Sister be united and happy."[78] He warned her, though, that not everyone in the community was happy with the potential union. Indeed, many of Dollcy's Quaker congregation openly disapproved of the courtship occurring so soon after her husband's death. Moreover, James Madison was not a member of their faith and marriage outside of the Quaker religion was a cause for expulsion. Wilkins ominously wrote: "...the Eyes of the World are upon you and your Enemies have already opened their Mouths to censure and Condemn you."[79]

HONORING HER SISTER'S WISHES, Dolley chose to be married at Harewood, the Virginia home of George Steptoe Washington. Located near Berkeley Springs, it was planned to be a small, intimate affair since it was Dolley's second marriage and the wedding was occurring a scant eleven months after her previous husband death.

Dolley Payne Todd made the arduous 200 mile journey from Philadelphia with Anna and Payne in a barouche loaned by Thomas Jefferson. James Madison and several of their friends accompanied the wedding party riding alongside on horseback. The actual ceremony was performed in the Harewood parlor on September 15, 1794 with Episcopalian minister, Dr. Alexander Baldwin, of Winchester, presiding.[80] Among the gathered witnesses were Madison's sister, Frances, and the American patriot, Congressman Light Horse Harry Lee.[81]

Shortly after the conclusion of the brief ceremony, Dolley took a moment to compose a heartfelt letter to her close friend, Eliza Collins Lee. She wrote: "...to tell you in short, that in the course of this day I give my Hand to the Man who of all other's I most admire— You will not be at a loss to know who this is as I have been long ago

Harewood, the home of George Steptoe Washington and Lucy Payne. James Madison and Dolley Payne Todd were married here on September 15, 1794. Dolley's son, John Payne Todd, was just two years old at the time. (Library of Congress)

gratify'd In having your approbation—In this Union I have every thing that is soothing and greatful in prospect." She then added poignantly, "...& my little Payne will have a generous & tender protector."[82] Dolley forgetfully signed her letter "Dolley Payne Todd" but then hastily appended it with "Dolley Madison! Alas!"[83]

The newlyweds decided that after their marriage ceremony, they would visit Madison's sister, Nelly Conway Hite, at her new home, Belle Grove, in the northern Shenandoah Valley.[84] En route, though, they stopped to overnight in the nearby town of Winchester where Dolley became seriously ill with a high fever. Madison used the unforeseen interlude to write to his father and explained that his new wife had "...a regular ague and fever. The fits were so severe that I thought it prudent to call a physician…Dr. Baldwin attended and—the administration of the Bark soon expelled the complaint." The unexpected illness precluded any plans for a quick visit to Montpelier so Madison apologized and explained that: "…In about eight or ten days we expect to set out for Philadelphia, and your daughter-in-law begs you and my mother to accept her best and most respectful affection, which she means to express herself by an early opportunity."[85]

The Madison's returned to Philadelphia for the remaining session of the third Congress and would eventually rent a house on Spruce Street. Just a few weeks later, as news of their marriage quickly spread, Dolley's Quaker congregation met on December 26 and expelled her for the transgression of marrying outside of her religion. She was accused of callously "disregard[ing] the wholesome order of our discipline in the accomplishment of her marriage to a person not in membership with us before a hireling priest."[86] It was then succinctly and indelibly recorded that "Dorothy Madison was disowned Twelfth Month, 1794."

More tragic news followed. Her brother, William Temple Payne, died unexpectedly in early 1795 from an unidentified illness while living in Norfolk. He had joined the United States Navy as an ensign and had been expelled by the Quakers for "…accept[ing] a Commission in the Army" in violation of their pacifist beliefs. Likewise, brother Isaac, had also been ousted from his meetinghouse but for the serious offenses of "…resorting to houses of ill fame and gaming." He was the reprobate of the Payne family and he continued to struggle with alcoholism. His fondness for drink contributed to a feud where he "…offended a man in Virginia, who sometime afterward shot him with a pistol, of which wound he died."[87]

While Dolley grieved for her lost brothers, Madison was absorbed in organizing the opposition against the recently negotiated Jay's Treaty with England.[88] The treaty was an attempt to solve many of the festering issues with Great Britain that stemmed from the American Revolution. Among these were the need to withdraw all British troops from western frontier outposts, boarder adjustments with neighboring Canada, and a normalization of trade relations. It was also an attempt to avert American involvement in an ongoing Anglo-French conflict and had the enthusiastic support of the Secretary of the Treasury, Alexander Hamilton, and the Federalists,

For Madison, Jefferson, and their political allies, though, Jay's Treaty amounted to an open betrayal of France, an ally whose timely intervention during the Revolution had literally saved American independence. Moreover, they believed that the treaty was part of a thinly veiled Federalist conspiracy to economically return the United States to virtual colonial status with Britain, albeit with an autonomous government. In the end, after a bitter and divisive debate, the treaty was ratified by the United States Senate by a 20 to 10 margin but it would continue to be a source of contention and would serve as a catalyst for the development of two distinct American political parties.

With the federal government now fully functioning, George Washington decided not to seek reelection to a third term of office. The 1796 election thus became the first presidential contest to be openly contested by two opposition political candidates: Federalist John Adams versus Republican Thomas Jefferson. There was no popular vote at this time for electors for president and the issue would be ultimately decided in each of the 16 individual state legislatures. The Federalist strength was centered primarily in New England, New York and a few Middle Atlantic states while the Republicans were strong in Pennsylvania, the South and the new western states of Kentucky and Tennessee. The electoral returns from the states took weeks to be officially recorded and James Madison wrote to Jefferson in early December that "*Exitus in dubio* (The issue is doubtful) is still the Motto to the election. You must reconcile yourself to the secondary (the vice presidency) as well as the primary station, if that should be your lot."[89] Just nine days later, it was becoming increasingly clear that Jefferson would not prevail and would, indeed, be forced to settle for the vice presidency, an office with little political consequence or authority. Madison again wrote to Jefferson urging that he accept the results and advising that "You must prepare yourself therefore to be summoned to the place Mr. Adams now fills." He did, however, acknowledge Jefferson's reluctance to accept such a meaningless position, especially with a hostile administration, writing: "I am aware of the objections arising from the inadequateness of the importance of the place to the sacrifices you would be willing to make to a greater prospect of fulfilling the patriotic wishes of your friends; and from the irksomeness of being at the head of a body (the Senate) whose sentiments are at present so little in unison with our own. But it is expected that as you had made up your mind to obey the call of your Country, you will let it decide on the particular place where your services are to be rendered."[90] Jefferson finally replied to Madison, "I can particularly have no feelings which would revolt at a secondary position to mr. Adams. I am his junior in life, was his junior in Congress, his junior in the diplomatic line, his junior lately in our civil government." [91]In the end, Adams won the presidency, albeit narrowly, with 71 electoral votes, just three more than Thomas Jefferson. Jefferson would become the nation's second vice president.

James Madison, though, had finally decided to retire from the constant turmoil of political life. After four terms in Congress, he yearned to return home to Virginia and a quiet, domestic life with his new family. He wrote to his father, James Madison, Sr., that red clover seed were currently for sale and offered some advice on the forthcoming planting of the spring crops. He went on to explain: "We are all well & anxious to be on the Journey, which will be thro' Berkely & Fredk."[92] A new chapter in James and Dolley Madison's married life was beginning and it would also bring about major changes for little Payne Todd.

———————————

James Madison's parents, Nelly Conway and James, Sr. After his retirement from Congress, James Madison, Jr. returned to Montpelier with his new wife, Dolley, and her son, John Payne Todd. He immediately began renovations of the Montpelier manor house to transform it into a duplex to house separately the two families. Madison's father died in 1801 while his mother lived until 1829 and died at the age of 98. (Library of Congress)

ON APRIL 20, 1797 James Madison and his family arrived home at Montpelier. Dolley's teenage sister, Anna, had once again accompanied them. It was, in many ways, a triumphal return to Virginia for James Madison. He had accomplished much during his 20 years in public service and his place in history was undoubtedly secure. It seemed apropos that he could finally enjoy the tranquility of a privileged existence as an elite member of the Virginia gentry. John Adams, though, was deeply skeptical of such pseudo-retirements. In a letter to his wife, Abigail, he prophetically observed, "It seems the Mode of becoming great is to retire. Madison I suppose after a Retirement of a few Years is to become President or V.P. It is marvelous how political Plants grow in the shade."[93]

Madison's parents, James, Sr. and Nelly, although elderly by the standards of the day, were still very much alive. His father remained the undisputed patriarch of Montpelier and was responsible for making the day-to-day decisions on the plantation and for supervising and managing its diverse operations. There were now two distinct households living in residence under the same roof and this arrangement quickly became problematic. The younger Madison quickly decided that it was imperative to make significant structural alterations to the brick manor house in order to transform the structure into a duplex. He began by adding a 30-foot extension which allowed for the creation of separate entrances into the house while duplicate kitchen and living facilities provided both families a degree of autonomy and privacy. It was during this first extensive renovation of Montpelier that a distinctive, two story portico was added to the front facade of the great house complete with four classical Doric columns.[94]

Although James Madison had assumed the responsibilities of fatherhood late in life due to marriage, he always treated Dolley's son, Payne, as if the boy was his own natural child. As one observer noted, Madison was a dutiful parent and he performed "every act and service of parental guidance."[95] He also accepted the responsibility for tutoring the boy during his early schooling even though Payne showed little interest or academic inclination. He seemed to prefer frolicking around the plantation, playing with the slave children, and attending to the plantation's horses rather than studying.[96] This growing proclivity towards idleness was a matter of some concern, and it was during this Montpelier interlude that Payne first began to exhibit some disturbing character flaws. He could be stubborn and willful at times, but his mother seemed incapable of disciplining the child and would frequently excuse his youthful transgressions.[97] She was understandably overprotective and indulgent, since Payne was her sole tangible link to her first marriage with John Todd. As historian Virginia Moore writes: "[Dolley was horrified] to think that yellow fever might have snatched him away."[98]

Everyone who knew James Madison, however, was delighted that he had finally found true contentment with a new wife. Senator Charles Pinckney of South Carolina wrote to Madison: "My best respects to your Lady. You recollect we used often to talk about Matrimony & I have much curiosity to see your Lady. I have heard every thing I could wish of her—for certainly if ever a man deserved a good Wife you did." And then he inquired: "Have you any little Madisons running about & giving you a feeling which I assert is not otherwise found in human nature?"[99] The Madison's were, in fact, destined to remain childless and there would never be any siblings for little Payne. He alone would be force to bear the entire responsibility for the Madison family legacy.

Regardless of his public pronouncements to the contrary, Madison was determined to remain informed and involved in the major political developments of the day. He was, after all, Thomas Jefferson's closest friend and political ally and would regularly confer and advise the Vice President either through the mail or by regular visits to each other's homes. Jefferson had plenty of time for political intrigue since his sole constitutional duty was to preside over the Senate. He and Madison were covertly organizing the opposition to the Adams administration, especially after the passage of the hated Alien and Sedition Acts in 1798.[100]

The laws were passed by the Federalist Congress in an effort to preserve American neutrality in the ongoing conflict between Britain and France. The legislation gave the President extraordinary powers to expel dangerous foreigners as well as to arrest those who "utter[ed] or publish[ed] any false, scandalous, and malicious writing or writings against the government of the United States, or either house of the Congress of the United States, or the President of the United States." [101] The new laws were a clear violation of the principles articulated in the First Amendment and seemed to confirm Jefferson's and Madison's worst fears about the new administration. Jefferson observed: "…a little patience…we shall see the reign of witches pass over, their spells dissolved, and the people recovering their true sight, restoring their government to its true principles."[102]

Madison despised the laws claiming that they were "…a monster that must forever disgrace its parents."[103] He secretly composed the Virginia Resolution which was adopted by the Virginia state legislature and which expressed the Commonwealth's strong objections to the federal laws. It was becoming increasingly clear that Madison's "retirement" at Montpelier was to be short-lived. Instead, he began to orchestrate the Republican efforts to elect Thomas Jefferson president in the forthcoming 1800 election.

ON DECEMBER 14, 1799, George Washington died at his Mount Vernon estate at the age of 67. His death marked the end of the 18th century and metaphorically, an end of a remarkable era which had transformed the American republic. No other American was held in such high esteem or enjoyed the stature of General Washington. He was a singular figure in the history of the nation and represented a

The death of George Washington. Washington's died at Mount Vernon on December 14, 1799. His passing marked an end of an era in American history. (Library of Congress)

uniquely unifying figure, revered by both Federalists and Republicans. James Madison, who was then serving in the Virginia State Legislature in Richmond, eulogized: "Death has robbed our country of its most distinguished ornament, and the world of one of its greatest benefactors. George Washington, the Hero of Liberty, the father of his Country, and the friend of man is no more. The General Assembly of his native state were ever the first to render him, living, the honors due to his virtues. They will not be the second, to pay to his memory the tribute of their tears."[104]

A new generation of Americans was coming of age. They had been born after the fight for independency and even the struggles for the adoption of a new Constitution were rapidly becoming a distant memory. These young citizens had grown comfortable and complacent with the liberty and freedom that had been won by their patriot parents. As with most things that had not been earned, they took these rights for granted. A new era was about to begin and Payne Todd's life would be forever altered when his step-father re-entered public life after the critical presidential election of 1800.

ENDNOTES

Epigraph: Dolley Payne Madison quoted in Catherine C. Allgor (2006). *A Perfect Union: Dolley Madison and the Creation of the American Nation.* New York, Henry Holt and Company, p. 32.

1 The census is mandated under Article I, Section 2 which states: "The actual Enumeration shall be made within three Years after the first Meeting of the Congress of the United States, and within every subsequent Term of ten Years, in such Manner as they shall by Law direct." Its primary purpose is to determine the allotment of representatives each state is entitled to in the House of Representatives.

2 "Heads of Families at the First Census of the United States in the Year 1790," available at http://www.census.gov/prod/www/abs/decennial/1790.html.

3 See Article I, Section 2 of the United States Constitution which originally read, "Representatives and direct Taxes shall be apportioned among the several States which may be included within this Union, according to their respective Numbers, which shall be determined by adding to the whole Number of free Persons, including those bound to Service for a Term of Years, and excluding Indians not taxed, three fifths of all other Persons."

4 *Ibid.*, p. 5.

5 Rhode Island's ratification of the Constitution came on May 29, 1790. James Madison had earlier proposed a series of amendments to the Constitution during the initial sessions of the first Congress. Eventually ten of these amendments were ratified in late 1791 and would become known collectively as the Bill of Rights, appeasing many critics of the new Constitution.

6 The census showed that there were 4,421 slaves in Orange County and 4,500 free inhabitants. See the Historic Census Browser at the University of Virginia available at http://mapserver.lib.virginia.edu/php/state.php.

7 "Heads of Families," p. 5.

8 The population of Paris in 1790 was 524,186 while London's population in 1801 was 959,300. The combined total of residents living in the five largest American cities was just 126,105 people, which represented just 24% of the population of Paris.

9 Benjamin Franklin had died in Philadelphia on April 17, 1790. He is buried on the grounds of Christ Church located at the corner of 5th and Arch Streets.

10 Philadelphia's population was approximately 30,000 in 1793 making it the largest city in the United States. Joseph Wheelan. (2003). *Jefferson's War: America's First War on Terror 1801-1805.* New York, Carroll & Graf Publishers, p. 63.

11 Thomas Jefferson letter to James Madison, 12 September 1793, quoted in Thomas Mason, Richard Rutland, and Jeanne Sisson, Ed. (1985). *The Papers of James Madison: 24 March 1793-20 April 1795*, Vol. 15. Charlottesville, University Press of Virginia, p. 106.

12 John Todd, Dolley P. Todd, J. Madison Jr., Paul G. Sifton (April 1963). "'What a Dread Prospect...': Dolley Madison's Plague Year." *The Pennsylvania Magazine of History and Biography* 87(2), 182.

13 Dolley Payne Todd letter to James Todd, 4 October 1793, quoted in David B. Mattern and Holly C. Shulman, Ed. (2003). *The Selected Letters of Dolley Payne Madison*. Charlottesville, University of Virginia Press, p. 24.

14 Interestingly, in Dolley Todd Madison's obituary published in New York, the editor remarked about the coincidence of Dolley's birth in North Carolina. He reported: "...although accidently born in another State [she] claim[ed] the title so dear to all who possess it, of being a Virginian." (1849). *The Weekly Herald*, New York. XV, p. 231.

15 In a manumission document witnessed by John Payne, a friend expressed Quaker sentiments eloquently swearing that: "being fully persuaded that freedom is the natural birthright of all mankind and that no Law moral or divine has given me a right to [hold] property in the persons of any of my fellow creatures, and being desirous to fulfil the injunction of our Lord and Savior Jesus Christ by doing to others as I would be done by...release [Betty from bondage]," quoted in Elizabeth Stephens Arnett. *Mrs. James Madison: The Incomparable Dolley*. Greensboro, Piedmont Press, p. 25.

16 Anthony Morris Letter to Anna Cutts 26 June 1837 quoted in Peter, Grace Dunlop (1944). "Unpublished Letters of Dolly Madison to Anthony Morris Relating to the Nourse Family of the Highlands." *Records of the Columbia Historical Society* 44-45, p. 219.

17 Allgor, p. 20.

18 Dolley Madison letter to Anna Cutts 19 August 1805 quoted in Mattern, p. 63.

19 (1837). Mrs. James Madison. *The Madisonian*. Washington, D.C., p. 1.

20 Mattern, p. 14.

21 (1790). *Pennsylania Mercury*. Philadelphia, p. 4.

22 AmericanCatholic.org writes: "[Saint Oswald] was widely known for his sanctity, especially his love for the poor. The final winter of his life was spent at the cathedral in Worcester that he so loved. At the start of Lent in February of the year 992, he resumed his usual practice of washing the feet of 12 poor men each day. On Leap Year Day, February 29, he died after kissing the feet of the 12th man and giving a blessing." The famous Italian composer, Gioacchino Rossini, was born on the same day as Payne Todd. Likewise, Peter Jefferson, Thomas Jefferson's father, was born on February 29, 1708.

23 John Payne died on October 24, 1792. Arnett, p. 47.

24 Kenneth R. Foster, Mary F. Jenkins and Anna Coxe Toogood (1998). "The Philadelphia Yellow Fever Epidemic of 1793." *Scientific American*, p. 89.

25 J. H. Powell (1993). *Bring Out Your Dead: The Great Plague of Yellow Fever in Philadelphia in 1793*. Philadelphia, University of Pennsylvania Press, p. 2.

26 *Ibid.*, p. 17.

27 Dr. Benjamin Rush (1794). *An Account of the Bilious remitting Yellow Fever as it Appeared in the City of Philadelphia in the Year 1793*. Philadelphia, Thomas Dobson: p. 11-12. The Boston Public Library has a copy of the pamphlet that was given by Dr. Rush to Vice President John Adams. It is inscribed: "For John Adams, (to whose worth and fame titles can add nothing) from his old friend: the Author." An online edition of this pamphlet is available at http://ia351426.us.archive.org/3/items/accountofbilious00rush/accountofbilious00rush.pdf.

28 *Ibid.*, p. 113.

29 Thomas Jefferson letter to James Madison, September 1 & 2, 1793, quoted in James Morton Smith, (1995). *The Republic of Letters: The Correspondence between Thomas Jefferson and James Madison 1776-1826.* New York, W.W. Norton & Company: p. 814.

30 Mark A. Smith (Oct. 1996). "Andrew Brown's 'Earnest Endeavor': The *Federal Gazette's Role* in Philadelphia's Yellow Fever Epidemic of 1793." *The Pennsylvania Magazine of History and Biography* 120(4), p. 321.

31 Thomas Jefferson letter to James Madison, 1 September 1793, quoted in Mason, p. 90.

32 Powell, p. 22.

33 *Ibid.*, p. 332.

34 Paul Preston (1914). "Some Incidents of the Yellow Fever Epidemic of 1793." *The Pennsylvania Magazine of History and Biography* 38(2), 238.

35 According to the Journal of American Pediatrics: "Bishop George Berkeley (1685-1753), the Anglo-Irish philosopher and Bishop of Cloyne, a remote diocese in County Cork, published a remarkable book in 1744 on the panacean value of tar-water. Berkeley recommended that tar-water be prepared by pouring a gallon of water over a quart of tar, then stirring and mixing thoroughly for three or four minutes with a ladle or flat stick. After standing for 48 hours to allow the tar to settle, the clear supernatant layer was poured off and kept for use. Berkeley claimed that a pint of tar-water a day would cure almost every disease then known." Available at: http://pediatrics.aappublications.org/cgi/content/abstract/66/6/839.

36 Smith, p. 329.

37 Powell, pp. 11-12.

38 Rush, p. 12.

39 Foster, p. 89. Saint Domingue is now known as Haiti. It was an incredibly profitable French colony providing almost 40% of the entire world's sugar supply. Inspired by the ideals of the French Revolution, however, the slave populations first rebelled in 1791 and large numbers of the French landowners fled the island over the ensuing years. Blacks outnumbered their white overseers by a ration of 10 to 1. Ultimately, France ended slavery in 1794 but unrest continued on the island into the 19th century.

40 Powell, pp. 4-5.

41 Smith, p. 326. The true source of the yellow fever epidemic was the female *Aedes Aegypti* mosquito. It was transmitted only when an infected mosquito bit someone. Patients were not contagious but the spread of the disease was rampant during the hot summer months with the insects were abundant. Dr. Walter Reed is credited with discovering the nature of the disease during the Spanish-American War.

42 Benjamin Rush available at http://www.geocities.com/bobarnebeck/acct99.html.

43 *Ibid.*

44 Thomas Jefferson letter to James Madison, 1 September 1793, quoted in Mason, p. 90.

45 Paul Preston (1914). "Some Incidents of the Yellow Fever Epidemic of 1793." *The Pennsylvania Magazine of History and Biography* 38(2), p. 233-234.

46 Foster, p. 90.

47 Thomas Jefferson letter to James Madison, 8 September 1793, quoted in Mason, p. 104. Madison had left Philadelphia after the Congress adjourned in late winter and returned to Montpelier on March 17.

48 Thomas Jefferson letter to James Madison, 12 September 1793, quoted in Mason, p. 106. Jefferson finally left Pennsylvania for Monticello on September 17, the sixth anniversary of the signing of the United States Constitution.

49 Thomas Jefferson letter to James Madison, 8 September 1793, quoted in Mason, p. 104.

50 Thomas Jefferson letter to James Madison, 12 September 1793, quoted in Mason, p. 106.

51 Arnett, p. 51.

52 James Todd quoted in Todd, p. 184-185. According to Lucia B. Cutts, Dolley Madison's grand-niece, when John Todd arrived at Gray's Ferry, he was met by his mother-in-law and reportedly said, "I feel the fever in my veins, but I must see *her* [Dolley] once more." This seems to be romantic hyperbole rather than an accurate historical account. See Lucia Cutts (1887). *Memoirs and Letters of Dolly Madison: Wife of James Madison, President of the United States.* Boston, Houghton, Mifflin and Company, p. 12-13.

53 James Todd quoted in Arnett, p. 51.

54 Todd, p. 182.

55 Mary Coles Payne quoted in Arnett, p. 52.

56 George Washington letter to James Madison, 14 October 1793, quoted in Mason, pp.126-127.

57 *Ibid.*, pp. 126-127.

58 *Ibid.*, pp. 126-127.

59 *Ibid.*, pp. 126-127.

60 James Madison letter to George Washington, 24 October 1793, quoted in Mason, p. 129.

61 John Beckley letter to James Madison, 20 November 1793 quoted in Mason, pp. 140-141.

62 John Todd quoted in Allan Clark (1914). *The Life and Letters of Dolly Madison.* Washington, D.C., W.F. Roberts Company, p. 502.

63 *Ibid.*, p. 502.

64 Since both of John Todd's parents had died the previous year from yellow fever, Dolley also stood to inherit from that estate as well. This exacerbated the conflict with her brother-in-law, James Todd.

65 Dolley Madison letter to James Todd, 7 February 1794, quoted in Arnett, p. 54.

66 Dolley Madison letter to James Todd quoted in Mattern, *Selected Letters*, p. 25.

67 Anthony Morris quoted in Mattern, p. 16.

68 Will of Dolley Payne Todd, 13 May 1794, quoted in Mattern, p. 27.

69 Eliza Collins quoted in Clark, p. 19.

70 William Hutchinson , Ed. (1969). *The Papers of James Madison* Vol. VI *1783 January 1—30 April 1783*, Vol. 6. Chicago, University of Chicago Press, p 182.

71 James Madison letter to Thomas Jefferson, 22 April 1783, quoted in Hutchinson, p. 481.

72 Ketcham, p. 110. Kitty Floyd did, in fact, marry her new paramour, 19-year old medical student, William Clarkson. The couple had three children. Clarkson died in 1817; Kitty died in 1832 at age 62 and was buried in Brooklyn.

73 Thomas Jefferson letter to James Madison, 31 August 1783, quoted in Hutchinson, p. 298.

74 Dolley Payne Todd quoted in Clark, p. 19.

75 Brandt, p. 407.

76 Martha Washington quoted in Moore, p. 11.

77 Brandt, p. 413.

78 William Wilkins letter to Dolley Payne Todd, 22 August 1794, quoted in Mattern, *Selected Letters*, p. 29.

79 *Ibid.*, p. 29-30.

80 Eliza Washington Wills, "The Wedding of Dolly Payne Todd and James Madison," *Magazine of Jefferson County Historical Society*: Vol 1, Dec. 1935, p. 28.

81 Light Horse Harry Lee would eventually father Robert E. Lee, who would gain fame as the Confederacy's most renowned general during the American Civil War.

82 Dolley Payne Madison to Eliza Collins Lee, 16 September 1794, quoted in Mattern, *Selected Letters*, p. 31.

83 *Ibid.*, p. 31.

84 Ketcham, p. 282.

85 James Madison quoted in Willis, p. 29.

86 Moore, p. 48.

87 Holly Shulman, "History, Memory, and Dolley Madison," in Catherine Allgor, Ed. (2012). *The Queen of America: Mary Cutt's Life of Dolley Madison*. Charlottesville, University of Virginia Press, pp. 48-49.

88 The full name of the treaty was actually the Treaty of Amity, Commerce, and Navigation, Between His Britannic Majesty and The United States of America.

89 James Madison letter to Thomas Jefferson, 10 December 1796, quoted in J.C.A. Stagg, Ed. (1989). *The Papers of James Madison 27 April 1795—27 March 1797*, Vol. 16. Charlottesville, University Press of Virginia, pp. 422-423.

90 James Madison letter to Thomas Jefferson, 19 December 1796, quoted in Stagg, p. 433.

91 Thomas Jefferson letter to James Madison, 1 January 1797, quoted in Stagg, p. 440.

92 James Madison letter to James Madison, Sr., 19 March 1797, quoted in Stagg, p. 501.

93 John Adams letter to Abigail Adams quoted in Mattern, *Selected Letters*, p. 19.

94 Bryan Clark Green, Ann L. Miller, and Conover Hunt (2007). *Building a President's House: The Construction of Montpelier*. Orange, Virginia, The Montpelier Foundation, p. 5. The Madison family had lived in Orange County for over six decades. In 1732, James Madison's grandfather, Ambrose, first settled on the estate which he initially christened Mount Pleasant. It was a primitive settlement, very much a frontier outpost located in the colony's isolated piedmont region, far from the great estates of the First Families of Virginia located along the banks of the James, York, Rappahannock, and Potomac Rivers. Ambrose Madison had 29 slaves working on the new plantation. However, within a few months, Madison became extremely sick and unexpectedly died on August 28, 1732 apparently after having been poisoned. Three slaves—Pompey, Turk, and Dido—were accused of "feloniously Conspiring the Death of Ambrose Madison" and placed on trial. Pompey was convicted and promptly executed while the other two slaves were deemed to have been in collusion and sentenced to 29 lashes each. See Douglas B. Chambers (2005). *Murder at Montpelier: Igbo Africans in Virginia*. Jackson, MI., University Press of Mississippi, pp. 5, 198.

95 Mark Knukel quoted in Moore, p. 148.

96 *Ibid.*, p. 148.

97 *Ibid.*, p. 144.

98 *Ibid.*, p. 164.

99 Charles Pinckney letter to James Madison, 26 October 1800, quoted in David Mattern, Ed. (1991). *The Papers of James Madison: 31 March 1797—3 March 1801*, Vol. 17. Charlottesville, University Press of Virginia, pp. 427-428

100 Under the original provisions of the Constitution, the state electors for president cast two votes but were unable to distinguish between their preference for president and vice president. The individual who finished second in the overall electoral balloting for president would automatically become the new vice president. In 1796, the Federalist, John Adams, received 71 electoral votes while the Republican, Thomas Jefferson, finished second with 68. This proved to be an extremely awkward situation since the two men were political opponents and represented different political parties. This issue was resolved with the ratification of the XII Amendment to the Constitution in 1803 which now provides for separate balloting for president and vice president.

101 The Alien and Sedition Acts. See the Avalon project at http://avalon.law.yale.edu.

102 Thomas Jefferson quoted in Ketcham, p. 394.

103 James Madison quoted in Mattern *Selected Letters*, p. 21.

104 James Madison quoted in Mattern, Vol. 17, p. 295.

Chapter Two

1800 - 1809

"I regret that I am now to die in the belief that the useless sacrifice of themselves, by the generation of 76, to acquire self government and happiness to their country, is to be thrown away by the unwise and unworthy passions of their sons and that my only consolation is to be that I live not to weep over it."

Thomas Jefferson

T*he Constitution had been ratified by the prerequisite nine states in 1788, just twelve years earlier. At the advent of the 19th Century, the United States of America was still politically immature. The British viewed their former colonies with a mixture of contempt and arrogance while George III's nemesis, France, conversely saw the infant American republic as forgetful and ungrateful. Indeed, the Americans seemed oblivious to the pivotal role that France had played during the struggle for independency during the American Revolution.*

Thomas Jefferson's election to the presidency in 1800 was viewed by his many supporters as the ultimate triumph of republicanism. The rival Federalist Party had been conquered and vanquished and the nation's future seemed to be securely in the hands of the champions of the agrarian famer and in the noble ideals of the Enlightenment. The Jeffersonians foresaw an entirely new epoch in world history, one in which peace and prosperity would reign, free from monarchies, high taxes and crippling debt.[1] But like many idealists and great thinkers, Thomas Jefferson himself failed to comprehend

*the more mundane aspects of human
nature, and this inevitably made him
a poor politician and an even worse
governor. His presidency would last
eight years but his noteworthy accomplishments were confined to his
first term. Indeed, the purchase of the
vast Louisiana Territory (1803) from
the financially needy Napoleon effectively doubling the size of the United
States and it was acquired for a pit-
tance—just three cents an acre. Fourteen new states would ultimately be
carved from this land mass and the
nation's westward expansion as well
as its manifest destiny was secured.
Jefferson's other memorable triumph
was sponsoring the Lewis and Clark*

Thomas Jefferson, the nation's third President of the United States. His election was
often referred to as the Revolution of 1800
and the triumph of republicanism. (Library
of Congress)

*expedition. The so-called Corps of Discovery departed St. Louis on
May 14, 1804, and for the next two years, the explorers traversed
and explored the vast continent in what historian Gordon Wood
aptly describes as "the greatest adventure of exploration in American history."[2] The explorers returned with botanical samples, ani-
mal skins, and incredible stories of the vast unexplored lands to the
west. Jefferson even proudly displayed a caged grizzly bears on the
grounds of the President's Palace to the delight and amazement of
area residents.[3]*

*Ironically, the peace-loving Jefferson administration would also
wage the country's first major foreign war, a conflict against a group
of rogue Islamic states in the western Mediterranean.[4] Despite the
obvious need for a suitable military, the President persistently disparaged standing armies and the military. He instead approved the
construction of several small, poorly armed, shallow water coastal
skiffs rather than building powerful, heavily-armed seafaring frig-*

ates. *This ill-advised policy ultimately left the United States unprepared to counter growing threats to its neutrality and its essential mercantile trade, as both the French and the British violated American shipping rights with impunity. Jefferson's inept solution was to self-impose an economic embargo, a policy that further crippled the country's fragile economy while alienating and infuriating New England merchants.*

During Jefferson's administration, his native state of Virginia continued to decline in both political and economic importance. The "Old Dominion" was supplanted by New York as the country's most populous state, while its financial influence waned as the state's plantation economy completely collapsed. Tobacco, once the valued cash crop that had funded and fueled the American Revolution, had by now so depleted the soil that vast acreages of land remained unproductive and fallow while the once great manor houses of the Tidewater gentry were neglected and slowly rotting away. Still, slaves constituted almost 40% of the Virginia population but most were unproductive and inefficient. Ironically, in 1808 after the abolition of the international slave trade, slaves became even more valuable as a commodity since the supply was curtailed. Large plantation owners in the old tobacco regions began to traffic in human cargo, selling domestically bred slaves to the deep cotton south.[5]

In 1809, Jefferson's close friend, James Madison, succeeded him to the presidency. The author of the Declaration of Independence gladly retired to his home in Charlottesville noting that: "I look with infinite joy to the moment when I shall be ultimately moored in the midst of my affections, and free to follow the pursuits of my choice."[6] He left Madison with a series of pressing economic and foreign policy problems. With Napoleon dominating the European continent and Britain determined to impress American sailors into service, the nation was perilously close to being dragged into a major conflict which it had little interest or stake. Still, in his State of the Union address delivered on November 29, 1809, Madison opti-

*mistically stated: "In the midst of the wrongs and vexations experi-
enced from external causes there is much room for congratulation
on the prosperity and happiness flowing from our situation at home.
The blessing of health has never been more universal. The fruits of
the seasons, though in particular articles and districts short of their
usual redundancy, are more than sufficient for our wants and our
comforts. The face of our country every presents evidence of laud-
able enterprise, of extensive capital, and of durable improvement."[7]*

WASHINGTON CITY WAS STILL unfinished when President John Adams arrived on November 1, 1800 to take up
residence at the newly built, albeit unfinished, President's House.
The next day he wrote in a letter to his wife, Abigail: "I pray heaven to bestow the best of blessings in this house and all that shall
hereafter inhabit. May none but honest and wise men ever rule under this roof."[8] The First Lady joined her husband two weeks later
on November 16, delayed after having become hopelessly lost in
Maryland. Apparently, few citizens knew the exact location of the
new federal capital. Abigail was sorely disappointed by the primitive conditions she saw after finally reaching the city. She lamented:
"Washington City [is] not a city at all."[9] Albert Gallatin, who was
then serving as a member of Congress, confirmed her bleak assessment writing that: "Our location is far from being pleasant or even
convenient. Around the Capitol are seven or eight boarding houses,
one tailor, one shoemaker, one printer, a washing-woman, a grocery
shop, a pamphlets and stationery shop, a small dry goods shop, and
an oyster house. This makes the whole of the Federal City as connected with the Capitol."[10] Another young Congressman, John Randolph of Roanoke, was disgusted with Washington, asserting that it
consisted of "bad accommodations, worse roads, extravagant bills,
yea, and even of drunken society."[11]

Abigail Adams was also distressed by the recent news of the deteriorating health of her severely depressed and alcoholic son, Charles. She wrote that he was "laid upon a Bed of sickness, destitute of a home. The kindness of a friend afforded him asylum. A distressing cough, an affection of the liver and a dropsy will soon terminate a life."[12]

The President and First Lady were also anxiously awaiting the final state returns from the recent presidential contest. They were preparing themselves for bad news which seemed to be increasingly inevitable. Adams' Federalist Party was in a state of political decline while Thomas Jefferson and his Republican Party was in its ascendency. The Republicans enjoyed considerable support throughout the various state legislatures where the selection of the presidential electors would ultimately be determined.[13] In the interim, a letter arrived on December 3 which informed John and Abigail that their 30-year old Charles had, in fact, died two days

President John Adams. In December 1800, Adams learned that he had lost his bid for re-election and that his son, Charlie, had died from alcoholism. (National Archives)

earlier from complications of his alcoholism.[14] The young man had been a constant source of embarrassment and heartache for the first couple throughout their marriage but it was nevertheless shocking and horrific news. His precipitous emotional and physical decline had begun early while attending Harvard. There, Charlie had almost been expelled for his garish behavior when he and a group of his roguish friends were accused of running through Harvard Yard naked in a drunken stupor.[15] As an adult, Charlie spent lavishly and foolishly, which led Abigail to bitterly complain that "his conduct does not meet my wishes."[16] His exasperated father was typically more blunt and laconic in his assessment writing: "[My son is a] Madman possessed by the Devil…[a] mere rake, buck, blood, and beast…I renounce him."[17] In a subsequent letter he wrote: "I cannot bear the trouble with children at my age…[My] son bring[s] down my gray hairs with sorrow to the grave."[18] Now in her grief, though, Abigail was a more forgiving mother. She confided to her sister that Charles final illness "was rapid, and through the last part of his life, dreadfully painful and distressing…His mind at times was much deranged…[but] he was no man's enemy but his own."[19]

Adding to John and Abigail's distress was that by the end of the year, it was apparent that Adams had indeed failed to win re-election. For the first time in America's brief history, an incumbent president had been defeated. Although Adams' fate was no longer in question, there was a serious constitutional crisis developing caused by a procedural quirk which had resulted in an electoral tie between Thomas Jefferson and his vice presidential choice, Aaron Burr.[20] In such a case, the Constitution empowered the House of Representatives to select the new president. It still took 36 ballots and until February 17 to break the deadlock with Jefferson elected as the nation's third president. During the turmoil, the lame duck, John Adams, continued to make a series of controversial lifetime appointments to the federal judiciary which included that of John Marshall as the new Chief Justice of the United States Supreme Court.

On inauguration day, John Adams quietly and without ceremony left Washington during the early morning hours of March 4, 1801. He was well en route back to his Massachusetts home when Thomas Jefferson was formally sworn in at the new Capitol as president.[21] Adams was a bitter and disillusioned man. For years, he had been mercilessly abused, slandered, and maligned by his political opponents so he was now ready to retire to the peace and tranquility of his home in Quincy. It would be there that he would await the ultimate judgment of history and his final vindication.

JEFFERSON WAS AT HIS rhetorical best in delivering his first inaugural address, although it was easy to be magnanimous in victory. Before the gathered members of Congress, he proclaimed: "But every difference of opinion is not a difference of principle. We have called by different names brethren of the same principle. We are all Republicans, we are all Federalists. If there be any among us who would wish to dissolve this Union or to change its republican form, let them stand undisturbed as monuments of the safety with which error of opinion may be tolerated where reason is left free to combat it. I know, indeed, that some honest men fear that a republican government can not be strong, that this Government is not strong enough; but would the honest patriot, it the full tide of successful experiment, abandon a government which has so far kept us free and firm on the theoretic and visionary fear that this Government, the world's best hope, may by possibility want energy to preserve itself? I trust not. I believe this, on the contrary, the strongest Government on earth."[22] Margaret Bayard Smith who was in attendance in the Senate Chambers during Jefferson's speech, observed: "I listened to an address containing the principles the most correct, sentiments the most liberal, and wishes the most benevolent conveyed in the most appropriate and elegant language and in a manner mild as it was firm. If doubts of the integrity and talents of Mr. Jefferson ever existed in the minds of one, methinks this address must forever eradicate them."[23]

The very next day, Jefferson sent his appointment of James Madison as the nation's new Secretary of State to the Senate for confirmation. James and Dolley Madison, though, were still at Montpelier. Madison's father had died just a few days earlier and as the executor of the estate, he was preoccupied with personal and family matters.[24] It would not be until May that Madison, accompanied by his wife Dolley, stepson Payne, and sister-in-law Anna, would arrive in Washington.

The family was initially invited to stay at the President's Palace with Jefferson but within a few weeks, they relocated to temporary lodgings at 2113 Pennsylvania Avenue in one of the Six Buildings located between 21st and 22nd Streets. They would later move to an impressive brick house at 1333 F Street just two blocks east of the President's Palace.[25]

A Civil War era photograph (circa 1865) of the Madison's home at 1333 F Street, NW. The Madisons lived here during the Jefferson administration. During the Civil War it served as the headquarters for the Sanitary Commission which was chartered to help sick and wounded soldiers.(Library of Congress)

DURING THE WINTER OF 1803, Payne Todd turned eleven years old and it was becoming increasingly obvious that the boy was reaching a critical juncture in his intellectual development. At a similar age in 1762, his stepfather was attending Donald Robertson's boarding school in King and Queen County, Virginia. It was there that a young "Jemmy" Madison was able to partake in his teacher's extensive private library and where he was first introduced to such important Enlightenment thinkers as John Locke, Charles-Louis Montesquieu, and Jean-Jacques Rousseau. [26] Robertson's influence on Madison's academic and intellectual life was profound and he would always remember his first teacher fondly, once writing that: "All that I have been in my life, I owe largely to this man." [27]

Yet despite Madison's best efforts to tutor Payne personally, his new position as Secretary of State precluded him from devoting sufficient time to properly monitor his stepson's schooling. Madison once lamented that "I am endeavoring to keep him in some sort of attention to his books [and to keep him] in the path of the Student. The close employment of my time, at this juncture leaves much to his own disposition." [28] It was obvious that the undisciplined boy needed far more structure and discipline in his schooling. There was, however, a promising alternative located just across the Potomac River—the Alexandria Academy. [29]

The school had been initially founded by George Washington in 1785 and was considered to be a remarkably progressive institution for its time. Washington had always been self-conscious and uncomfortable about his own lack of formal education so during his initial retirement from public service, he devoted himself to chartering a school that would educate and improve young children. He generously endowed the new academy with a pledge of £1000 sterling with the caveat that along with its traditional enrollment, the school would be expected to accommodate the academic needs of poor children as well as those of orphans of Continental soldiers who had sacrificed their lives during the American Revolution. Washington further directed that these penurious students would be taught "that kind of education which would be most extensively useful to people of the lower class of citizens, viz.—reading, writing & arithmetic, so as to fit them for the mechanical purposes." [30] It was his hope that the Alexandria Academy would cultivate and nurture what Thomas Jefferson had once referred to as the "genius buried in poverty." [31]

The Alexandria Academy. Originally founded by George Washington, Payne Todd attended classes here for two years while his father was serving as Secretary of State. (Philip Bigler)

During his lifetime, Washington was kept closely informed about the school's progress and its policies. James Muir and Samuel Hanson, two members of the board of trustees for Academy informed the General that: "[We] are happy in reporting that the Pupils acquit themselves very well, and that the plan of teaching appears to us good, and well executed." They did discover, though, that among many of the indigent students, there was a persistent problem with truancy. The two men reported that: "The Teacher informs us that many of them attend very irregularly, owing, as he believes, to the necessity their Parents are under of employing them at home to procure fuel; and for other necessary purposes." To ensure "punctual attendance," the academy initiated a strict policy which forgave only a single unexcused absence while any subsequent missing of classes was cause for immediate expulsion.[32] The teachers and the trustees took their educational responsibilities seriously and they were determined to provide a structured environment that was conducive to learning. The Alexandria Academy seemed to be an ideal placement for the academically indifferent Payne.

James Madison was further pleased that the school was staffed primarily by teachers from his own alma mater, Princeton. These educators were well-renowned for their academic prowess as well as their intellectual rigor. Moreover, the academy offered a challenging classical curriculum which would help young Payne in his ongoing preparation for his future college entrance exams. Although while attending the school Payne would be living apart from his parents, he would still be supervised by several friends and relatives who lived in close proximity to the academy.[33]

WITH PAYNE FINALLY ENSCONCED in school, Madison was able to focus on the conduct of the nation's complicated diplomacy. His position as Secretary of State was considered to be the most critical post in the Jefferson administration and there were numerous delicate and unresolved foreign policy issues that required Madison's attention. [34] The most immediate was the ongoing conflict with the rogue Barbary States of Algiers, Morocco, and Tunis. Their pirate corsairs were continually preying upon vulnerable, unarmed mercantile shipping in the western Mediterranean. Without a powerful naval presence in the region to counter the Arab threat, the various pashas felt emboldened and regularly seized American vessels. They were able to do this without serious consequences and the captured sailors were held hostage under brutal conditions while ransom demands were made and tribute extorted. The American crews, during their prolonged and pitiful captivity, were forced into virtual slavery and had to endure unimaginable physical hardships. Many were compelled to convert to Islam prompting the American consul to Tunis, William Eaton, to inform the State Department that the sailors were being "dragged to Slavery and goaded to a lingering death under the bastinade of merciless robbers."[35]

Meanwhile, Napoleon Bonaparte was successfully consolidating his personal and political power in France while advancing his considerable military ambitions. To finance his growing megalomania, the French government was actively engaged in negotiations with American diplomats for the purchase of the vast French-held Louisiana territory. The British were understandably concerned and hoped to thwart Napoleon's global aspirations. But in order to maintain the nation's military superiority, the royal navy was compelled to engage in its noxious policy of impressing American seamen to fully crew its massive fleet of warships. This practice was an ongoing source of contention between the American and British governments and both Jefferson and Madison hoped to reach a quick diplomatic solution to end the despicable practice.

In 1803, the British crown appointed Anthony Merry to serve as their "Envoy Extraordinary and Minister Plenipotentiary to the United States."[36] Merry was, in fact, an experienced diplomat but this new assignment was his first posting since his recent marriage to Elizabeth Leathes. James Monroe, the American minister to England, was initially optimistic about the new appointment and informed Secretary of State Madison that: "Mr. Merry appears to me to be a man of candour & good views, and I think the more full & frank you are with him…the better the effect will be."[37]

The Merry's arrived in the United States via the port of Norfolk on November 4, 1803. After a brief respite, they continued their journey on to Washington in Merry's words: "anxious to fulfill the Commands of the King my Master, who has been graciously pleased to appoint me His Minister to the United States of America."[38] Upon their arrival in the embryonic capital, the new British minister immediately requested an audience with Secretary of State Madison and President Jefferson in order to formally present his diplomatic credentials.

The Jefferson administration, however, in fidelity to their proclaimed egalitarian republican principles had abolished much of the formal diplomatic protocol that had been established during the earlier Federalist administrations of Washington and Adams. Jefferson naively believed that all individuals should be treated equally regardless of their office or official rank. He personally dispensed with any superfluous decorum or artificial ceremony and did so without any regard or concern for long-standing European traditions, customs, and protocol. Thus, when Ambassador Merry was finally able to call upon the President at his Pennsylvania Avenue residence on November 29, he was astonished that Jefferson greeted him informally while casually dressed "…[in] an old brown coat, red waistcoat, old corduroy small clothes much soiled, woolen hose and slippers without heels." [39] It was a violation of all diplomatic convention and Merry took this unceremonious reception as a personal slight as well as an insult to his Majesty, George III.[40]

Matters got progressively worse when Anthony and Elizabeth Merry were invited to attend an official dinner hosted by Jefferson at the executive mansion on December 2. Etiquette dictated that the

President, as the nation's head-of-state, escort the wife of the senior ambassador to the dinner table, but Jefferson, oblivious to such niceties, instead spontaneously offered his arm to Dolley Madison.[41] Other government officials followed his example and selected their escorts without any regard to diplomatic rank or status. This same *pêle mêle* seating was repeated a few days later at a dinner hosted by the Madison's at their F Street home.[42] Afterwards, the much insulted Elizabeth Merry observed with scorn that the occasion was "more like a harvest-home supper, than the entertainment of a Secretary of State."[43] Her husband concluded that these personal snubs were, in fact, intentional and "a studied Design (possibly with some view to their internal Politics) to degrade the Character of a Foreign Minister." He conveyed his concerns to his superiors in England.[44]

An invitiation to dinner at the Madison's home, May 1807. The Madison's were gracious hosts while living in Washington, D.C., but they often failed to follow traditional European protocals. This offended the British ambassador, Anthony Merry, and his wife, Elizabeth. Mrs Merry denounced one Madison dinner as little more than a "harvest-home supper." (Greensboro Historical Museum)

There was already a widely held suspicion among the British delegation that the new Republican administration retained strong pro-French sympathies. These misgivings were apparently confirmed when the Baltimore-born Elizabeth "Betsy" Patterson married Jerome Bonaparte, the French emperor's younger brother (See Appendix F). Jefferson personally hosted a reception in honor of the young couple's wedding and the event was widely attended and well publicized. At this and other soirees, the beautiful and vivacious Betsy Bonaparte scandalized many of the invited guests by wearing so little that, as one individual observed: "she makes no secret of her anatomy."[45] Vice President Aaron Burr noted that: "I am sure that I could stuff all of her dresses together into my pocket and mistake them for my handkerchiefs."[46] The newlyweds presently became close friends of the Madison's and even spent a few days with them at their Washington residence during their extended honeymoon.[47]

During the cold Washington winter of 1804, the Merry's were invited to attend a gala ball hosted by the Secretary of the Navy, Robert Smith. Elizabeth Merry fully expected to be the evening's center of attention and she arrived elegantly costumed and adorned for the special occasion. To her shock, she was upstaged by the appearance of the stunning Betsy Bonaparte, who, once again, was scantily dressed. One of the party guests, Margaret Smith, observed that "mobs of boys have crowded round her splendid equipage to see what I hope will not often be seen in this country, an almost naked woman."[48] She continued: "her appearance was such that it threw all the company into confusion, and no one dar'd to look at her but by stealth; the window shutters being left open, a crowd assembled round the windows to get a look at this beautiful little creature, for every one allows she is extremely beautiful. Her dress was the thinnest sarcenet and white crepe without the least stiffening in it…there was scarcely any waist to it and no sleeves; her back, her bosom, part of her waist and her arms were uncover'd and the rest of her form visible."[49] On a subsequent occasion, another witness observed: "The state of nudity in which she appeared attracted the attention of the Gentlemen, for I saw several of them take a look at her bubbies while they were conversing with her."[50] A young Phoebe Morris, though, was completely captivated and enthralled by the beautiful Mrs. Bonaparte writing, that she had "never beheld a human form so faultless…[it was] impossible to look at any one else."[51] Elizabeth Merry, as well as many other Washington wives, were furious and perhaps a bit jealous of Betsy. They steadfastly refused to attend any further social functions with Mrs. Bonaparte until she "put more clothes on."[52]

Elizabeth Merry was rapidly becoming disillusioned and dispirited by her husband's diplomatic posting. Washington, D.C. defied all of her European sensibilities with its primitive living conditions and pedestrian social scene. She wrote privately expressing her utter disgust with the city, stating: "The Capital—good heavens, what a profanation!! Here is a creek, too—a dirty arm of the river—which they have dignified by calling it the Tiber. What patience one need have with ignorance and self-conceit."[53]

As an ominous diplomatic rift between Britain and the United States widened, the Merry's chose to socially isolate themselves and refused further social invitations from administration officials. The ambassador, to his credit, continued to conduct his official business in a professional manner, but Secretary of State Madison was still concerned about the potential adverse impact that the series of diplomatic blunders and *faux pas* would have on Anglo-American relations. He felt compelled to inform the American ambassador to England, James Monroe, of all that had recently transpired. In a truly remarkable, extensive multi-page communiqué, Madison began: "I think it proper therefore, nauseous as such a subject is, to put you in full possession of it, that misconceptions may be rectified if any should prevail where you are, that you may in particular, obviate political inferences from this frivolous incident."[54] He then proceeded to provide an extensive chronicle of the misunderstand-ings between the American government and the ambassador beginning with Merry's first introduction to President Jefferson. Madison explained, "I found [Merry] had been deeply wounded, and into a recital of causes, some of which had never been dreampt of. His first complaint was that althou' he had according to instructions waited on the President at his audience, in the fullest dress, he had been recd, not even in such a dress as the P. generally has on in the afternoon, but in the plainer dress of the morning. He was told that the P. did not observe these distinctions of dress, more than others in this country, and that he had recd. A Danish Minister, the only one who had come hither during his administration, in the same plain manner."[55] A clearly irritated Madison concluded that: "I blush at having put so much trash on paper."[56]

The secretary to the British legation felt that the Merry's had, indeed, been slighted and disparaged. He concluded that the United States "is indeed a country not fit for a dog."[57] It was an inauspicious beginning for Madison's tenure as the nation's Secretary of State.

AROUND THIS SAME TIME, the renowned portrait painter, Gilbert Stuart, had arrived in Washington, D.C. He had just turned 48-years old in December 1803, and with the assistance of Benjamin Latrobe, the architect of the Capitol, was able to set up a small studio where he could work and solicit clients.[58] For the next twenty months, Stuart would successfully capture the images of many of the new republics most notable and prominent citizens and he did so for a considerable fee of $200.[59]

Stuart's growing body of artistic work was greatly admired throughout the country. His portraits of George Washington were particularly popular since the General had become virtually a secular icon and symbol for the infant nation. Stuart successfully capitalized and profited on the public's insatiable demand for Washington's likeness but despite his fortune and fame, Stuart had earned a reputation of being temperamental and difficult man. Charles Willson Peale recalled that the painter was, in fact: "an indolent, thoughtless being." His excessive drinking further exacerbated his many personality flaws.[60]

Stuart refused to listen to any criticism or to take advice claiming that he could not "paint by direction."[61] When one dissatisfied customer complained that Stuart had failed to accurately depict his wife in a painting, the artist angrily retorted: "What damned business is this of a portrait painter. You bring him a potato and expect he will paint a peach."[62] Still, there were few people who would deny this petulant and irascible painter's considerable talent and Stuart remained in much demand. One patron wrote to Dolley Madison: "Stuart is all the rage. He is almost worked to death and everyone is afraid they will be the last to be finished."[63]

In order to produce his portraits more quickly, Stuart chose to paint only the heads of his subjects from live sittings. To save time and effort, he would later line up a series of unfinished canvases and paint-in nearly identical backdrops and add generic torsos. It was a clever way of mass producing portraits, but to mollify his customers' considerable egos, he always inserted a few personalized items to distinguish each painting.[64]

Dolley Madison became one of Stuart's greatest patrons and advocates. She encouraged her friends and acquaintances to frequent his studio and have their portraits done. In 1804, Dolley and her husband sat for their own personal portraits. At age 35, Dolley was elegant and sophisticated, at the peak of her beauty and Stuart successfully captured this on his canvas. In June of that year, Dolley wrote that "Stuart has taken an admirable likeness of Mr. Madison; both his and mine are finished."[65] The two finished portraits became among the most cherished possessions of the Madison's and they were prominently displayed in the drawing room at their Montpelier home in Virginia.[66]

The Gilbert Stuart portrait of Dolley Madison. The painting was one of her favorites and was displayed in the drawing room at Montpelier. Today, it is exhibited in the Red Room at the White House. (White House Historical Association)

ON MARCH 30, 1804, Dolley's beloved sister, Anna, married Congressman Richard Cutts of Massachusetts at the Madison's home in Washington, D.C.[67] Dolley had been her sister's constant companion and guardian for well over twelve years and during that time, the two sisters had been virtually inseparable. So the occasion proved to be bittersweet, filled with joy but also tempered by an impending sense of loss. Although Anna and Dolley would maintain a regular correspondence over the years, their relationship would be forever altered as Dolley later lamented in a letter to her now absent sister: "If Payne was a Man Married & gone from me I could not feel more sensibly every thing that regarded him than I do."[68]

Just a few months after the Cutts marriage, ominous news reached the capital that the incumbent Vice President of the United States, Aaron Burr, had shot and killed Alexander Hamilton in a duel held at Weehawken, New Jersey. It was a contemptible and vile act, but for the Madison's there was a family matter of more immediate concern. Their son, Payne Todd, was dangerously ill and bedridden. Dolley was horrified at the prospect that she might lose her sole surviving child and she blamed the stagnate, stale summer air in the nation's capital for causing the boy's sickness. She pined to return to Montpelier and the more genteel climate of the Virginia Piedmont but it was obvious that Payne's health was far too fragile to risk such an arduous journey. In another letter to her sister Anna, she confided that: "Payne continues weak and sick. My prospects rise and fall to sadness as this precious child recovers of declines."[69] Fortunately, the boy illness eventually ran its natural course and Payne recovered sufficiently to return to school in Alexandria.

That fall, Thomas Jefferson was re-elected in a historic electoral landslide. His Federalist opponent, Charles Cotesworth Pinckney, carried just two states (Connecticut and Delaware) and lost in the Electoral College by a lopsided vote of 162 to 14. Jefferson saw his reelection as a vindication of his professed republican principles and ideals. In his less than memorable second inaugural address delivered on Monday March 4, 1805, in the Senate chambers, the President claimed that his administration had "endeavored to cultivate the friendship of all nations."[70] It was, in truth, a hollow declaration since the French and British were now fully engaged in renewed hostilities while American neutrality and mercantile rights were being violated with impunity by both warring countries. Within just two years, the United States Frigate, *Chesapeake*, would be attacked off of the Virginia coast by a British warship. The incident left four American sailors dead and the ship's commander shamefully surrendered the vessel after firing just a single return shot. The entire humiliating episode brought the two nations precariously close to war. Jefferson's anemic response was to declare an economic embargo, but the policy did little to deter the British, and had the adverse effect of crippling New England shipping and mercantile interests. Jefferson's popularity waned as his presidency limped towards an ignominious conclusion.

In June 1805, Dolley Madison developed an ominous looking ulcer on her knee. The doctors were perplexed as to its cause but they ordered bed rest and tried to immobilize the infected leg using tight splints. They feared that with an open wound, Dolley could eventually develop gangrene and this would necessitate amputation, a life-threatening procedure under the best of circumstances.[71] Dolley was dejected and in constant pain. Once again she confided to her sister, Anna Cutts: "I wrote to you from my bed, to which I have been confined for ten days with a bad knee; it has become very painful." She continued, "Two doctors have applied caustic with the hope of getting me well, but Heaven only knows. I feel as if I should never walk again."[72]

Despite her physicians' best efforts, the knee stubbornly refused to respond to any known medical treatments. In late July, James Madison finally decided that his wife's best chance for a cure and recovery was in Philadelphia under the care of the country's leading doctor and surgeon, Philip Syng Physick.[73] Madison arranged for a horse-drawn carriage to transport the couple to Pennsylvania. Driven by a slave, Peter, the grueling journey took four days of travel over rough and nascent roads. En route, the Madison's stopped briefly at Gray's Ferry for breakfast. For Dolley, it was an unhappy reminder of the loss of her first husband and their newborn son, William, during the yellow fever epidemic some 12 years earlier.[74]

After finally arriving in Philadelphia, the Madison's took lodging on Sansom Street. Dr. Physick promptly arrived and examined Dolley's diseased leg. He was optimistic that he could heal her as Dolley explained in a letter written shortly after their arrival: "Doctor Physick has seen it, & says he will cure me in a month—this aught to comfort me—but Anna, if I was not afraid of death I could give way to most immoderate gr[ief]—but fool that I am—here is my beloved Husband siting anxiously by me & who is my unremitting Nurse—but you know how delicate he is I tremble for him—on our way one night he [was]taken very ill with his old bilious complaint I thought all was over with me, I could not fly to him & aid him as I used to do—but Heaven in its mercy restored him next Morning & he would not pause until he hear[d] my fate from Doctor Physick."[75] In fact, Madison loyally refused to leave his beloved wife's bedside and he personally tended to her needs over the next three months. During this prolonged absence from Washington, he attempted to conduct his State Department business through letters, couriers, and written instructions but Dolley's recovery proved to be delicate and prolonged. By October, Madison felt compelled to return to the capital to attend to ongoing foreign policy issues and he reluctantly left Dolley in Philadelphia. It would be the first time in the couple's 12-year marriage that they would be separated for an extended period of time.[76]

During this interlude, the two exchanged numerous letters. Shortly after returning to Washington, Madison somberly wrote to his wife: "I reached the end of my journey on Saturday evening; without accident and in good health. I found your friends here all well. Payne arrived about an hour after I did. I enclose a letter from him with several others." Madison then told Dolley about his efforts to enroll their teenage son at Saint Mary's College in Baltimore so he could continue his studies and eventually enter Princeton upon reaching an appropriate age. He continued: "During my halt at Baltimore, I made two efforts to see Bishop Carroll, but without success...I could do nothing therefore towards getting a b[erth] for Payne in the seminary of Mr. Dubourg. I have lost no time however in making an attempt for the purpose, by a request which is gone in a letter to Bishop Carroll, and if his answer authorizes me, I shall take immediate steps for preventing any further loss of time."[77] On November 1, Dolley wrote to Madison: "Kiss my child for me, and remember me to my friends."[78] She also kept him informed about her progress informing him that "the knee is acquiring strength every day but my nerves are often weak—the Doctor ordered me some drops yesterday which I took—he also directed me to eat meat and drink porter, I take but a morsel of either, having no appetite. I walk about the room and expect a few days more will enable me to ride, no inflammation and the little incision nearly fast, so you may expect me to fly to you as soon—ah!"[79] Still, Dolley's recovery was slow and uneven. On November 14, she wrote to Madison that she felt so poorly that she had trouble writing but that her spirits had been lifted by a welcomed visit from her sister, Anna, and her husband. Two weeks later, though, in late November, Dr. Physick deemed Dolley healed sufficiently to allow her to return to Washington. Dolley eagerly informed her husband: "I will make my preparations to set of[f] on monday. The weather for 3 days has been bad for the roads but hope to get along as far as Chester the first night & by small stages, for as long as I can bear until I am safely lodged in your arms."[80] She would arrive home in time for only a brief reunion with Payne Todd who was now scheduled to begin his studies at Saint Mary's on December 1.

FATHER WILLIAM DUBOURG WAS one of many French émi-
grés who fled to Maryland after the onset of a series the violent slave
rebellions in the Caribbean sugar islands. As a Sulpician priest,
Father DuBourg established a Catholic seminary in Baltimore for
young men to study for the priesthood. A companion academy was
also created to educate young students. This parochial school was
staffed primarily by the seminary but its faculty also included a few
ordained priests as well as some laymen. The school was designed
to provide young children with structure and discipline and featured
a rigorous academic curriculum.[81]

DuBourg's Academy had been renamed Saint Mary's College
in 1801. It initially consisted of just two modest buildings and a
handful of Cuban students. By the time Payne Todd registered for
classes in late 1805, though, the enrollment had swelled to 125 students and most were now native-born Americans.[82] There was, however, a strong public prejudice about educating Protestant boys in a
Catholic school environment. Indeed, throughout the United States,
there existed a fervent anti-Catholic sentiment and many citizens
openly denounced all "Romish" schools and institutions. Written
condemnations of the Pope, priests, and nuns were commonplace in
the nation's newspapers, even those published in Baltimore, a city
with a relatively large Catholic population.[83] To their credit, James
and Dolley Madison did not share in this conventional bigotry.
They were, in fact, remarkably enlightened in their own personal
views concerning religion. Madison had authored one of the most
impressive manifestos for religious tolerance, "the Remonstrance,"
in 1785 and this document had directly led to the passage of the Virginia Statute on Religious Freedom. Similarly, Dolley's own Quaker
background and cosmopolitan upbringing in Philadelphia, meant
that she had no overt objections to her son, Payne, being educated
by Catholic priests and seminarians as long as they provided him
with a quality education and allowed the boy to retain his own personal faith without any proselytizing or theological coercion. Father
DuBourg did accommodate Protestant students by excusing them

St. Mary's College in Baltimore, Maryland. The Catholic school was run by Father William DuBourg, a French priest and educator. Payne Todd studied here for almost seven years. Although he was an undistinguished student, he learned to speak French fluently. (Library of Congress)

from attending daily Mass at St. Mary's but they were still expected to engage in regular prayer. Moreover, the school's rules required all students to show: "a high respect for religion, a great regard for morality, respectful docility to their teachers, [and] union with their fellow students."[84]

The highly structured atmosphere at St. Mary's seemed to be a perfect environment for the increasingly distracted Payne. Dolley desperately hoped that Father Dubourg would be able to focus her son's attention on his education and force him to abandon his bad habits. She confided to her husband: "I am very [grateful] for the prospect you have opened for our child, & shall now look forward to his Manhood, when he will bless—and do honor to his guardians."[85]

For Saint Mary's College to have the distinguished Secretary of State's stepson in attendance added to its prestige and to the delight of Father DuBourg. James Madison wrote to the priest and headmaster: "It affords me great pleasure to learn that the dawn of my son-in-law's deportment is found to be so acceptable. I was fully aware of the little progress he had made in his studies, and was the more anxious on that account that in the future he might have the aids which I doubt not he will experience under your superintendence." Madison then requested that a private tutor be engaged to improve Payne's meager language skills: "I entirely approve the expedient of engaging a female teacher of French, in order to bring him up in that necessary part of his instruction, and will be thankful if you will have one provided. The expense will be attended to in the remittance otherwise to be made."[86]

The curriculum at St. Mary's emphasized the traditional Greek and Latin classics. It also included instruction in natural philosophy, physical science, mathematics, geography, and history. Students were taught penmanship and could elect to take instruction in music and dancing. The school remained in session for 10 months a year with classes beginning on the first Monday in September and continuing until mid-July.[87] Classes began at 8:30 AM and continued until 6:00 PM, with the students allotted a two-hour afternoon break. Strict silence was maintained in all of the classrooms and study areas while the school's written regulations declared that "All games, or diversions of a dangerous tendency, or contrary to good-breeding are forbidden; such as cards, dice, bandies, sticks, slings, bows and arrows, twisted or knotted handkerchiefs, &c. &c. Also the use of fire arms and gunpowder—throwing stones or snow-balls, wrestling, &c. &c. Smoking and chewing—also, all vociferous noise in play."[88] Students were also expected to behave in a gentlemanly manner, not "vandalize" the desks and to show "...a high respect for religion, a great regard for morality, respectful docility to their Teachers, union with their fellow Students."[89]

Over the ensuing years, Madison would regularly send checks to St. Mary's to cover Payne's tuition and considerable living expenses. Once such itemized list included payments of "$79.50 for ta[i]lor and $20 for shoe maker and $3 pair of sheet and $4 for blanket; $12 for washing."[90] Likewise, Payne had to regularly purchase books, postage, slates, and quill pens while living away at school.[91] Father DuBourg, though, was pleased with Payne's initial progress at St. Mary's and in a letter to the Secretary of State, assured Madison that the boy was adjusting very well. DuBourg wrote that: "it is with very great pleasure I repeat the impression of my Personal satisfaction at his application and deportment."[92]

DOLLEY MADISON'S YOUNGEST sibling and her last surviving brother, John C. Payne, was struggling with acute alcoholism. Like his ill-fated brother, Isaac, John's excessive drinking, gambling and reckless lifestyle had only exacerbated his growing financial difficulties and personal problems. His health and emotional well-being was a source of constant worry for Dolley. [93] In an effort to help, Mr. Madison decided to intercede on behalf of his brother-in-law. In 1806, he appointed the 24-year old to serve with a newly formed American diplomatic mission to Tripoli. Although John Payne's secretarial position would have only modest responsibilities and duties, Madison hoped that this overseas posting would isolate him from some of his debauched cronies while providing John with a modicum of self-respect as well as a renewed sense of purpose in life.

On July 12, the American counsel, George Davis, wrote to Dolley Madison from the port of Norfolk to inform her that John had arrived safely. Together they were awaiting ship passage to Gibraltar and then on to Tripoli. Davis reassured Dolley that he would look after her brother's welfare writing: "[I] feel confident, that his new situation however unimportant in itself, will at least call forth those energies of mind, which have been cramped for a want of action; and open an extensive field for advancement. You may rest assured his Interest and happiness is very dear to me; to hasten the one, & secure the other, will be the Ambition of those friends you have committed him to; who in thanking you for this mark of confidence, reciprocate unfeignedly, the prayers you have offered for their well being"[94]

The next year while John was abroad, Dolley's 62-year old mother suffered a "violent stroke of the dead palsy." She died on October 21, 1807 at the Clarksburg residence of her youngest daughter, Mary "Polly" Jackson.[95] In anguish, Dolley wrote: "Deep affliction my dear friend has for some time past arrested my pen! My beloved & tender Mother left us forever, on the 20th [sic] of October last—she was in Virgi[nia] with my youngest sister where she died without suffering or regret—The loss is only ours, & for that only ought we, her children mourn!"[96] To further compound the family tragedy was news that her sister, Polly had also succumbed to illness just four months later at the age of 27.[97]

While Dolley's grief was inconsolable, John Payne remained blissfully ignorant of all that had transpired. He rarely wrote while living in Tripoli and Dolley complained that she did not receive a single letter from her brother in over two years. Finally, in 1809, exasperated and annoyed, she wrote to John about all that had happened during his lengthy absence: "I have written you vols. since your departure…[there have been] many & sad changes in your family, you are yet to weep over—Alas! My Dear John nearly two years have elapsed since the loss of our beloved & sainted mother! Our tender & amiable sister, Polly remained but a few weeks after! Mama was ill but a few days—Polly appeared to be in a decline for some months—she left only one child, little Mary."[98] She added later, perhaps a little sardonically, "Mr. M. who you *must know*, is President of the U.S."[99]

THE ELECTION OF 1808 was to be determined in the various seventeen state legislatures who still retained their power to select electors for president. The heir apparent to Thomas Jefferson was clearly James Madison, the President's closest friend and advisor. The anemic Federalist Party once again chose Charles Cotesworth Pinckney of South Carolina as its candidate. Pinckney's primary political support came from a loose coalition of New England states that had been devastated by the hated Jefferson embargo. The American economy was in shambles. Some 30,000 sailors were idled and unemployed and these angry, crude, and sometimes violent men haunted the nation's closed seaports occupying their time by drinking and whoring. John Randolph of Roanoke called the Jefferson imposed embargo: "the most fatal measure that ever happened to this country."[100]

Despite the nation's discontent, Madison and the Republicans were still able to win a decisive electoral victory. Madison won 122 electoral votes, 33 more than the minimum necessary while Pinckney received just 47 votes. The aged 69-year old George Clinton was reelected as the nation's vice president.

Three days before the advent of the Madison administration, Congress wisely repealed the unpopular embargo act. John Randolph acerbically observed that the Jefferson administration had proven to be an unmitigated disaster. He wrote: "[N]ever has there been any Administration which went out of office & left the nation in a state so deplorable and calamitous as the last." [101]

On inauguration day, March 4, 1809, canons were fired from the Washington Navy Yard and nearby Fort Warburton to salute the president-elect.[102] Madison graciously requested that Thomas Jefferson accompany him in the presidential carriage to the Capitol for the formal ceremonies but the outgoing president politely declined. He instead chose to follow Madison's entourage on horseback "un attended by even a servant, undistinguished in any way from his fellow citizens."[103] Over 10,000 cheering citizens lined the streets to cheer Madison en route to the swearing-in ceremonies.

The formal ceremony was held in the hall of the House of Representatives (now Statutory Hall). The Chief Justice, John Marshall administered the constitutionally prescribed oath-of-office to Madison. Margaret Bayard Smith observed that the new President looked pale and uncertain as he began to deliver his carefully prepared inaugural remarks.[104] After a bit of hesitancy, though, Madison seemed to gain confidence declaring that the Constitution of the United States was the "cement of the Union" and that the federal government's responsibility was "to respect the rights and authorities reserved to the states and to the people...[and] to avoid the slightest interference with the right of conscience or the functions of religion."[105]

Later that evening, the Madison's hosted the nation's first ever inaugural ball. It was held at Long's Hotel on Capitol Hill and was billed as "A Dancing Assembly." Young Payne Todd, on short recess from school, was there to celebrate alongside his parents.[106] Although Dolley did not dance due to her Quaker upbringing, the guests were impressed with the new first lady's impeccable sense of style and elegance. One observer noted: "[Mrs. Madison] looked like a queen...her head dress a turban...with two superb plumes of the bird of paradise feathers...unassuming dignity, sweetness, grace. It seems to me that such manners would disarm envy itself and conciliate even enemies."[107] For the now ex-president Jefferson, though, there was an enormous sense of relief. He remarked: "There is good reason for my happy & his serious looks, I have got the bur[d]en off my shoulders, while [Madison] has now got it on his.'"[108]

A few days later on March 17, Thomas Jefferson, now a private citizen, recounted to Madison his difficult trip back to Charlottesville. In a letter to the new President, he wrote: "I had a very fatiguing journey, having found the roads excessive bad, altho' I have seen them worse. The last three days I found it better to be on horseback, and travelled 8 hours through as disagreeable a snow storm as I was ever in. Feeling no inconvenience from the expedition but fatigue, I have more confidence in my vis vitae than I had before entertained. The spring is remarkably backward. No oats sown, not much tobacco seed, & little done in the gardens."[109] While Jefferson's attentions were now redirected to planting and farming rather than politics, Madison was facing the dangerous consequences of the deterioration of foreign relations between the United States and France and Britain.

An early view of the United States Capitol. There was no dome on the structure in 1809 when James Madison was inaugurated as the nation's fourth President. The new federal capital was still primitive and unfinished. (Library of Congress)

ENDNOTES

Epigraph: The complete quote from Jefferson is as follows: "I regret that I am now to die in the belief that the useless sacrifice of themselves, by the generation of 76, to acquire self-government and happiness to their country, is to be thrown away by the unwise and unworthy passions of their sons and that my only consolation is to be that I live not to weep over it." See Thomas Jefferson letter to John Holmes April 22, 1820 quoted in Virginia Scharff (2010). *The Women Jefferson Loved.* New York, Harper Collins Publisher, p. 361. It is excerpted from the famous "Fire Bell in the Night" letter concerning the Missouri Compromise.

1 Gordon S Wood (2009). *Empire of Liberty: A History of the Early Republic, 1789-1815.* New York, Oxford University Press, p. 277.

2 *Ibid.*, p. 381.

3 Constance McLaughlin Green (1962). *Washington: Village and Capital, 1800-1878.* Princeton, Princeton University Press, pp. 49.

4 One of the best books available on the Barbary Wars is Joseph Wheelan (2003). *Jefferson's War: America's First War on Terror 1801-1805.* New York, Carroll & Graf Publishers.

5 The Constitution authorized Congress to ban the international slave trade in Article I, Section 9: "The Migration or Importation of such Persons as any of the States now existing shall think proper to admit, shall not be prohibited by the Congress prior to the Year one thousand eight hundred and eight, but a Tax or duty may be imposed on such Importation, not exceeding ten dollars for each Person."

6 Thomas Jefferson letter to Martha Jefferson Randolph, 27 February 1809, quoted in Dumas Malone (1974). *Jefferson the President: Second Term 1805-1809.* Boston, Little, Brown & Company, p. 665.

7 James Madison State of the Union Address available at: http://www.answers.com/topic/james-madison-s-first-state-of-the-union-address#ixzz2Znrl82ML.

8 John Adams letter to Abigail Adams, November 2, 1800, quoted in David McCullough, (2001). *John Adams.* New York, Simon & Schuster, p. 551.

9 Abigail Adams quoted in Philip Bigler (1988). *Washington in Focus: The Photo History of the Nation's Capital.* Arlington, VA, Vandamere Press, p. 14.

10 Albert Gallatin quoted in Bigler, p. 14.

11 John Randolph quoted in David Johnson (2012). *John Randolph of Roanoke.* Baton Rouge, Louisiana State University Press, p. 49.

12 Abigail Adams quoted in Jack Shepard (1975). *The Adams Chronicles: Four Generations of Greatness.* New York, Little, Brown & Company, p. 210.

13 There was no popular vote for presidential electors at the time.

14 John and Abigail had five children: Abigail (1765-1813), John Quincy (1767-1848), Susanna (1768-1770), Charles (1770-1800), and Thomas (1772-1832). John Quincy would be the most successful of the offspring and would be elected president in 1824.

15 McCullough, p. 411.

16 Abigail Adams letter to John Quincy Adams quoted in McCullough, p. 514.

17 John Adams quoted in Paul C. Nagel (1983). *Descent from Glory: Four Generations of the John Adams Family*. New York, Oxford University Press, p. 79.

18 John Adams letter to Abigail Adams quoted in Nagel, p. 77.

19 Abigail Adams letter to Mary Smith Cranch quoted in McCullough, p. 555.

20 State electors were each allotted two votes to cast in the election. The Constitution provided that the individual who received the majority of electoral votes would be elected president while the candidate that came in second would become the vice president. In the past, one party elector would intentionally throw away one of his votes so that the preferred vice president would receive one less vote than the president. This did not happen in 1800, which resulted in Jefferson and Burr both receiving the same electoral tally. In such a circumstance, the House of Representatives in empowered to choose the new president. Because of the 1800 electoral controversy, the XII Amendment was ratified in 1804, which provides for separate balloting for president and vice president.

21 McCullough, p. 564.

22 Thomas Jefferson quoted in *Inaugural Addresses of the Presidents of the United States from George Washington 1780 to George Bush 1989* (1989). Washington, D.C., Government Printing Office, p. 15.

23 Margaret Bayard Smith letter to Susan B. Smith, 4 March 1801, quoted in Gary Hunt, Ed. (1906). *The First Forty Years of Washington Society Portrayed by the Family of Letters by Mrs. Samuel (Margaret Bayard) Harrison Smith*. New York, Charles Scribner & Sons, pp. 25-26.

24 James Madison, Sr., March 27, 1723 – February 27, 1801.

25 Virginia Moore (1979). *The Madison's: A Biography*. New York, McGraw-Hill Book Company, p. 159 and David Mattern (2003). The Selected Letters of Dolley Payne Madison. Charlottesville, University of Virginia Press, p. 40.

26 William Hutchinson, Ed. (1962). *The Papers of James Madison 1751 March 16—16 December 1779* Vol. I. Chicago, University of Chicago Press, p. 5.

27 James Madison quoted in Ralph Ketcham (1990). *James Madison: A Biography*. Charlottesville, University of Virginia Press, p. 21.

28 James Madison quoted in Catherine Allgor (2006). *A Perfect Union: Dolley Madison and the Creation of the American Nation*. New York, Henry Holt and Company, p. 112.

29 Alexandria was part of the original 10-mile square District of Columbia. It was returned to Virginia in the 1840's.

30 George Washington quoted in Dorothy Twohig, Ed. (1999). *The Papers of George Washington: Retirement Series April-December 1799*. Charlottesville, University of Virginia Press, p.495.

31 "Genius buried in poverty" is a phrase attributed to Thomas Jefferson. T. Robinson Ahlstrom, Headmaster of the Alexandria Academy, interview by Philip Bigler, July 30, 2010, Alexandria, VA.

32 James Muir and Samuel Hanson quoted in Dorothy Twohig, Ed. (1998). *The Papers of George Washington: Presidential Series December 1790-March 1791*. Charlottesville, University of Virginia Press, pp. 552-553.

33 Moore, p. 173.

34 There were only five cabinet positions at the time: State (James Madison); Treasury (Albert Gallatin); War (Henry Dearborn); Navy (Benjamin Stoddert); and Attorney General (Levi Lincoln).

35 William Eaton quoted in Joseph Wheelan (2003). *Jefferson's War: America's First War on Terror 1801-1805*. New York, Carroll & Graf Publishers, p. 139.

36 Ketcham, p. 432.

37 James Monroe letter to James Madison, 18 September 1803, quoted in David Mattern (2000). *The Papers of James Madison: Secretary of State Series 16 May--31 October 1803*, Vol. 5. Charlottesville, University Press of Virginia, p. 448.

38 Anthony Merry quoted in Mary Hackett, ed. (2002). The Papers of James Madison: Secretary of State Series 1 November 1803--31 March 1804, Vol. 6. Charlottesville, University Press of Virginia, p. 17.

39 Green, pp. 46-47.

40 Mattern. *The Selected Letters*, p. 45.

41 Jefferson had personally drawn up his own "Canons of Etiquette." It stated "At dinners, in public or private, and on all other occasions of social intercourse, a perfect equality exists between the persons composing the company, whether foreign or domestic. To give force to the principle of equality, or pêle mêle, and prevent the growth of precedence out of courtesy, the members of the Executive, at their own houses, will adhere to the ancient usage of their ancestors,--gentlemen en masse giving place to the ladies en masse." See Arnett, p. 143.

42 *Pêle mêle* is of French origin and means literally chaotically or without any order.

43 Elizabeth Merry quoted in Ketcham, p. 46.

44 Anthony Merry quoted in Hackett, p. 187.

45 Claude Bourguignon-Frasseto (2003). *Betsy Bonaparte: The Belle of Baltimore*. Baltimore: The Maryland Historical Society, p. 43.

46 Aaron Burr quoted in Bourguignon-Frasseto, p. 43.

47 *Ibid.*, p. 266. Jerome Bonaparte's brother refused to accept the marriage. Napoleon would deny Elizabeth entry into France. The marriage ultimately ended in divorce. See Appendix F for more information. The Maryland Historical Society is the repository for many items, artifacts, and manuscripts associated with Elizabeth Bonaparte. See http://www.mdhs.org/betsy-bonaparte/.

48 Margaret Smith quoted in Clark, p. 59.

49 Margaret Smith quoted in Arnett, p. 153-154.

50 Helen Jean Burn (2010). *Betsy Bonaparte*. Baltimore, Maryland Historical Society, p. 63.

51 Phoebe Morris quoted in Moore, p. 257

52 Arnett, p. 154.

53 Elizabeth Merry letter to Tom Moore quoted in Clark, p. 59.

54 James Madison letter to James Monroe, 19 January 1804, quoted in Hackett, p. 361.

55 *Ibid.*, p. 362.

56 *Ibid.*, p. 366.

57 Augustus John Foster quoted in Allgor, p. 95.

58 Gilbert Stuart, December 3, 1755 – July 9, 1828.

59 Charles Merrill Mount. "Gilbert Stuart in Washington: With a Catalogue of His Portraits Painted between December 1803 and July 1805," *Records of the Columbia Historical Society*. Vol. 71/72, p. 90.

60 Charles Willson Peale quoted in Mount, p. 81.

61 Gilbert Stuart quoted in Mount, p. 96.

62 *Ibid.*, p. 99.

63 Mount, p. 94.

64 *Ibid.*, p. 91.

65 Dolley Madison quoted in Mount, p. 90.

66 The painting was at Montpelier until after James Madison's death in 1836. Dolley then had them removed to her home in Washington, D.C. After her death, the painting were inherited by Payne Todd and auctioned off. Fortunately, Dolley's niece, Annie Payne Causten was able to successfully bid on the portrait. See "Dolley Madison," available at the White House Historical Association http://www. whitehousehistory.org/whha_about/whitehouse_collection.

67 Moore, pp. 176-177.

68 Dolley Payne Madison letter to Anna Payne Cutts quoted in Allgor, p. 106.

69 Dolly Payne Madison letter to Anna Payne Cutts, 16 July 1804, quoted in Moore, p. 182.

70 Thomas Jefferson quoted in *Inaugural Addresses*, p. 18.

71 Moore, p. 186.

72 Dolley Payne Madison letter to Anna Payne Cutts, 4 June 1805, quoted in Clark, p. 77.

73 Allgor, p. 108.

74 Moore, p. 188.

75 Dolly Payne Madison letter to Anna Cutts, 29 July 1805, quoted in Richard N. Cote (2005). *Strength and Honor: The Life of Dolley Madison*. Mount Pleasant, SC, Corinthian Books, p.242.

76 Allgor, p. 110.

77 James Madison letter to Dolley Payne Madison, 16 October 1805, quoted in Mattern, *Selected Letters*, p. 66.

78 Dolley Payne Madison letter to James Madison, 1 November 1805, quoted in Clark, p. 83.

79 Dolley Payne Madison letter to James Madison, 30 October 1805, quoted in Mattern, *Selected Letters*, pp. 67-68.

80 Dolley Payne Madison letter to James Madison, 23 November 1805, quoted in Mattern, *Selected Letters*, p. 77.

81 The best history of Saint Mary's College is the master's thesis written by Father James Kortenick. It is available at the Saint Mary's Seminary and University Marion Burk Knott Liberty in Baltimore, Maryland. See Rev. James Joseph Kortendick (1942). *The History of St. Mary's College: Baltimore 1799-1852*. Unpublished Master's Thesis in History, Catholic University, pp. 3, 5, and 37.

82 *Ibid.*, pp. 10, 25.

83 *Ibid.*, pp. 27-28.

84 *Ibid.*, pp. 38-39.

85 Dolley Payne Todd quoted in Allgor, p. 112.

86 James Madison letter to Father William DuBourg, 21 December 1805, quoted in Kortenick, pp. 37-38.

87 Kortenick, p. 43.

88 *Ibid.*, pp. 38-39.

89 *Ibid.*, pp. 39.

90 James Madison letter to Father William DuBourg, 10 December 1811, Saint Mary's Seminary archives.

91 J.C.A. Stagg (1992). *The Papers of James Madison: Presidential Series 1 October 1809--2 November 1810*, Vol. 2. Charlottesville, University Press of Virginia, pp. 370-372.

92 Father William DuBourg letter to James Madison, 26 December 1806, letter book #3 at the Saint Mary's Seminary archives.

93 Allgor, p. 208.

94 George Davis letter to Dolley Payne Madison, 12 July 1806, quoted in Mattern, *Selected Letters,* p. 79.

95 Moore, p. 210-211.

96 Dolley Madison quoted in Clark, p. 90.

97 Mary "Polly" Payne Jackson, (Day of Birth unknown) 1781- February 13, 1808.

98 Dolley Payne Madison letter to John C. Payne, 21 September 1809, quoted in Mattern, T*he Selected Letters*, p. 128.

99 *Ibid.*, p. 129.

100 John Randolph quoted in Johnson, p. 134.

101 *Ibid.*, p. 129.

102 Maud Wilder Goodwin, (1897). *Dolly Madison: Women of Colonial and Revolutionary Times*. New York, Charles Scribner's Sons, p. 124.

103 Margaret Bayard Smith quoted in J. Jefferson Looney, Ed. (2004). *The Papers of Thomas Jefferson: Retirement Series March 1809-November 1809*. Princeton, Princeton University Press, p 8.

104 Smith, p. 59.

105 James Madison quoted in Inaugural Addresses of the Presidents of the United States from George Washington 1780 to George Bush 1989 (1989). Washington, D.C., Government Printing Office, p. 27.

106 Moore, p. 222.

107 Smith quoted in Moore, p. 223.

108 Smith quoted in Looney, p. 9.

109 Thomas Jefferson letter to James Madison, 17 March 1809, quoted in Rutland, Robert A., Ed. (1984). *The Papers of James Madison: Presidential Series 1 March--30 September 1809*, Vol. 1. Charlottesville, University Press of Virginia, p. 59.

Chapter Three

1810 - 1819

"Bonaparte hates our government because it is a living libel on his, [and] the English hate us because they think our prosperity filched from theirs."

Thomas Jefferson

James Madison became the third Virginian elected to America's nascent presidency in December 1808.[1] Many critics, especially in the New England states, decried what they perceived to be a de facto Virginia dynasty ruling the country, but in truth, the United States was rapidly changing demographically. The 1810 census revealed that the country's population had increased to just over seven million people while new states were being added on a regular basis slowly shifting political power away from the original 13 colonies. Over the ensuing decade, six more states (Louisiana, Mississippi, Alabama, Illinois, Indiana, and Maine) would be added to the union as Americans continued their relentless migration westward. Meanwhile, New York City remained the country's most important economic port and its most populous city, with 96,373 residents in 1810.

Despite the end in 1808 to the international slave trade by Congressional fiat (2 Stat. 426), slavery as an institution continued to flourish.[2] At the beginning of the decade, there were 1,191,362 enslaved people living within the United States, with Virginia continu-

87

ing to hold the dubious distinction of being the largest slave-holding state. Indeed, slaves constituted one-third (392,518) of the Old Dominion's population despite a precipitous decline in tobacco prices and its production. Most of the state's plantation owners were shifting to growing wheat and grain crops that were far less labor intensive, but this change only augmented the state's growing surplus of slaves. The demand for chattel labor was shifting increasingly to the warmer climates of the Deep South with its long growing season. Furthermore, Eli Whitney's invention of the cotton gin (1793) had revolutionized the region's agriculture by mechanizing the removal of seeds from cotton fibers. The crop was now the staple of the economy of the agrarian south, with slavery at its core.

During the era of James Madison's presidency (1809-1817), a new generation of Americans was reaching political maturity. These young, determined, and ambitious men had all been born after the conclusion of the American Revolution and had no direct memories of the divisive philosophical debates over the ratification of the United States Constitution. They had grown accustomed, even complacent, concerning the liberties and rights that had been hard-won during the nation's perilous founding years. They were fierce advocates of continued, unobstructed westward expansion, and patriotic defenders of international navigation rights. Among this new generation of political neophytes were Henry Clay (April 12, 1777-June 29, 1852) of Kentucky, Daniel Webster (January 18, 1782 - October 24, 1852) of Massachusetts, and John C. Calhoun (March 18, 1782 - March 31, 1850) of South Carolina. These three exceptional men were destined to dominate politics and the legislative branch for over four decades and they would define the new character of American politics.

Chief Justice John Marshall, the most notable of John Adams' "midnight appointments," was continuing to make landmark rulings which effectively secured the Supreme Court's place as a co-equal branch of government. Marshall greatly expanded the scope and nature of federal powers in 1819 in the landmark decision, Mc-Culloch v. Maryland (17 US 316), which established the doctrine of implied powers, authorizing broad Congressional discretion and action under the auspices of the Constitution's necessary and proper clause (Article I, Section 8).

While serving as the nation's fourth president, James Madison presided over the republic's first congressionally declared war. Euphemistically referred to as America's Second War for Independence, the War of 1812 pitted a weak, ill-prepared United States against Great Britain, the most powerful military power in the world. Much of the fighting took place on the Great Lakes and along the country's western frontiers. The American military campaigns were often marked by incompetence and failure, leading vocal opponents of the war to brand the entire fiasco as "Mr. Madison's War."

In August 1814, to the country's everlasting shame and humiliation, the new federal capital was unceremoniously sacked and burned by British troops. A group of angry, disgruntled New England Federalists met in convention that December in Hartford, Connecticut, to protest the ineptitude of the Madison administration and became the first group to raise the potential specter of secession from the union. Almost simultaneously, the Treaty of Ghent was signed in Belgium, effectively ending the war on terms that were, in essence, a return to the status quo antebellum. *The treaty was quickly approved and ratified by the United States Senate, and the fact that the United States had survived yet another conflict with Great Britain was deemed significant enough to proclaim victory. Two important military heroes with political ambitions did emerge from the war: William Henry Harrison and Andrew Jackson. Harrison had gained honor and fame for his military actions at Tippecanoe against the Shawnee Indians, and later for the Battle of the Thames where the famous Indian chief, Tecumseh, was killed. Likewise, Jackson became a national hero for his spirited defense of New Orleans where he defeated a much larger British force in January 1815. It mattered little to the American people that the battle was politically inconsequential and had no impact on the outcome of the war. It had, in fact, taken place after the peace treaty had already been negotiated and signed in Ghent, albeit before Senate ratification.*

*In 1816, another Virginian, James Monroe, succeeded Madison
to the presidency. James and Dolley were finally able to retire to private life and the peace and tranquility of their beloved home, Montpelier. A now elderly John Adams declared that "notwithstanding a
thousand Faults and blunders [Madison's] administration has acquired more glory and established more Union than all of his three
predecessors, Washington, Adams and Jefferson, put together." It
was a generous assessment but the nation was entering into a new
era, its own* Pax Americana. *It would prove to be a prolonged period
of peace, free from international interference and intrigue, allowing
the nation to at last to concentrate on its domestic pursuits and its
economic prosperity.*

––––––––––––––––––

IN DECEMBER 1809, Father William DuBourg wrote from St.
Mary's College to James Madison to inform the President that
his stepson would be released from school and allowed to return to
Washington to spend the Christmas holidays with his family at the
President's House. Payne would, however, be required to return to
Baltimore no later than December 27th to attend the school's winter
commencement ceremonies.[3] In his letter, Father DuBourg apologized to Madison for being unable to accompany Payne personally
to D.C., but explained that he was currently "being confined to my
room" by an illness and this would preclude any travel. The priest
then used the remainder of his correspondence "...to make interest
in favor of a beloved brother Major Peter F. DuBourg of Orleans, for
the office of Collector of that Port."[4] The extensive letter went on to
list Major DuBourg's many qualifications and accomplishments for
the posting. Apparently this personal lobbying and intercession was
successful, since Father DuBourg's brother was eventually granted
the coveted Presidential commission.

Payne continued to be a merely adequate student while in attendance at St. Mary's. Over the six years that he was in attendance,
Madison would send quarterly bank drafts to Father DuBourg to
cover the boy's tuition costs and his considerable living expenses.

A bank draft for $175.33 sent to St. Mary's College by President Madison dated December 20, 1810. Madison sent regular payments to the college for Payne Todd's tuition, books, and incidental expenses. (St. Mary's Theological Seminary)

The amount of these payments varied greatly depending upon individual circumstances but the price of "Six Months board and Tuition" was consistently around $115.[5]

While away at school, Payne had matured into a fine-looking, debonair young man. His mother was overly proud of her son's physical and social development. Dolley boasted to her sister, Anna, that: "Payne is in Baltimore yet, and as much admired and respected as you could wish."[6] In truth, the boy had acquired little of his stepfather's scholarly interests, nor did he exhibit much in the way of ambition. Madison biographer, Ralph Ketcham, observes succinctly that Payne Todd was "handsome, dashing, competent, though not brilliant."[7]

While residing in Baltimore, though, Payne had successfully mastered French. He became fluent and was able to speak the language without any discernable accent.[8] Likewise, while under the strong tutelage of the predominately French clergy at St. Mary's, Todd became an enthusiastic Francophile and developed a strong appreciation for the nation's culture, its elegance, and its sophistication. This admiration of France was further encouraged by his regular association and visits with the Madison's family friend and socialite, Betsy Bonaparte.

Throughout the period of Payne's schooling, the effervescent Betsy was residing in Baltimore with her young son, Jerome Napoleon "Bo" Bonaparte. Dolley was forever grateful to her for looking after Payne's well-being, once writing "…Mrs. Patterson (Betsy's mother) and Mrs. Bonaparte are very attentive to him, and [Payne] is invited to all their great houses there." She added somewhat optimistically, "We intend to send him in a few months to Princeton."[9]

Betsy Bonaparte's influence over the impressionable Payne would have lasting implications. She had been deeply hurt and embarrassed by her husband's abandonment of her and their infant son. This personal and public humiliation was further compounded by the Emperor Napoleon, her brother-in-law, who banned her from France, effectively sentencing her to exile in America. As one of Betsy's friends astutely observed, though: "nature never put so much beauty & wit together to languish away in obscurity."[10]

Despite Betsy's eventual divorce from her husband, she stubbornly continued to use his surname, Bonaparte. Furthermore, she retained her delusions that her son was of noble lineage and was a legitimate heir to the French throne. Betsy insisted that the boy be treated with all of the respect and veneration due that of a European prince, even though these aristocratic pretentions ran counter to the American republic's disdain for hereditary titles and inherited entitlements. For the receptive Payne Todd, it was easy for him to imagine that he, too, should be revered as the sole stepson of the President of the United States, the highest elected official in the country. His growing sense of entitlement and conceit were not supported by merit or reality. Payne had yet to accomplish anything of substance and was increasingly relying upon his striking good looks and considerable charms to manipulate his way in the world. It would soon develop into a disturbing pattern of behavior that would continue throughout his adult life.

AFTER THE DEATH OF his father, James Madison had become the sole owner of the Montpelier plantation. Although his mother, Nelly, was still residing on the estate, the duplex configuration of the manor house no longer seemed practical and was proving to be quite inconvenient. Shortly after his election to the presidency, Madison decided to begin a full scale renovation of the house in order to enlarge and enhance the structure and make it more befitting the status of the nation's chief executive. During this major construction period, Madison solicited the aid of Thomas Jefferson's personal architect and skilled craftsman, James Dinsmore. Dinsmore oversaw the construction of two wings to the mansion as well as the addition of a rear colonnade. Chimneys were added and many of the existing rooms were renovated and enlarged.[11] Nearby, a magnificent, classical, temple-like structure was erected over the plantation's ice house and this edifice quickly became a much admired and distinguishing feature of the Montpelier estate.[12]

The ice house at Montpelier. The structure was built during the extensive renovation of the manor house and grounds during Madison's presidency. (Library of Congress)

Yet even with all of the ongoing construction work, Montpelier continued to serve as a welcomed sanctuary for Madison throughout his presidency. James and Dolley spent every summer on the estate, since it was still wise to abandon the nation's capital during the hot and humid seasonal months when the city's surrounding marshes and swamps produced swarms of disease-laden mosquitos. After one welcomed sojourn away from Washington, Dolley wrote: "we passed two months on our mountain in health and peace, returning the first of October to a sick and afflicted city. The unfinished canal caused a bilious fever to prevail through all its streets, many died, and Congress convened in dread of contagion."[13]

But when the Madison's were in Washington, Dolley was determined to bring a new elegance and refinement to the President's House and to capital society. She began by re-decorating and re-furnishing the executive mansion, aided by a generous Congressional appropriation of $5,000. Soon the President's Palace became the center of social activity and James and Dolley regularly welcomed large gatherings of politicians and dignitaries to their home. Family and friends often visited for extended periods of time as one guest observed in 1812: "The House was crowded with company from top to Bottom, the chambers & every room was occupied with Ladies & Gentlemen and all descriptions of persons."[14] The numerous guests were apparently oblivious to Benjamin Franklin's axiom from *Poor Richard's Almanack* that "fish and visitors smell after three days."[15]

In truth, Dolley loved entertaining, socializing, and city life. She began a regular practice of hosting large social gatherings and dinners at the President's Palace. On these much anticipated occasions, she served her guests plentiful amounts of food, cakes and sweets along with ample quantities of "Roman Punch," a concoction of sugar, lemons, brandy and rum.[16] Although President Madison was uncomfortable and reserved in such social circumstances, Dolley was able to charm, flatter, and enchant their many visitors.[17] Her "levées" became highly anticipated affairs in Washington and were well attended by Congressmen, Senators, and Cabinet members as well as foreign dignitaries and other acquaintances. These events also proved to be politically advantageous since they allowed government officials to relax and socialize while subtly building political alliances and assuaging partisan disagreements. Margaret Bayard Smith observed that Dolley's parties "oftener succeed[ed] in neutralizing the bitterness of opposition."[18]

One of Dolley Madison's fashionable gowns. Dolley Madison loved to entertain while in Washington and these social occassions became highly anticpated affairs bringing togehter politicians, diplomats, and other dignitaries. (Greensboro Historical Museum)

The First Lady impressed everyone with her sense of refinement and good taste. She always appeared dressed in the most fashionable clothing and was mindful of the latest styles and trends.[19] On one occasion, she asked Betsy Bonaparte to shop for a chic, new turban to add to her expansive wardrobe, writing: "I will avail myself of your taste in case, you meet with any thing elegant in the form of a Turban, or even any thing brilliant to make one, such as gau[z]e or lace flower'd with Gold or Silver."[20] But unlike the more ostentatious Mrs. Bonaparte, Dolley was more cautious and conservative in her daily appearance. She inevitably "wore a modest Quaker cap and shielded her bosom with a kerchief."[21]

By 1812, Payne had, at last, finished his formal schooling at St. Mary's and had returned to live with his parents in Washington. To their dismay, he showed no inclination to furthering his education at his stepfather's alma mater, Princeton, nor was he motivated to pursue a career. Even more alarming than his lack of ambition was the growing realization that Payne's behavior was becoming increasingly irresponsible. He was drinking excessively and his reckless gambling was becoming problematic, but the narcissistic Payne well understood that his doting parents would overlook his repeated trespasses. Indeed, there would be few consequences for his self-indulgent behavior. Dolley, in particular, was unmindful to his misconduct while his stepfather seemed reluctant to interfere or intervene. Historian Catherine Allgor explains: "Payne was developing along worrisome and, considering his uncle, ominously familiar lines. Dolley could not discipline him; something within her collapsed at the prospect of restricting her only child. James could or would not either. He may have felt the delicacy of his position as Payne's step-, rather than 'real,' father. In this culture of early death, however, many families were blended, and, for all the cultural preoccupation with blood, other men unambiguously ruled over stepchildren. More likely, James wanted to 'spare' Dolley, and the two of them began a pattern of bailing Payne out of his various scrapes, each sometimes hiding their efforts from the other. Payne soon figured this out and played on their dynamic."[22]

Although Washington City was still rustic and incomplete, there were ample temptations, enticements, and vice for the impetuous 20-year old Payne. As Virginia Moore writes: "Though smaller, Washington was socially gay as Baltimore, and to the stepson of the President of the United States every door was open. During off-hours, he rode horseback, bet on the races, danced, and had tête-à-têtes with an assortment of pretty girls."[23]

Still, Dolley retained her dreams that Payne would soon marry and settle down with a stable, loving wife. She actively began searching for a suitable match for him and one of the most promising candidates was Phoebe Pemberton Morris. She was the eligible, attractive daughter of one of Dolley's oldest and dearest friends, Anthony Morris.[24] During the winter of 1812, Dolley invited Phoebe to come to Washington and live with the family. The prospect excited the young girl and she wrote with anticipation to Dolley: "Oh! My dearest Mrs. Madison, I shall certainly embrace you in a few days, the 3rd or 4th of January, I think at the latest…I am full of joy…I am now busy in making preparations for my departure. I shall bring you some Parisian snuff from Mmme. Poletica."[25] Dolley immediately responded: "My husband and myself will receive you with open arms."[26] Shortly after her arrival, Phoebe wrote enthusiastically to her sister: "I have a dear little room, with an alcove bed."[27]

Dolley was exceeding fond of Phoebe and treated her like a surrogate daughter. Phoebe and Payne were friendly and frequently attended the same social functions at the President's Palace. It was apparent that she was attracted to Payne who, despite his faults, was handsome, urbane, and charming.[28] On March 29, 1812, the two participated in the wedding of Dolley's recently widowed sister, Lucy, to Supreme Court Justice, Thomas Todd, at the President's House.[29] Judge Todd was seventeen years older than his new bride and had five children from his previous marriage, but Phoebe explained that "[he] is so estimable & amiable a man that every person respects & admires him; he is very rich, very handsome."[30]

Regardless of Phoebe's budding romantic interest in Payne, he remained aloof and indifferent. Apparently even the beautiful Phoebe's charms were no match for the variety of libertine women that were readily available to Payne in antebellum Washington.

AT THE SAME TIME that the Madison's were celebrating Judge Todd's and Lucy's marriage at the President's House, 72-year old Vice President George Clinton was confined to his bed and near death. Dolley noted the precarious state of his health in a letter and added that despite the impropriety, several people were already positioning themselves to replace Clinton on the Republican ticket for the upcoming election. She wrote in disgust: "…electioneering for office goes on beyond description."[31]

George Clinton was a distinguished American patriot. He had been a member of the Continental Congress before serving as a Brigadier General during the Revolution. After the war, he was elected as New York State's first post-colonial governor and would serve in the important post for the next 24 years. In 1804, Governor Clinton was chosen to replace the disgraced Aaron Burr as Thomas Jefferson's Vice President. Clinton hoped to be eventually elected as Jefferson's successor. The Republican caucus instead decided to nominate Secretary of State, James Madison, while Clinton was re-elected as Vice President, the only man who would ever serve in that position for two different presidential administrations.

Clinton's health declined precipitously while in office and he died on April 20, 1812 at his residence, the O'Neal's Hotel on Pennsylvania Avenue. He was the first Vice President in history to die in office. The *Daily National Intelligencer* reported somberly: "It is with feelings of unmixed veneration for the character of the Revolutionary Hero, the Patriot and Statesman combined in one, that we announce that the venerable GEORGE CLINTON IS NO MORE. He expired about nine o'clock yesterday morning at his lodgings in this city, after an illness of about four weeks continuance."[32] Congress immediately adjourned in Clinton's honor as the Vice President's body was transported to the United States Capitol to lay in temporary repose while the funeral arrangements were hastily finalized.

The Vice President's interment took place the very next day at Washington's new Congressional Cemetery. President Madison led a procession of distinguished mourners as reported in the newspaper: "The mortal remains of the late Vice President of the United States were on Tuesday evening interred at the burial ground near the Navy Yard in this city, in the presence of a concourse of people greater than ever has been gathered together in this city on any similar occasion. The shops were shut at an early hour; and a general gloom pervaded all ranks of Society. The hearse with its escort reached the Capitol about 4 o'clock, and the procession moved thence in about half an hour afterwards, in the order which was announced in our last. The scene was awful and impressive. The martial parade, the glistening arms and nodding plumes of the military corps which preceded the hearse--the solemn melody of the martial band, which attuned all

Vice President George Clinton and his originnal gravesite at Congressional Cemetery. Clinton was the first Vice President to die while in office. His remains were disinterred in 1908 for reburial in Kingston, New York. His successor, Elbridge Gerry, would also die in office in 1814. (Library of Congress)

hearts to melancholy--the sable hearse, attended by eight veteran pall-bearers, who partook of the toils of the revolution--the well-known carriage of the deceased--the Chief Magistrate of the Nation mourning the loss of one of its noblest sons--the Senate deploring the loss of a revered President--But why particularly describe the lengthened train? Suffice it to say, that this assemblage of mournful and interesting objects inspired feelings suited to the occasion. When a Clinton descends to the tomb of his ancestors, it is fit that the whole nation bewail the general loss, and history immortalize his name. Hallowed be the ashes of the honored dead!"[33]

The business of politics, however, continued unabated. Soon thereafter, the Republican Congressional caucus met and chose New Hampshire Governor, John Langdon, as its new vice presidential candidate for the upcoming 1812 election. But Langdon, due to his advanced age, surprisingly refused to accept his party's nomination and it eventually was passed on to Elbridge Gerry of Massachusetts.[34] Regardless, Madison's political coalition of southern and western states was more than enough for the president to win re-election that fall by a comfortable 128 to 89 electoral vote margin against New York mayor, DeWitt Clinton.

While the political maneuvering and campaigning was continuing, Dolley received a disturbing letter from Nelly C. Willis, her brother-in-law's daughter. It contained more tragic family news.[35] Willis reported that she had recently learned that Reuben Conway, who was married to Madison's niece, Lucie, was in ill-health due to his excessive and abusive drinking. The couple had been married for only a year and were living at Greenwood Plantation in Orange County quite near the Willis' own estate and to Montpelier.[36] Nelly confided to Dolley: "I believe I mentioned in a former letter something about Reuben Conway's indisposition and the course of it. Poor fellow he is in a most deplorable situation and if he does not become more temperate must surely die very soon. I never in my life heard any person drinking to such excess as he does. Poor Lucy I feel for her most sincerely"[37] The scourge of alcoholism was once again disrupting the Madison family's delicate harmony but there was little that Dolley could do since the United States was preparing to wage war against the mighty British empire.

JAMES MADISON SENT HIS carefully prepared war message to Congress on June 1, 1812. He had initially intended to expound on the continuing hostility and antagonism that Britain had shown towards the American republic since the Revolution, but instead chose to confine his written remarks to a catalog of the many offenses that had occurred since 1803. In truth, the French had been an equal offender of American neutrality rights as Nathaniel Macon of South Carolina astutely noted: "the Devil himself could not tell what government, England or France, is most wicked."[38] But for Madison and his Republican party, their deep-rooted distrust of the British and George III superseded all other foreign policy slights. The most outrageous violation of American sovereignty was the continued impressment of U.S. sailors on the high seas by the British navy and this was the *prima facie* case for war. There was, though, a strong suspicion that the English were fostering Indian unrest on the nation's western frontiers where American settlers lived in constant fear of being slaughtered in their homes. In his war message to Congress, Madison accused the British of encouraging and abetting the hostilities, claiming that on "our extensive frontiers a warfare which is known to spare neither age nor sex, and to be distinguished by features particularly shocking to humanity [is being waged]."[39]

The Constitution in Article I, Section 8 grants only Congress the power to declare war and Madison willingly deferred to the collective judgment of the House and Senate on the matter. There was, however, a strong anti-war sentiment in the country, emanating primarily from New England, a region that had greatly suffered during the Jefferson self-imposed economic embargo. The merchants had never fully recovered and any renewed hostilities with the British would inevitably disrupt trade and threaten shipping.

A political cartoon (1812) entitled "A scene on the frontiers as practiced by the 'humane' British and their 'worthy' allies." The British were accused of inciting Indian insurrection on the frontier by President Madison in his war resolution to Congress. (Library of Congress)

Madison's war resolution passed comfortably in the House of Representatives with its strong Republican majority by a vote of 79 to 49, but the bill was narrowly approved by the Senate by a margin of just 19 to 13.[40] The official declaration of war was signed by Madison on June 18 and then publically printed and disseminated the following day.

A new war with Great Britain was an audacious and perilous action. It was predicated more upon patriotism than upon military preparedness. The Federalist press immediately denounced President Madison and the congressionally declared war. Alexander Hanson, the editor of Baltimore's *Federal Republican & Commercial Gazette* wrote that "Silence would be treason" and continued to claim that it was foolhardy to go to war against the world's greatest military power "without funds, without an army, navy or adequate fortifications."[41]

Such unpatriotic sentiments seemed like sedition to many including Mathew Carey, a rabid Republican publisher. He personally wrote to President Madison to urge the suppression of the opposition press arguing that: "The press, one of the greatest blessings of mankind, when properly conducted, has for four or five years been the greatest curse & scourge of this Country…many of Our printers have abandoned all sense of honour, shame, or decency. There is no falsehood too base for them to assert…It is easy to point out an evil--&, in many cases, not very difficult to point out remedies."[42] In a subsequent letter, he continued his tirade: "A corrupt or wicked press…write down a government of angels & archangels that did not use the proper means to defend itself. Had Mr. Jefferson been a Nero, & you a Caligula, you could not be more completely abhorred & detested than you are in such parts of New England as are under the influence of the *Boston Gazette & the Repertory*. A law of ten lines, making any attempt to dissolve the union, a high crime & misdemeanor, subject to severe penalty, wd. Have probably arrested even in an early stage. Better late than never. Such a law ought to be one of the first enacted at next session."[43]

To his credit, the President resisted partisan demands to suppress public discourse and he steadfastly refused to order any restrictions upon political liberties or free speech. He well remembered the repulsive Alien and Sedition Acts which had been passed during John Adams' presidential administration, and was determined that no one should be arrested for their political opinions, no matter how vile or loathsome. Once again James Madison refused to allow political expediency to trump his deeply held philosophical beliefs or fundamental constitutional principles.

Despite the impetus for the war, Madison wanted to open diplomatic channels with Britain in hopes of negotiating a quick and amenable settlement. John Quincy Adams, who was then serving as the American Ambassador to Russia, was approached by Count Nikolai Romanzoff who offered Russian mediation in the conflict. He assured Adams of Russia's continuing friendship and of Tsar Alexander I's desire to maintain his trade relationships with the United States.[44] These overtures were accepted by Madison and soon the President appointed Albert Gallatin and James Bayard to serve as members of a new United States diplomatic peace mission and ordered them to Russia to pursue the Tsar's offer of intercession. It also afforded him the opportunity to give his stepson, Payne, a chance at meaningful employment. Payne's excellent French language skills could be invaluable to the American delegation since French was the preferred language of the Russian aristocracy as well as that of international diplomacy..[45] Indeed, it was only the *moujik* (peasants) who regularly spoke vernacular Russian.

Madison had high hopes that the appointment of Payne to the peace commission would give him some direction and purpose in life. As historian Ralph Ketcham observed, the commission would provide "a steady occupation…to counterbalance the attentions of a doting mother and the flattery of the belles of Baltimore and Washington, to whom he was an American prince."[46]

Payne was officially assigned to serve as a personal attaché to Albert Gallatin and was correspondingly given the rank of a third lieutenant in the cavalry.[47] This entitled Payne to wear a military uniform and gave him additional cachet while further contributing to his already bloated ego. His first assignment was to deliver some presidential dispatches to Gallatin and to rendezvous with the peace delegation in Philadelphia yet even this simple task proved problematic. Payne

Mr. Todd

Attaché à la Mission Extraordinaire des États-Unis d'Amérique.

John Payne Todd's calling card while serving with the diplomatic mission during the War of 1812. (Greensboro Historical Museum)

was forced to delay his departure due to a painful boil, for which Madison apologized to Gallatin, explaining that it was "not being healed, though relieved by the salutary maturation & discharge."[48]

Madison was careful to ensure that his stepson had adequate personal funds to cover his expenses during his sojourn abroad. Not trusting Payne's frugality, though, Madison secretly entrusted most of the money to Gallatin, explaining: "I inclose a draft for $800 dollars to be a fund in your hands for J.P. Todd. He has in his own $200 more; which our estimate called for." He added: "Should the whole be judged, on a better calculation, to be deficient, be so good as to convert a draft on me into a supply of the deficiency."[49]

A few days after Payne's belated arrival, the peace mission embarked on May 9 onboard the *Neptune* from New Castle, Delaware. The captain had to carefully avoid prowling British warships off the American coast. The arduous, transatlantic voyage took six weeks to complete. Dolley reported with some satisfaction that Payne had borne the difficulties of sea travel well: "he is charmed with his voyage so far, and has escaped sea-sickness, though all the party has succumbed."[50]

Gallatin, Bayard, Todd, and other members of the delegation arrived in St. Petersburg in mid-summer after completing their journey via Gothenburg and Copenhagen. To their surprise and dismay, Tsar Alexander I was absent from the city and engaged in ongoing military operations against Napoleon's retreating army.[51] Compounding the mission's problems was the fact that the British government refused to accept the Russian mediation in their ongoing conflict with America so there was little for the commissioners to do but await further developments and instructions.

Few countries in Europe were as socially stratified as 19th century Russia. Indeed, most of the peasants were poor, landless serfs, while a small hereditary nobility lived in splendor, blissfully ignorant of the suffering and hardships of the masses. The Tsar was the absolute, autocratic ruler of the empire and was unrestrained by law, Parliaments, or the inconveniences of representative government.

The titled nobility lived an isolated, privileged existence in St. Petersburg. The princesses wore splendid gowns and priceless jewels while the men were resplendent in garish uniforms decorated with medals and ribbons that had been conferred for fidelity and heredity rather than for battlefield glory or personal valor. Collectively, they spent their ample idle time attending lavish balls and other leisurely activities, always fueled by copious amounts of vodka. For young Payne Todd, it was an exhilarating and licentious existence. Rather than trying to escape from the shadow of his famous parents, he relished the attention and opportunities his birthright provided. Payne was charmed, flattered, and seduced by Russia's regal society and was treated by the court effectively as President Madison's regent, an American royal. His fellow American diplomats conversely were regarded as mere commoners. Henry Clay later chastised Payne for his cavalier behavior writing: "Do you remember when you were with us in Russia that John Quincy Adams and the rest of us sat in the gallery, and apart from you, and watched you dance with the Princess, we being disbarred because we were not royalty?"[52]

Payne relished the attention and enjoyed the drinking and the dancing. He loved to flirt with beautiful girls and reportedly entertained and caroused with all types of women, including many of questionable virtue.[53] It was even rumored that during his time in the Russian capital, Payne had become romantically involved with a Russian princess despite the disapproval of the girl's father.[54] For unknown reasons, perhaps to avoid a scandal, Payne suddenly left St. Petersburg and traveled to Paris in advance of the diplomatic delegation.[55]

THERE WAS NO REGULAR mail service in the early 19th century. Letters to and from Europe were often entrusted to acquaintances who were making the transatlantic voyage. It could take well over three months for a letter to arrive at its destination and much correspondence sent in this manner simply disappeared in transit. News from abroad was thus difficult to obtain under the best of circumstances.

To Dolley's dismay, the self-absorbed Payne was an irregular correspondent while living in Europe. His silence was maddening but Dolley continued to write to him, although to no avail. Upset and frustrated, she finally scolded: "Not a line from you has reached us since you left St. Petersburg. How impatient I am, you [o]ught to imagine—I am consoled for your absence & your silence by the impression that you are engrossed by the variety of objects in Europe which are to enlighten & benefit you the rest of your life."[56]

Dolley was anxious. She craved news about her son's health and well-being but she was able to receive only sporadic information about his whereabouts indirectly, usually through the intersession of Albert Gallatin's wife, Hannah. In one sympathetic letter, Hannah wrote to Mrs. Madison: "I understand, my dear, that you did not receive any letters from Payne by the last arrivals...Mr. Gallatin says...[that] Todd & Millegen left St. Petersburg before them, & took the Sweden route...Payne had gone on a visit to Paris...He will have a very pleasant jaunt, no doubt."[57]

With little to do in Russia, the peace commissioners decided to abandon St. Petersburg and eventually arrived in Ghent. Henry Clay and Jonathan Russell had belatedly joined the delegation as did John Quincy Adams who was reassigned from his diplomatic posting. Payne, though, was still neglecting his modest duties and was slow to travel to Belgium. He much preferred to remain in Paris where he was free to drink, gamble, and carouse. A clearly irritated Albert Gallatin scolded Payne: "Permit me...to urge the propriety of your leaving Paris where you have remained long enough for every useful purpose...I would be very sorry that either your property should be injured or your time improperly wasted by your trip to Europe; and you must ascribe my anxiety solely to my attachment to you, your mother, and Mr. Madison."[58]

Payne was totally enraptured by French society and began to purchase large amounts of art, sculpture and other luxuries. These tasteful but expensive items would eventually be shipped back to the Madison's home at Montpelier, but Payne's extravagant lifestyle meant that his debts continued to accumulate.[59] This necessitated Madison eventually to issue an additional bank draft for $6,500 to help pay for his son's extravagances. Madison privately complained that he was "not prepared for a heavy demand for the expenses of J.P. Todd."[60] Thus began a troublesome pattern where Madison would come to Payne's financial aid after his debts accumulated until they became insurmountable.[61] His monetary difficulties did not humble or deter Payne's behavior and Madison's intercession seemed only to encourage further fiscal irresponsibility.

ON MARCH 31, 1814, Paris fell to the triumphant armies of Tsar Alexander I. Emperor Napoleon was forced to abdicate eleven days later and was exiled to the island of Elba. The end of the Napoleonic Wars was welcomed by Thomas Jefferson, then living in retirement at Monticello. He wrote: "I rejoice…in the downfall of Bonaparte."[62]

But the defeat of Napoleon was ominous news for American military forces who were still at war with the British. For much of the War of 1812, the intermittent fighting had been a mere sideshow for the English, more of a nuisance than anything else. The early efforts by the United States to conquer its so-called "14th Colony" (Canada) had been easily repulsed. Even the periodic naval battles where the Americans enjoyed some success were inconsequential to the eventual outcome of the war. But with Napoleon now banished from the continent of Europe, the full might of the British army and navy could finally be unleashed to punish the upstart Americans. The British began by tightening its naval blockade of the Atlantic coast and launching a series of new military offensives. This included a bold expedition up the Chesapeake Bay towards Washington, D.C. and the critical port of Baltimore.

On August 19, a powerful British armada consisting of 20 warships as well as numerous infantry transports, landed 4,500 regulars at Benedict, Maryland. These troops began a march overland towards the nation's capital. Initially, there was little panic within the city since most citizens optimistically believed that any overland attack would be repulsed by American troops and militia.[63] The Secretary of State, James Monroe, was more realistic. After conducting a personal reconnaissance mission, he wisely decided to take precautions to safeguard important governmental documents. He ordered the immediate evacuation of the State Department's archives including the original Declaration of Independence, the Articles of Confederation, portions of George Washington's official correspondence, the journals of Congress, important international treaties, as well as other essential books and documents. Stephen Pleasonton, a clerk at the department, undertook the task of supervising the packing of these irreplaceable documents, all of which were carefully sewn into linen bags for safe evacuation. He then ordered them conveyed across the Potomac where the cache of documents were temporarily stored in an old, abandoned grist mill just two miles northwest of the city. After commandeering additional wagons, Pleasonton then had the documents moved further inland to Leesburg, Virginia, to avoid capture or destruction by the British.[64]

In reality, the city of Washington was only lightly defended by ill-trained militia companies and vulnerable to attack. With news of the impending invasion, an American army of 6,000 men was quickly mustered into service and this force did include a small but significant contingent of regular army troops, sailors, and marines. The soldiers marched out to Brandywine, Maryland, some 25 miles southeast of the capital, where they set up defensive fortifications designed to intercept the British force. President Madison, armed only with two dueling pistols, rode out to oversee the impending battle.[65]

Despite the impending danger, Dolley insisted on remaining at the President's House where she anxiously awaited further news from her husband. She professed confidence in "the success of our army" but she had already been cautioned by the President to be ready to evacuate the premises quickly if "the enemy seemed stronger than had at first be reported."[66] In a letter to her sister, Anna, Dolley confided that "I am accordingly ready; I have pressed as many Cabinet papers into trunks as to fill one carriage; our private property must be sacrificed, as it is impossible to procure wagons for transportation. I am determined not to go myself until I see Mr. Madison safe so that he can accompany me, as I hear of much hostility towards him."[67] While Dolley periodically scanned the horizon through a telescope for news of her husband, she busied herself with preparing a dinner for forty people. In the distance, she could hear the distinct thunder of artillery.[68]

The Battle of Bladensburg was fought on August 24 in the oppressive summer heat. It lasted just three hours and despite being outnumbered, the well-trained British force quickly outflanked and routed the American defenders, who fled the battlefield in a panic. It was an ignoble and embarrassing defeat, prompting one eyewitness to observe that the American troops "ran like sheep chased by dogs."[69] Likewise, Margaret Bayard Smith lamented: "Oh how changed are my feelings, my confidence in our troops is gone."[70] She rationalized, "[The British] army composed of conquering veterans, ours of young mechanics & farmers, many of whom had never before carried a musket."[71]

News of the defeat arrived quickly back in Washington and a general panic ensued. Residents were urged to flee their homes since there was no other line of defense available to save the city. Wagons were hastily procured and loaded with personal goods, while all who could fled to the safety of the Virginia or Maryland countryside.[72] Still, Dolley Madison delayed steadfastly refusing to leave the President's House until she had made arrangements to rescue Gilbert Stuart's full length portrait of George Washington.[73] The huge painting was firmly secured and mounted to a wall so the frame had to be broken and the canvas cut out. As Dolley related to Anna: "It is done! and the precious portrait placed in the hands of two gentlemen of New York, for safe keeping. And now, dear sister, I must leave this house, or the retreating army will make me a prisoner in it by filling up the road I am directed to take. When I shall again write to you, or where I shall be to-morrow, I cannot tell!"[74]

The Gilbert Stuart painting of George Washington. Dolley Madison rescued the portrait from destruction before leaving Washington during the War of 1812. (White House Historical Association)

WHEN THE PRESIDENT RETURNED to Washington, he was dismayed to see his retreating troops in total disarray. The soldiers were unable, or unwilling, to further defend the federal capital. To avoid his own capture, Madison and several of his advisors hastily procured a boat and were rowed safely across the Potomac River into Virginia where they sought shelter near Little Falls.[75]

Now completely uncontested, the British army jubilantly entered the federal capital. The Washington Navy Yard was already engulfed in flames, having been set afire by the Americans in an effort to prevent the crucial facility from falling into enemy hands. The yard's stockpiles of mast, rope, pitch, and tar readily fueled the raging fires which quickly consumed the military base while the remaining sailors and marines hastily scuttled several moored ships to avoid their capture.[76]

The British admiral, Sir George Cockburn, dispatched an advance contingent of 50 soldiers and sailors to torch the city's federal buildings including the Treasury, War, and State Departments as well as United States Capitol. The President's House on Pennsylvania Avenue was seized and looted for souvenirs while Admiral Cockburn and several of his aides feasted upon the dinner Dolley Madison had abandoned in her haste to escape. They drank mock toasts to their absent host, "Jemmy," while Cockburn personally absconded with one of the President's hats and a fashionable cushion from one of the mansion's chairs. The building was then ordered to be torched.[77]

Washington was of little militarily importance and the British had no intentions of occupying the city. After a sudden, violent summer thunderstorm quenched the raging fires, the British returned to their awaiting vessels on the Patuxent River, leaving behind the charred rubble of the federal government and a ravaged city. One anonymous soldier left a mocking graffiti on a charred wall of the Capitol saying: "George Washington founded this city after seven years' of war with England—James Madison lost it after a two years' war with England."[78]

A British cartoon entitled "The Fall of Washington--or Maddy in Full Flight." It lampooned President Madison's hasty evacuation after the American defeat at Bladensburg. (Library of Congress)

A lithograph showing the destruction of Washington by British forces in August 1814. (Library of Congress)

The United States Capitol in ruins. A British solider wrote on one of its charred walls: "George Washington founded this city after seven years' of war with England--James Madison lost it after two years' war with England. (Library of Congress)

Over the next few days, residents slowly returned to Washington and were horrified by what they encountered. Margaret Bayard Smith observed: "We afterwards look'd at the other public buildings, but none were so thoroughly destroy'd as the House of Representatives and the President's House. Those beautiful pillars in the Representatives Hall were crack'd and broken, the roof, that noble dome, painted and carved with such beauty and skill, lay in ashes in the cellars beneath the smouldering ruins, were yet smoking. In the P[resident's] H[ouse] not an inch, but its crack'd and blacken'd walls remain'd."[79] She continued, "I do not suppose the Government will ever return to Washington. All those whose property was invested in that place, will be reduced to poverty...The consternation about us is general. The despondency still greater."[80] Secretary of State, James Monroe, angrily published an open letter to Admiral Cockburn condemning the British actions: "In the wars of modern Europe, no examples of the kind, even among nations the most hostile to each, can be traced— We must go back to distant and barbarous ages, to find a parallel for the acts of which I complain."[81]

The President returned to the capital on August 27 and he and Dolley eventually took up residence at the nearby Octagon House, the home of Colonel John Tayloe. Margaret Bayard Smith observed that Dolley was devastated by the destruction of the city: "Mrs. M. seem'd much depress'd, she could scarcely speak without tears."[82]

The disaster did have one personal, positive outcome for the Madison's. It finally compelled Payne Todd to break his long silence and to write to his parents. He addressed the letter "Dear Papa" and wrote: "We received…very painful intelligence of the destruction of the public buildings in Washington. This barbaric act meets with universal excoriation…My absence from Washington I most deeply regret if for no other reason [than that] I might at least have been useful to you and my mother."[83]

AS THE RESIDENTS OF WASHINGTON continued to return to their burned out city, welcomed news was received. The British armada, after continuing up the Chesapeake Bay, had failed to take Baltimore. Fort McHenry, which guarded the entrance to the harbor, successfully withstood a fierce naval bombardment while brazenly flying a huge 15-star, 15-stripe garrison flag to taunt the invaders.[84] The historic event was witnessed by a Washington attorney, Francis Scott Key, who commemorated the defense of Ft. McHenry in verse and later published the poem in the newspapers. It would eventually be adapted to music as "The Star-Spangled Banner."[85]

Despite the severe damage that the capital had sustained, President Madison reconvened his cabinet and was determined to rebuild the federal city. Margaret Bayard Smith, who by now had safely returned to Washington, wrote: "I trust we will retrieve our character and restore our capital…This is not the first capital of a great empire that has been invaded & conflagrated. Rome was reduced still lower by the Goths of old." There were many politicians who favored relocating the capital inland to safer confines but Smith dismissed these arguments explaining: "Romans would never be driven from their homes, Rome should never be destroy'd. May a Roman spirit animate our people, and the Roman example be followed by the Americans."[86]

Meanwhile, the peace negotiations in Ghent remained stalemated. The British refused to make any concessions on the critical issues of American neutrality rights and the impressment of sailors. The Secretary of State, James Monroe, conveyed President Madison's instructions to the American commissioners to remain firm: "On impressment, as to the right of the United States to be exempted from it, I have nothing new to add. The sentiments of the President have undergone no change on that important subject. This degrading practice must cease; our flag must protect the crew; or the United States cannot consider themselves as an independent Nation."[87]

Payne Todd was oblivious to the diplomatic intricacies and contributed little to the eventual outcome of the diplomatic discussions. He was content to waste his time drinking, gambling, and playing cards often with Henry Clay.[88] The more sober and scholarly John Quincy Adams was dismayed by his behavior.

After almost 25 years of continuous warfare, the continent of Europe was in political turmoil despite Napoleon's defeat and subsequent exile. National boundaries had been disrupted and altered while ethnic divisions festered. To address the situation, the Congress of Vienna had been convened as Austria, Russia, Britain, and France attempted to restore some sense of political equilibrium. This conference rightly became the central foreign policy priority for the British government. In reality, the constant warfare had severely depleted the treasury and the British population was unenthusiastic about the prospects of being further taxed to support military operations in a pointless conflict with America. In November, 1814, a major breakthrough occurred when the British negotiators were instructed "to bring the American war if possible to a conclusion" without any territorial concessions. They would offer essentially a return to the *status quo antebellum*. It would be as if the two years of fighting and bloodshed between the United States and Great Britain had never occurred.[89]

The American diplomats seized upon the opportunity to end the interminable war and agreed to the essentially honorable terms. After all, the nation had once again defended its honor on the battlefield and had once again asserted its right to independency. They signed a tentative peace agreement on Christmas Eve and the treaty was immediately dispatched by ship to the United States for consideration and final approval by the United States Senate.

The Treaty of Ghent arrived in Washington on February 13 and was submitted to the Senate, which quickly ratified it by a unanimous vote of 35-0. The War of 1812 was officially over and regardless of the realities, President Madison declared outright victory, claiming that the war was "highly honorable to the nation, and terminates, with peculiar felicity, a campaign signalized by the most brilliant successes...[It] has been waged with a success which is the natural result of the wisdom of the Legislative councils, of the patriotism of the people, of the public spirit of the militia, and of the valor of the military and naval forces of the country."[90]

With the conclusion of the war, Dolley anticipated the imminent return of her son Payne, but he once again disappointed her. Todd chose to extend his sojourn in Europe by a few months, and did not to depart with his fellow peace commissioners. He did, however, make arrangements to ship back home his personal belongs which now included an extensive collection of artworks which had cost his father a small fortune.[91]

It would not be until the summer of 1815 that Payne finally returned to America. He showed up unannounced one day at Montpelier. His parents were ecstatic by his return but surprised by the remarkable metamorphosis Payne had undergone while in Europe. He was, of course, older and physically more mature but his demeanor seemed aloof, even haughty. His manner and bearing were more French than American.[92] Still, it was a joyous family reunion and Payne eventually returned with his parents that fall to Washington for what would be the denouement of the Madison presidency.

Madison biographer Ralph Ketcham describes the 23-year old Payne as: "...uneducated, unwed, and unemployed, but [still] much impressed with his own social standing."[93] Although he would occasionally serve as his father's secretary while in Washington, it wasn't long before Payne reverted to his old bad habits. "[He] was restless," writes historian Virginia Moore. "He danced, hunted, played cards, vacillated between high and low company, drank heavily in taverns, rode horseback in Maryland and Virginia and around Tiber Creek… he had no long term goals."[94]

In the fall of 1816, Secretary of State, James Monroe, won election to the presidency by defeating the Federalist Party candidate, Rufus King, in an electoral landslide 183 to 34. Monroe successfully maintained Virginia's presidential dynasty while Madison was anxiously anticipating a blissful retirement from decades of public service. Madison wrote to Albert Gallatin: "I am in the midst of preparations to get to my farm, where I shall make myself a fixture; and where I anticipate many enjoyments, which if not fully realized, will be a welcomed exchange for the labors and solicitudes of public life."[95]

During the extended lame duck period, James and Dolley found time to sit for their portraits by Joseph Wood, the famed, albeit troubled, miniaturist. [96] Madison, who was then approaching his 66th birthday, appears in the final painting as an aging but dignified patriarch. Eliza Lee Collins, a childhood friend of Dolley's who eventually received the paintings as a gift, lauded the Wood portrait in a letter to Dolley: "The likeness of your dear Husband almost expresses much of the serenity of his feelings at the moment it was taken, in short, it is *himself*."[97] Other family members would later recall: "We have a good likeness of Mr. M—taken in 1817—by Wood—it is like him as we recalled him."[98]

Joseph Wood's portrait of James Madison, 1817. (Virginia Historical Society)

For her own portrait, Dolley wore a typically fashionable gown as well as her signature turban. She was now a middle-aged woman at 48 but still very much in her prime. Eliza, though, expressed disappointment with the quality of the image: "Your likeness my

Dolley Madison at age 48 as painted by Joseph Wood. The two Madison portraits were given to Dolley's friend, Eliza Lee Collins. (Virginia Historical Society)

dear friend," she wrote to Dolley, "is sufficient, and instantly recognized—but I lament the absence of the expression of your eye,
which speaks *from*, and *to*, the Heart—the want of which robs your
countenance of its richest treasure. And tho, whilst memory lasts, I
shall always be able to supply, to myself,
the deficiency."[99]

Wood was also commissioned
by the Madison's to paint a miniature portrait of Payne Todd.
Dolley's son was 25-years old,
handsome and debonair, as
Wood's small (2.6 x 2 inches),
oval watercolor on ivory accurately depicted. Ironically, it
was destined to survive as the
only known existing image of
Payne.[100]

The Madison's stayed on in Washington after the inauguration of
James Monroe on March 4 as the
nation's fifth president. For the

The only known image of John Payne Todd.
(Copyright © Metropolian Museum of Art)

next few weeks, the couple was celebrated with a series of balls and
galas held in their honor. Thomas Jefferson, anticipating the Madison's return home, wrote from Monticello: "Congratulating you on
the riddance of your bur[d]ens, I salute you affectionately and respectfully."[101]

The Madison's did not embark from Washington until early
April. They took a steamboat down the Potomac to Aquia Creek
and from there completed the remaining journey home by carriage,
arriving at Montpelier on Tuesday, April 6. Jefferson was elated to
have his closest friend nearby and wrote to Madison a few days
later: "I sincerely congratulate you on your release from incessant
labors, corroding anxieties, active enemies and interested friends on

Lines respectfully proposed to be inscribed beneath the Portrait of
Mrs. MADISON,
when exhibited at the Ball to be given her at GEORGETOWN
on Thursday, 13th March 1817. —

The Power divine, when Time begun,
Bade charming WOMAN and the SUN
Illumine the Terrestial Ball:
A charming WOMAN still we find,
Like the bright SUN, cheers all Mankind,
And, like IT, is admired by all! —

Washington City, March 11th 1817.

A verse "to be incribed beneath the Portrait of Mrs. Madison." The Madison's were celebrated after leaving office with a series of balls and galas including one held in Geogetown on March 13, 1817 in Dolley's honor. (Greensboro Historical Museum)

your return to your books and farm, to tranquility and independence. A day of these is worth ages of the former, but all this you know."[102]

WHEN DOLLEY AND JAMES returned to Montpelier, they were welcomed by his mother, Nelly, who, at age 86, was still in relatively good health and living on the 2,000 acre estate.[103] Payne predictably delayed his return and did not arrive home until later that summer.[104]

The Madison's were glad to be back home in their beloved Virginia piedmont. The major additions and alterations to the house were now essentially finished. Baron de Montlezun, a French expatriot and satirist, visited Montpelier while on a grand tour of the south and he recorded his impressions and observations in his travel diary.[105] He found the Madison's home to be pleasant but modest in comparison to the estates owned by European landed aristocrats. He wrote: "[Montpelier] is not at all pretentious, nor in consonance with what the high position of the owner would lead one to expect."[106] The acreage immediately surrounding the manor house was still mostly un-cleared land and covered by forest. There was, though, near the mansion a carefully laid out formal garden which allowed the Madisons to entertain and enjoy. Montlezun noted in his journal that the main drawing room at Montpelier was filled with paintings and artwork, including numerous busts of famous historical personages such as Homer, Socrates, Thomas Jefferson, and John Paul Jones. There were also a collection of family portraits that contained the cherished miniature of Payne Todd.[107]

After his introduction to James Madison, Montlezun observed that "years of study and toil have imparted an air of severity to his countenance" and he discovered that the President "does not speak French with ease."[108] As a result, he was forced to converse with him in English. Payne Todd, on the other hand, charmed and captivated Montlezun. "[Payne Todd] speaks French very well indeed and seems well educated," Montlezun wrote. "He is a young man of fine physique, with perfect manners; gentility is stamped on his face… he astonishes one by his knowledge, his balance and the solidity of his judgment at an age where men commonly have so little. He has travelled, and with much profit, in France, England, and Russia. To these advantages he joins those of fine physique, distinguished manners and urbanity. It is easy to see that he has frequented the good society of our European capitals."[109]

Payne had successfully mastered the ability to deceive people by using his wit, charm, status, and good looks to impress. His parents were frustrated by his lack of ambition and were desperate for him to settle down and find a career. According to Maud Wilder Goodwin, Dolley in particular was "still full of schemes for his future, and of hopes for his usefulness and prominence" but these hopes proved to be delusional.[110] In 1818, Payne's parents helped him purchase 104 acres of land from Richard Chapman for $540. The estate was located on the road to Gordonsville and in close proximity to Montpelier. It was already appropriately named Toddsberth, "Todd's Camp;" the land had originally been the site of an encampment for Governor Alexander Spotswood and the Knights of the Golden Horseshoe during their expedition to the Shenandoah Valley in 1716.[111]

Payne did not have either the temperament or inclination to become a traditional Virginia planter. Instead, he developed an elaborate scheme to use his newly acquired property to develop the silk worm industry in Virginia. It was an impractical, get-rich-quick scheme. Rather than first plant and cultivate the Mulberry trees that were necessary to feed silk worms, Payne instead impulsively hired a foreign farm manager along with several French workers and somehow paid for their travel expenses to Virginia. As historian, Allan Clark, notes: "[Todd] caught the mulberry epidemic and imported the Frenchmen to manufacture the silk."[112]

Silk manufacturing was a labor intensive and extremely delicate industry. Initially, Payne tried to make do by pilfering mulberry leaves from trees at Montpelier in a frenzied effort to feed his trays of silk larvae. Compounding his problems was the hot, muggy Virginia climate, which proved to be ill-suited for such an enterprise and soon all of the worms died. Payne was frustrated, impatient, and unwilling to put in the requisite time, effort, and sacrifice necessary to be successful in any legitimate enterprise. His desire for immediate gratification had caused this first business endeavor to collapse without ever producing any silk, textiles, or profit.[113] Payne responded by absenting himself from Toddsberth and chose to live a nomad's existence, traveling extensively and unpredictably to Richmond, Williamsburg, Philadelphia, and New York. He was drinking again and his gambling debts began to accumulate.[114] Dolley was dismayed since Payne's whereabouts were frequently unknown and she constantly feared for her son's safety. Senator William C. Rives was more dismissive in his assessment of Payne Todd, calling him "the snake in Eden."

ENDNOTES

Epigraph: Thomas Jefferson quoted Ralph Ketcham (1990). *James Madison: A Biography*. Charlottesville, University of Virginia Press, p. 504.

1 The Electoral College meets in December to cast its votes for president.

2 "The Act to prohibit the importation of Slaves" was signed into law by President Thomas Jefferson on March 2, 1807 and went into effect on January 1, 1808. It stated in part: "it shall not be lawful to import or bring into the United States from any foreign kingdom, place, or country, any negro, mulatto, or person of colour, as a slave, or to be held to service or labor." See "A Century of Law Making for a New Nation available at http://memory.loc.gov.

3 Father William DuBourg letter to James Madison, 15 December 1809, quoted in , J.C.A., Stagg ed. (1992). *The Papers of James Madison: Presidential Series 1 October 1809--2 November 1810*, Vol. 2. Charlottesville, University Press of Virginia, p. 131.

4 *Ibid*., p. 131.

5 "Account with St. Mary's College" quoted in Stagg, p. 370.

6 Dolley Payne Madison letter to Anna Payne Cutts, quoted in Virginia Moore (1979). *The Madison's: A Biography*. New York, McGraw-Hill Book Company, p. 267.

7 Ketcham, p. 552.

8 Moore, p. 238. Interestingly, James Madison learned French as a boy while at Donald Robertson's school. Emulating his teacher, he spoke the language with a considerable Scottish accent.

9 Dolley Payne Madison letter to Anna Payne Cutts, quoted in Virginia Moore (1979). *The Madison's: A Biography*. New York, McGraw-Hill Book Company, p. 267.

10 Charlene M. Boyer Lewis (2012). *Elizabeth Patterson Bonaparte: An American Aristocrat in the Early Republic*. Philadelphia, University of Pennsylvania Press, p. 42.

11 Bryan Clark Green, Ann L. Miller, and Conover Hunt (2007). *Building a President's House: The Construction of Montpelier*. Orange, Virginia, The Montpelier Foundation, pp 17-21.

12 See http://www.montpelier.org/mansion-and-grounds/landscape/mr-madisons-temple.

13 Dolley Madison letter of 15 November 1811 quoted in Allan Clark (1914). *The Life and Letters of Dolly Madison*. Washington, DC, W.F. Roberts Company, p. 123.

14 Phoebe Morris letter to Rebecca Morris, 1812, quoted in Clark, p. 125.

15 See http://www.pbs.org/benfranklin/l3_wit_franklin.html.

16 Ethel Stephens Arnett (1972). *Mrs. James Madison: The Incomparable Dolley*. Greensboro, Piedmont Press, pp. 170-171.

17 Allgor, p. 240.

18 Margaret Bayard Smith quoted in Catherine Allgor (2006). *A Perfect Union: Dolley Madison and the Creation of the American Nation.* New York, Henry Holt and Company, p. 72.

19 The term "First Lady" was first used in reference to Dolley Madison although it was not until after her death in 1849.

20 Dolley Madison letter to Betsy Patterson Bonaparte quoted in Charlene M. Boyer Lewis (2012). *Elizabeth Patterson Bonaparte: An American Aristocrat in the Early Republic.* Philadelphia, University of Pennsylvania Press, p. 45.

21 Allgor, p. 72.

22 Ibid., p. 181.

23 Moore, pp. 279-280.

24 There is only one known portrait of Phoebe Pemberton Morris (April 4, 1791 – May 30, 1825). It was done by Charles Willson Peale circa 1792 when Phoebe was just one year old. She is pictured with blond hair and dark brown eyes wearing a grey-white cap and a cream-white dress with pink rosebuds.

25 Phoebe Morris letter to Dolley Payne Madison, 19 December 1811, quoted in Peter Grace Dunlop (1944). "Unpublished Letters of Dolly Madison to Anthony Morris Relating to the Nourse Family of the Highlands." *Records of the Columbia Historical Society* 44-45: p. 231.

26 Dolley Madison quoted in Ketcham, p. 512.

27 Phoebe Morris letter to Rebecca Morris, 1812, quoted in Clark, p. 125.

28 Moore, p. 374.

29 Lucy's first husband, George Steptoe Washington had died three years earlier in 1809. Ketcham, *James Madison*, p. 520.

30 Phoebe Morris letter to Anthony Morris, 22 March 1812, quoted in Clark, p. 128. The marriage of Judge Todd to Lucy Washington was the first ever held at the President's House.

31 Dolley Madison quoted in Clark, p. 130.

32 Clinton died on April 20, 1812. See the Congressional Cemetery's website at: http://www.congressionalcemetery.org/vice-president-george-clinton. His body was reinterred to Kingston, New York in 1908.

33 *Ibid.*

34 Elbridge Gerry died in office on November 23, 1814. The *National Daily Intelligencer* reported, "His death was as sudden as it was unexpected. In apparent health, he presided in the Senate during an arduous sitting on the preceding day; fifteen minutes before his death, although in his seventieth year, he bade fair to outlive many of those who read these lines. At a few minutes warning, the thread of life was cut, and his spirit winged its flight to happier realms." Gerry's remains still rest at Congressional Cemetery in Washington, D.C. (R 29/9-11). Madison remains the only President in history to have had two vice presidents die while serving in office.

35 Nelly Conway Madison Willis was the daughter of James Madison's brother, Ambrose.

36 David Mattern and Holly Shulman provide an invaluable biographical index in their book, *The Selected Letters of Dolley Payne Madison*, pp. 393-416.

37 Neely Conway Willis letter to Dolley Payne Madison, 14 July 1812, from the Manuscript Collections of the Greensboro Historical Museum.

38 Nathaniel Macon quoted in Ketcham, p. 524.

39 James Madison quoted in J.C.A. Stagg, Ed. (1999). *The Papers of James Madison: Presidential Series 5 November 1811—9 July 1812*, Vol. 4. Charlottesville, University Press of Virginia, p. 436.

40 Stagg, *Papers of James Madison*, Vol. 4, pp. xxxi-xxxii.

41 Alexander Hanson quoted in Pitch, Anthony S. (1998). *The Burning of Washington: The British Invasion of 1814*. Annapolis, Md., Naval Institute Press, p. 1. One popular toast during the war was "*The President of the United States*—respect for the office, but contempt for the incumbent; an immediate resignation his first duty, the island of Elba his last retreat." See Moore, p. 302.

42 Mathew Carey letter of James Madison, 1 August, 1812 quoted in J.C.A. Stagg, Ed. (2004). *The Papers of James Madison: Presidential Series 10 July 1812—7 February 1813*, Vol. 5. Charlottesville, University Press of Virginia, p. 109.

43 Mathew Carey letter of James Madison, 12 August, 1812 quoted in Stagg, Vol. 5, p. 149.

44 Allan Nevins, ed. (1951). *The Diary of John Quincy Adams, 1794-1845: American Diplomacy, and Political, Social, and Intellectual Life, from Washington to Polk*. New York, Frederick Unger Publishing Company, p. 67.

45 Moore, p. 286.

46 Ketcham, p. 552.

47 Payne would eventually receive the rank of "colonel" and would use the rank as a title throughout his life.

48 James Madison letter to Albert Gallatin, 24 April 1813 quoted in J.C.A. Stagg, Ed. (2008). *The Papers of James Madison: Presidential Series 8 February—24 October 1813*, Vol. 6. Charlottesville, University Press of Virginia.

49 James Madison letter to Albert Gallatin, 26 April 1813 quoted in Stagg, *Papers of James Madison*, Vol 6, p. 237.

50 Dolley Madison letter, 10 June 1813, quoted in Lucie Cutts (1887). *Memoirs and Letters of Dolly Madison: Wife of James Madison, President of the United States*. Boston, Houghton, Mifflin and Company, p. 92.

51 Napoleon had taken Moscow in 1812, but was forced to retreat due to the horrendous Russian winter. The Grand Army took an estimated 380,000 casualties during the disastrous military campaign. Alexander I became known as the "Tsar Liberator."

52 Henry Clay quoted in Clark, p. 483.

53 Douglas Wead (2003). *All the President's Children: Triumph and Tragedy in the Lives of America's First Families*. New York, Atria Books, p. 333.

54 The girl's name was supposedly Olga but nothing more is known about this mysterious princess. Allegedly, her father removed her from St. Petersburg and Payne's grasp. Moore, p. 335.

55 *Ibid.*, p. 299.

56 Dolley Payne Madison letter to John Payne Todd, 6 August 1814, quoted in Moore, p. 328.

57 Hannah Gallatin letter to Dolley Payne Todd, 2 July 1814, quoted in Moore, p. 128.

58 Albert Gallatin letter to John Payne Todd, quoted in Moore, pp. 334-335.

59 Moore, p. 352.

60 Madison quoted in Moore, p. 354.

61 Stagg, *Papers of James Madison*, Vol. 6, p. 238 n. 1.

62 Thomas Jefferson quoted in Donald R. Hickey (2012). *The War of 1812: A Forgotten Conflict*. Chicago, University of Illinois Press, p. 183.

63 Margaret Bayard Smith in Gary Hunt, Ed. (1906). *The First Forty Years of Washington Society Portrayed by the Family of Letters by Mrs. Samuel (Margaret Bayard) Harrison Smith*. New York, Charles Scribner & Sons in Hunt, p. 98.

64 Anthony S. Pitch (1998). *The Burning of Washington: The British Invasion of 1814*. Annapolis, Md., Naval Institute Press, p. 48.

65 Hickey, p. 205.

66 Dolley Payne Madison letter to Anna Payne Cutts quoted in Cutts, pp. 108-109.

67 *Ibid.*, p. 109.

68 Pitch, p. 86.

69 Charles Ball quoted in Elizabeth Dowling Taylor (2012). *A Slave in the White House: Paul Jennings and the Madisons*. New York: Palgrave/McMillan Books, p. 50.

70 Smith in Hunt, p. 101.

71 Margaret Bayard Smith quoted in Hunt, p. 103.

72 *Ibid.*, p. 99.

73 The Gilbert Stuart painting of George Washington is now on display in the East Room of the White House.

74 Dolley Payne Madison letter to Anna Payne Cutts quoted in Cutts, p. 111. The portrait was transported and stored safely in a barn in Maryland.

75 See *The Writings of James Madison*, August 24, 1814, "Observations on the capture of Washington D.C. by British Troops available at http://memory.loc.gov.

76 Pitch, p. 101.

77 Margaret Bayard Smith quoted in Hunt, p 111.

78 Hickey, p. 209.

79 Margaret Bayard Smith quoted in Green, Constance McLaughlin (1962). *Washington: Village and Capital, 1800-1878*. Princeton, Princeton University Press, pp. 62-63.

80 Margared Bayard Smith quoted in Hunt, p. 109.

81 James Monroe quoted in Troy Bickham (2012). *The Weight of Vengeance: The United States, the British Empire, and the War of 1812*. New York: Oxford University Press, p 166.

82 *Ibid.*, p. 110.

83 John Payne Todd letter to James Madison, 9 October 1814, quoted in Moore, p. 338.

84 The flag is on permanent exhibit at the Smithsonian's American History Museum.

85 Hickey, p. 212. "The Star-Spangled Banner" did not become the official national anthem for the United States until 1931, during the Hoover administration.

86 Margaret Bayard Smith quoted in Hunt, p. 115.

87 James Monroe to the American Commissioners, January 24, 1814 quoted in James F. Hopkins and Mary W.M. Hargreaves, Ed. (1959). *The Papers of Henry Clay: Rising Statesman 1797–1814*. Lexington, University of Kentucky Press, p 857.

88 Bruce Chadwick (2014). *James & Dolley Madison: America's First Power Couple*. New York: Prometheus Books, p. 318.

89 Fred Kaplan,(2014). John Quincy Adams: American Visionary. New York, HarperCollins Publishers, p. 291.

90 James Madison quoted in Hickey, p. 300.

91 Moore, pp. 351-352; also see Wead, p. 334.

92 *Ibid.*, p. 353.

93 Ralph Ketcham (2009). *The Madisons at Montpelier: Reflections on the Founding Couple.* Charlottesville, University of Virginia Press, p. 11.

94 Moore, p. 358.

95 James Madison to Albert Gallatin, March 31, 1817 quoted in David Mattern, ed. (2009). *The Papers of James Madison: Retirement Series 4 March--31 January 1820.* Charlottesville, University Press of Virginia, p. 20

96 The paintings of James and Dolley Madison are on permanent display at the Virginia Historical Society in Richmond.

97 Eliza Collins Lee quoted in Clark, p. 207.

98 Mary Cutts quoted in Catherine Allgor, Ed. (2012). *The Queen of America: Mary Cutt's Life of Dolley Madison.* Charlottesville, University of Virginia Press, p. 200.

99 *Ibid.*, p. 207.

100 The Wood miniature of Payne Todd is in the collections of the Metropolitan Museum in New York City. It is not currently on display. Accession #36.73.

101 Thomas Jefferson letter to James Madison, 10 March 1817, quoted in David Mattern, ed. (2009). *The Papers of James Madison: Retirement Series 4 March 1817--31 January 1820*, Vol. 1. Charlottesville, University Press of Virginia, p 9.

102 Thomas Jefferson letter to James Madison, 15 April 1817, quoted in James Morton Smith (1995). *The Republic of Letters: The Correspondence between Thomas Jefferson and James Madison 1776-1826.* New York, W.W. Norton & Company, p 1785.

103 Nelly Conway Madison (January 9, 1731-February 11, 1829) lived to be 98 years old. She predeceased her son by just seven years.

104 Payne Todd finally left Washington on June 29.

105 Montzelun visited the Madison's at Montpelier from September 16 through September 23, 1816.

106 Baron de Montzelun quoted in L.G. Moffattand and J. M. Carrière. "A Frenchman Visits Norfolk, Fredericksburg and Orange County, 1816," *The Virginia Magazine of History and Biography.* Vol. 53, No. 3, July 1945, p. 198.

107 *Ibid.*, p. 202.

108 Montzelun quoted in Moffattand, pp. 199 and 202.

109 *Ibid.*, pp. 199, 212.

110 Maud Wilder Goodwin (1897). *Dolly Madison: Women of Colonial and Revolutionary Times.* New York, Charles Scribner's Sons, p. 149.

111 Moore, p. 379.

112 Clark, p. 484.

113 Chadwick, p. 321.

114 Moore, p. 382.

Chapter Four

1820 - 1829

"To Love liberty, a nation need but know it."

A Toast in 1825

P resident James Monroe was reelected in 1820 by a historic electoral landslide. He carried every state in the union and all of the electoral votes save one. A "faithless" New Hampshire elector chose to cast his vote for John Quincy Adams to ensure that George Washington would continue to hold the distinction of being the only person ever elected to the presidency unanimously.[1] The international crises that had preoccupied the United States since its founding had finally subsided with the end of the War of 1812 and President Monroe presided over the nation's increasing economic prosperity as well as the population's relentless migration westward. The decennial census recorded in 1820 that there were just under 10 million inhabitants in the United States, representing a staggering 33% increase in just ten years.

The Louisiana Purchase which was universally celebrated as the landmark achievement of the Jefferson administration, had effectively doubled the size of the United States at a minimal financial cost of just 42-cents an acre. The massive region was rapidly being settled and domesticated. Ultimately, portions of 14 new states would be carved from the gigantic land mass, but ironically, this *cherished land acquisition proved to be responsible for creating the major domestic policy crisis in 1820. The issue centered over the potential admission of Missouri to the union as a slave state as well as the potential future expansion of slavery into the remaining territories.*

There was a general consensus throughout the United States that slavery was a malicious system and that it would eventually be eliminated. But an immediate solution proved elusive if not impossible. Few southerners were willing to sacrifice their financial wealth and their personal well-being for a moral principle and chattel labor remained the basis for the region's lucrative cotton-based economy. Still, the nation's political leadership hoped to devise a new, national policy that would lead to the gradual elimination of slavery and one which would provide financial compensation to slave owners. Most Americans were reluctant to consign blame for a system that had existed for generations; no living American had been involved in its creation or imposition. As Eliphalet Nott noted: "Our Brethren of the South have the sympathies, the same moral sentiments, the same love of liberty as ourselves. By them, as by us, slavery is felt to be an evil, a hindrance to our prosperity, and a blot upon our character. But it was being when they were born and has been forced upon them by a previous generation."[2]

The American Colonization Society (ACS) had been chartered at the very end of the Madison administration. Its membership included such luminaries as Henry Clay, Daniel Webster, John Marshall, Francis Scott Key, James Madison, and James Monroe. The society encouraged southern plantation owners to emancipate their slaves and the ACS would help relocate these liberated individuals to the new western African colony of Liberia. Its capital, "Monrovia," had been christened in "honor" of the current president.[3]

The first expatriations did not begin until 1822. Liberia was, in reality, a wholly artificial place, created out of convenience and imagination rather than upon any logic or cultural history. Virtually none of the emancipated slaves scheduled for deportation from the United States had any ancestral roots or connections to the region. There were no efforts to take into consideration linguistic or cultural origins and, as a result, few slaves had any desire to resettle in a distant foreign land. This feeble effort to do something about slavery quickly proved impractical and the American Colonization Society would eventually transport just 15,000 emancipated slaves to Africa. At the same time, the domestic enslaved population within the United States increased from 1.5 to 4 million due to domestic birthrates.[4]

Thomas Jefferson was now an elderly man, living in quiet retirement and repose at his mountain-top refuge, Monticello. When the Missouri controversy erupted in Congress, the former president was dismayed. He foresaw that slavery had the potential to divide and even destroy the fledgling United States. Jefferson was convinced, though, that despite the crisis, under the United States Constitution, the federal government had no right to legislate any restrictions on slavery in the existing states or its new territories. By allowing the expansion of slavery into the western states, Jefferson rationalized that the system would be "diffused," and that this could actually result in an improvement in the living conditions of enslaved people by breaking up the monopoly of large plantations. Jefferson hoped that slavery would be "mitigated, weakened, and ultimately destroyed."[5]

The Speaker of the House, Henry Clay, was able to cleverly resolve the legislative controversy with a brilliant compromise. Missouri would be admitted to the union as a slave state while Maine would be similarly admitted as a free state.[6] This would establish a delicate balance of 12 slave and 12 free states and ensure that southerners would continue to maintain political power in the Senate and be able to block any potential efforts to regulate slavery.[7] Moreover, the compromise mandated that the latitude line of 36°30' would serve as a demarcation line across the remaining portions of the Louisiana Territory. All future states to the south would enter the union as slave-holding states while those to the north would be ad-

Henry Clay of Kentucky. Clay was primarily responsible for negotiating the Missouri Compromise which maintained the Senatorial balance between slave and free states. Thomas Jefferson prophetically warned: "I considered it at once as the knell of the Union. it is hushed indeed for the moment. but this is a reprieve only, not a final sentence. a geographical line, coinciding with a marked principle, moral and political, once conc[ei]ved and held up to the angry passions of men, will never be obliterated. " (Library of Congress)

mitted as free. The Missouri Compromise was destined to last for 30 years but it did nothing to resolve the fundamental issue of slavery. Thomas Jefferson was disheartened by all of the political machinations in Washington and in an evocative letter to Congressman John Holmes, he declared that the entire Missouri episode was: "like a fire bell in the night, awakened and filled me with terror. I considered it at once as the death knell of the Union. it is hushed indeed for the moment. but this is a reprieve only, not a final sentence. a geographical line, coinciding with a marked principle, moral and political, once conceived and held up to the angry passions of men, will never be obliterated...we have the wolf by the ear, and we can neither hold him, nor safely let him go. Justice is in one scale, and self-preservation in the other...I regret that I am now to die in the belief that the useless sacrifice of themselves, by the generation of [17]76, to acquire self government and happiness to their country, is to be thrown away by the unwise and unworthy passions of their sons, and that my only consolation is to be that I live not to weep over it. "[8]

———————

IN 1820, JOHN PAYNE TODD turned 28-years old. He had reached an age when most of his contemporaries had well-established careers and had started families, but Payne obstinately remained a blithe, directionless bachelor. After his disastrous failure at silk worm farming, he temporarily abandoned Toddsberth and left Orange County for extended periods of time. His actual whereabouts were frequently unknown to his increasingly alarmed parents. Indeed, James and Dolley Madison continually fretted over their troublesome son's future and his ultimate fate. Payne remained oblivious to their concerns and was apparently resigned to the fact that he would forever disappoint. Indeed, there could be no way that he could ever fulfill his parents' high expectations and he was fully cognizant of the reality that he would never duplicate his stepfather's intellectual accomplishments nor equal his mother's esteemed status in American society. It proved far easier to escape into his Bacchanal pursuits and to pursue his endless quest for fast, easy money.

In the late winter of 1820 during one of Payne's infrequent and unpredictable visits to Montpelier, he surprised his parents by announcing plans to take a trip to Pennsylvania to visit Phoebe Morris at her father's home, Bolton Farm. The two had remained distant friends over the years and for Dolley, the news revived her hopes that Payne would eventually marry Phoebe who she saw as the ideal spouse.[9] Once in a letter to her father, Phoebe candidly acknowledged that: "[Mrs. Madison] says that she indeed considers me as her daughter…she repeats to me very often her earnest hopes that I may one day be her daughter in reality."[10]

Dolley and Phoebe held each other in high regard and they corresponded frequently. In one letter, Phoebe wrote admiringly to Dolley: "When I review the incidents in my life which will appear to me among the most important in its varied character, I always trace your hand in their origin."[11] She continued to profess a fondness for Payne who still had the remarkable ability to charm and deceive. Phoebe gushed in a letter to Dolley that: "it is my delight, to know, that he inherits your engaging affability, & it shall be my prayer to Heaven, that he may add to the great blessings you possess, in the society of the best of Husbands, every source of joy and consolation which a Parents Heart can feel."[12] It was truly naïve and unmerited praise.

It had been a considerable time since Phoebe and Payne had actually seen one another and she was greatly anticipating a joyful reunion at Bolton. Inexplicably, though, weeks passed with no sign or word from Payne. Phoebe was crestfallen and her father was justifiably annoyed. Just as they were about to abandon any hopes of ever seeing Payne, he arrived in July. Anthony Morris shared the news immediately with Dolley writing: "Phoebe had delayd so long a reply to your most welcome letter of April in the daily expectation of seeing Mr. Todd that she was about concluding him a false Knight, and was actually preparing a denunciation of him to you, when he suddenly appeared at Bolton to speak for himself." Payne was amiable and affable, leading Morris to conclude that: "...he has silenced all censure, and made the most favorib[l]e impressions on our hearts, indeed my excellent friend I cant convey to you the pleasure his company afforded to us all."[13]

For a brief time, Phoebe and Payne enjoyed one another's company, taking long, leisurely rides on horseback through the countryside. Phoebe continually to probe Payne for information about his mother, so much so that he soon became exasperated. In a subsequent letter to Dolley, Phoebe explained: "I dare say he has been sufficiently wearied with my questions, for I was so glad to see him and to know every thing about you, how you looked, what you did, what you put on, &c &c all the minute details which I thought my long absence would make reasonable, however I think I have extracted this satisfaction from him, that you are still my own Mrs Madison, blooming, gay, and affectionate as ever." [14]

Despite Phoebe's blissful company, Payne quickly became restless and bored while at Bolton. He far preferred "the turbulent varieties of the gay world" and city life to the tranquil sanctuary of the countryside.[15] Suddenly and without adequate explanation, he departed despite both Phoebe and Anthony Morris's entreaties "... to induce Payne to remain for a longer time among us...but all our united attractions failed after two short days & he proceeded on his journey"[16] Phoebe was dejected; her promising romance had ended forever and she would never see her "false knight" again. Just five years later, she died from tuberculosis at the age of 34 having never married.[17]

———————————

IN JANUARY 1824, PHOEBE MORRIS was staying at one of the row of townhouses known as the Six Buildings in Washington,

D.C.[18] Everything about the nation's capital reminded her of the earlier good times she had spent in the company of the Madison's. In
a letter to the former first lady, she nostalgically remembered "the
happy period of my early youth which was rendered more joyous
by your protecting care."[19] The biggest news circulating throughout the capital that winter were rumors of a potential visit to the
United States by the Marquis de Lafayette. Phoebe enthusiastically
inquired of Dolley: "What do you think of the probability of having the Marquis de la Fayette for a visitor? For surely he will go to
Montpelier, should he visit the United States."[20]

The following month, Congress passed a resolution extending
an official invitation to the Marquis to come to America. President
James Monroe forwarded it with a letter to Lafayette urging him to
visit the "adopted country of your early youth, which has always
preserved the most grateful recollection of your important services."[21]

Lafayette remained a revered figure throughout the United
States. He was a genuine hero of the Revolution and a living icon
of American independency. Lafayette had voluntarily come to the
United States in 1777, an idealistic 20-year old French nobleman
enticed by the fledgling American nation's radical ideas concerning
self-government, individual freedom, and human liberty. For Lafayette, it was a refreshing and startling philosophical contrast to the
stratified, stagnate society that he had left behind in France during
the reign of Louis XVI.

Lafayette was soon commissioned by the Continental Congress
as a Major General in the American army and in that role, he would
participate in many of the most important campaigns and battles of
the Revolution. He became a close friend, confident, and surrogate
son to General George Washington, and Lafayette would exercise
his political influence to help sway the French government to militarily intervene on behalf of the United States in its ongoing strug-

gle against England. Ultimately, it would be Lafayette's forces that effectively cornered Lord Cornwallis' army at Yorktown in 1781, which leading to the climactic siege that would end the war and secure American independency.[22]

Now, almost five decades later, the generation of 1776 was rapidly passing into history. Lafayette hoped to pay a final visit to his surviving compatriots during his 1824-1825 grand tour of all of the nation's 24 states. On August 15, 1824 he arrived at Staten Island, New York and from there traveled to Quincy, Massachusetts for a reunion with the great John Adams. The two men spent an afternoon in animated conversation and reflection, but the curmudgeonly former President later remarked somewhat disappointedly: "That was not the Lafayette I knew."[23] In truth, both of their memories had been tempered and distorted by age and time. They were no longer the vigorous, bold patriots who had once been comrades in a principled revolution against British colonial rule; instead, they were old men facing the reality of their own imminent mortality. A few weeks later, James Madison would privately confide to his wife that Lafayette "is in fine health and spirits but so much increased in bulk and changed in aspect that I should not have known him."[24]

Still, Lafayette's visit to the United States proved to be an enormous success. In every city, town, and hamlet he visited, he was welcomed with elaborate celebrations and galas. While in Washington, D.C., the park located directly across from the President's House was renamed in his honor. Lafayette later spent the night just across the Potomac at the majestic Arlington House mansion as the honored guest of George Washington Parke Custis, the surviving step-grandson of General Washington. On October 17, he visited Mount Vernon to pay his respects at the tomb of his friend and the nation's first president, George Washington.[25] According to his secretary and traveling companion, Auguste Levasseur: "Lafayette descended alone into the vault, and a few minutes after re-appeared, with his eyes overflowing with tears. He took his son (George Washington Lafayette) and me by the hand, and led us into the tomb, where by a sign he indicated the coffin of his paternal friend...we knelt reverently near his coffin, which we respectfully saluted with our lips; rising we threw ourselves into the arms of Lafayette, and mingled our tears with his."[26]

From Mount Vernon, Lafayette traveled on to Yorktown and from there, made his way to Charlottesville, where he was scheduled to meet with both Thomas Jefferson and James Madison. Escorted by a contingent of Albemarle County's leading citizens, the Marquis de Lafayette arrived at Monticello on November 4th. He found Jefferson to be elderly and physically infirm but still in "full possession of all the vigor of his mind and heart."[27] James Madison, too, was in his twilight years but as Auguste Levasseur noted: "at the time of our visit [Madison] was seventy-four years (sic) of age, but his well-preserved frame contained a youthful soul full of sensibility, which he did not hesitate to show."[28]

The following day, Jefferson, Madison, and Lafayette traveled together by carriage the short distance to Charlottesville, where they attended a special dinner at the new University of Virginia. The college was still primitive and unfinished, but it was to become one of Jefferson's proudest accomplishments.[29] Chartered by the General Assembly in 1819, the grounds had been carefully surveyed and personally laid out by Jefferson.[30] He meticulously designed each of the campus' buildings and even supervised their construction. As Levasseur recorded in his journal: "Mr. Jefferson himself...passed several hours daily either among the workmen, or amidst the pupils and professors, who all profited by his wise counsel."[31]

The university had just 123 students enrolled in 1824. Its grounds consisted of ten, two-story, brick pavilions which served as both classrooms and residences for the professors. Interspersed among them were 54 student rooms which were symmetrically laid out in a horseshoe fashion separated into east and west wings by an open lawn.[32] There was also an outer crescent of classrooms and student

The Rotunda at the University of Virginia. It was here in the third floor dome room that a gala dinner was held in Lafayette's honor. The University was Jefferson's primary interest during his retirement years at Monticello. James Madison served on the Board of Visitors and would later serve as the college's president. (Library of Congress)

residences known as the range. At the center of the university was the domed Rotunda, a magnificent half-scale replica of the Parthenon in Rome. It would, in due course, house the school's library, the very heart and soul of the university. It was here in the uncompleted third floor dome room that was the site for the Lafayette banquet honoring him not only for his Revolutionary service but also as the first official guest of the University of Virginia.

Over 400 guests attended the celebratory dinner, which lasted for more than three hours. The lavish food courses were separated by speeches and punctuated by the traditional 13 toasts, one for each of the original American colonies.[33] It was a joyous, boisterous occasion but everyone present was well aware that they were, in fact, witnessing the final chapter in the lives of these great patriots.

PHEOBE MORRIS' EARLIER PROPHECY was proven true since Lafayette did, indeed, decide to visit the Madison's in Orange County. Jefferson was disappointed that he was too frail to accompany the Marquis to Montpelier, writing: "I would have accompanied the General to-day but…I have not strength."[34]

Lafayette left Charlottesville on November 15 and made the 30-mile journey to Montpelier after a brief stop en route at Thornton's Tavern in Gordonsville. He arrived later that evening and was warmly greeted by his hosts, James and Dolley Madison.[35] Payne Todd was not present on this occasion and his exact whereabouts were currently unknown, much to his parents' embarrassment. A few months earlier, Dolley had gently chastised her wayward son, writing: "I am impatient to hear from you, my dearest Payne, and had I known where to direct I should have written you before this; not that there anything particular to communicate, but for the pleasure of repeating how much I love you, and to hear of your happiness."[36] It was bewildering why Payne would miss the chance to meet Lafayette while he was staying at Montpelier. Indeed, Payne always relished the opportunity to converse in French and show off his European sophistication and to bask in the reflective glory of his distinguished parents. It was a missed opportunity and Todd's behavior was disconcerting and typically unexplained.

Lafayette spent four days at Montpelier enjoying Dolley Madison's legendary hospitality. There were several gatherings of neighbors and friends as well as plenty of time for rousing conversation.[37] The nightly discussions covered a wide range of political topics, including the issue of religious freedom as well as a lively interchange on the contentious issue of slavery. Lafayette openly loathed the entire system, which he viewed as completely incompatible with the ideals of the American Revolution. His liberal opinions on the subject were reinforced while at Montpelier after he visited the plantation's slave quarters. Most of these dwellings were consciously located a distance from the manor house, inconspicuous and out of

Montpelier as it appeared during James and Dolley Madison's retirement. Lafayette visted the Madison's at the estate during his grand tour of the United States. (Library of Congress)

sight. There, Lafayette freely mingled and talked with the enslaved residents. During a visit to the Walnut Grove quarter of the plantation, he was introduced to "Granny Milly." The old woman claimed to be 104 years old and she was a much-loved figure at Montpelier. Milly had been originally owned by Madison's father and first appeared in the Montpelier slave census in 1782. After the death of his father in 1801, Madison inherited Milly. At the time of Lafayette's visit, she was living in retirement with her daughter and her 70-year old granddaughter.[38] To Lafayette's surprise, Milly spoke passable French and could apparently read, proudly showing off her prized possession, a copy of the Greek myth, *Telemachus*.[39]

Lafayette readily conceded that Madison's slaves were well-clothed and well-fed. It was obvious that by the standards of the day, the former president was considered to be a benevolent master but to Lafayette, this did not exonerate Madison from his moral culpability. Indeed, the Marquis believed that no one had the right to own another human being.[40] He gently chided Madison and his fellow planters about their hypocrisy and there was a general consensus that the system of slavery demanded some future remedy, although no one could fathom exactly how that would be achieved. Lafayette's secretary, Levasseur, optimistically recorded in his journal that "all enlightened men condemn the principle of [slavery], and when public opinion condemns a principle, its consequences cannot long continue to subsist."[41]

It was a short but agreeable visit for Lafayette, a welcomed respite from his arduous travel schedule. He had found the elderly Madison to be still an impressive figure and an intellectual titan. "Mr. Madison," noted Levasseur, "stood out among all of them for the originality of his mind and the delicacy of his allusions."[42] On November 19, Lafayette and his entourage departed Montpelier for Fredericksburg. Madison accompanied them to the Orange County Court House where there was yet another banquet held in Lafayette's honor. After the prerequisite speeches and toasts, the pair bid one another adieu. Madison recorded that: "[Lafayette] took his final leave [carrying]…with him the unanimous blessings of the free nation which has adopted him, [and deserved honor]…due to the nobleness of his mind and the grandeur of his career."[43]

SHORTLY AFTER LAFAYETTE'S DEPARTURE from Montpelier, Dolley received two letters from her prodigal son, Payne Todd. In her response, Dolley wrote that they had recently entertained Henry Clay. The Speaker, who had been with Payne during his European sojourn, had graciously inquired as to Payne's well-being. Dolley was chagrined and had to make excuses for her son's insolence. "Mr Clay with 2 members of congress left us yesterday after passing 2 days," she wrote. "Mr. C. enquired affectionately after you, as, does all your old acquaintance whom I see—but my dear son it seems to be the wonder of them all that you shd. stay so long

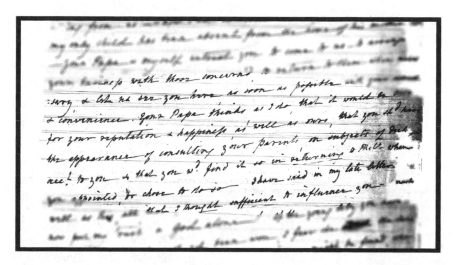

Dolley Payne Todd's plaintive letter to her son, John Payne Todd urging him to return home to Montpelier, 2 December 1824. Payne continued his roguish and self-destructive behavior, oblivious to the concerns of his parents. (Library of Congress)

from us! long my only child has been absent from the home of his mother![44]

Dolley urged Payne to put his affairs in order and to return home to Montpelier: "Your Papa & myself entreat you to come to us—to arrange your business with those concern'd to return to them when necessary, & let us see you here, as soon as possible with your interest & convenience. Your Papa thinks as I do, that it would be best for your reputation & happiness, as well as ours, that you shd have the appearance of consulting your parents, on subjects of deep acct. to you & that you wd. find it so in *returning* to Phila. when you appointed, or choose to do so."[45]

Payne remained oblivious to his parent's concerns and ignored their pleas. He continued unabated in his self-indulgent behavior. There had been persistent rumors that Payne was romantically involved with a woman, purported to be Anne Cole of Williamsburg. Whatever his affections may have been, they were clearly not reciprocated.[46] Dolley, realizing the futility of his quixotic pursuits, urged Payne to abandon his unattainable quest. "I have said in my

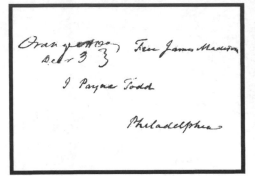

A free-franked envelope signed by former President James Madison addressed to his stepson, John Payne Todd in Philadelphia. (Greensboro Historical Museum)

late letters, as well as this, all that *I thought sufficient* to influence you—I must now, put my trust in God alone! If the young lady you have followed so long, has not yet been won, I fear she (hasn't) the character to form your happiness here after, tho others might be found, who would."[47] It seemed that Payne was destined to remain a bachelor, albeit a rapidly aging one. In historian Maud Wilder Goodwin words, Payne chose to "drown his sorrow, if indeed his nature was capable of any real grief, in the wine-cup, and continued to amuse himself with other kindred spirits around the gaming-table."[48] His itinerant existence continued as he wandered and traveled throughout the east coast, rarely writing his anxious parents.

WITH THE FINAL POLITICAL demise of the Federalists, the nation was reduced to just one major party, the Democratic-Republicans. In 1824, without any formal nomination process, several state legislatures independently chose their own favorite son candidates for the presidency. These included Andrew Jackson of Tennessee, John Quincy Adams of Massachusetts, and Henry Clay of Kentucky. In Washington the Congressional caucus selected its own candidate, the current Secretary of the Treasury, William Crawford of Georgia. There were 24 states in the union in 1824 with a combined total of 261 electoral votes; an absolute majority of 132 was required to elect a new president.[49] If none of the candidates received the prerequisite number of votes, the House of Representatives was, under the provisions of the XII Amendment, empowered to select the president from the top three electoral vote getters.[50]

The power to determine how electors for president were selected was expressly granted to the individual state legislatures by the Constitution. For the first time in the nation's short history, a majority of the states (18) had adopted new laws that allowed the people to vote directly for a candidate's slate of electors. A majority of the popular vote within the state would then democratically determine which candidate would win the state's entire allotment of electors. The traditional system of having electors appointed by the state legislature was still retained by the remaining six states.[51]

In creating a republican form of government, the Founding Fathers had never envisioned individual citizens voting within their states for the president. Instead, the system they had designed and implemented instituted an indirect election process whereby a group of wise individuals would choose a president based upon merit rather than popularity or impulse. This would help ensure that a president would remain above the crass politics of the day and would be dedicated to promoting the general welfare of the people.

In Federalist #10, James Madison expressly warned against the dangers of America's democratic propensities, claiming that popularly elected governments were always "spectacles of turbulence and contention...incompatible with personal security or the rights of property."[52] Moreover, in another essay, he expressed his fear that politicians would become unprincipled "courtiers of popularity."[53] John Adams agreed with Madison's assessment but was even more candid, definitively declaring that "Democracy never lasts long. It soon wastes, exhausts, and murders itself. There is never a democracy that did not commit suicide."[54]

Despite these forewarnings, the country's rapidly changing demographics impacted politics. The era of Washington, Adams, Hamilton, Jefferson, Madison and a dispassionate natural aristocracy was over as lesser figures commanded the national stage. Of the four candidates running for president in 1824, Andrew Jackson was the most problematic. "Old Hickory" was popularly acclaimed to be the true champion of the common man. His military triumphs and reputation as a fierce Indian fighter were legendary and had made him famous, even revered, among the masses. In truth, Jackson could be crude, uncouth, hot tempered, and vindictive. His sordid history as a dueler and brawler led his opponent, John Quincy Adams, to privately dismiss Jackson as "a barbarian who could not write a sentence of grammar and hardly could spell his own name."[55]

John Quincy Adams was by far the most qualified and most experienced candidate for president in 1824. Having served with distinction in the government for decades, he was currently acting as President James Monroe's Secretary of State and his heir apparent. But to Adams' dismay, Monroe refused to endorse his candidacy, feeling that it was undignified for the president to engage in partisan politics and was "unjust to the people…to throw the weight of his name and character to either side of any contest."[56]

The remaining two candidates were Henry Clay and William Crawford. Both were experienced and well-known politicians. Clay was the Speaker of the House and the author of the "American System," a bold plan calling for a federal tariff, a sound national bank, and nationally funded internal improvements while Crawford had been a senator, a diplomat, and a cabinet secretary. The Georgian, though, was openly ambitious and occasionally unprincipled leading John Quincy Adams to note that Crawford had "immense patronage throughout the Union, which he exercises to promote his purposes without scruple and without restraint."[57] Prior to the actual election, though, Crawford suffered a debilitating stroke which left him partially blind and slightly paralyzed. Despite his precarious health and physical infirmities, he steadfastly refused to withdraw his name from contention.

During this antebellum period, none of the candidates personally campaigned for the presidency since it was seen as unseemly to openly solicit votes. Thus, it was left to surrogates to advocate for the candidates and these partisans could be ruthless, devious, and amoral. They flooded the newspapers with anonymous letters, salacious rumors, and fictitious stories which helped feed the public's insatiable appetite for scandal. Crawford, for instance, was falsely accused of illicitly trading slaves and mishandling treasury department funds, while Adams was alleged to go to church barefooted and to refuse to wear undergarments.[58]

With four candidates running, the election results were predictably inconclusive. Jackson had won a clear plurality of the popular vote (41%) but this was irrelevant since he had received only 99 electoral votes, far short of the required absolute majority. John Quincy Adams had finished second in the balloting with 84 electoral votes followed by Crawford with 41 and Clay with 37. For the first time since the disputed election of 1800, the House of Representatives would have to determine the new president. The state representatives would have to select from the top three electoral vote getters with Henry Clay eliminated from consideration. The Speaker, though, would ultimately play a pivotal role in the election's final outcome.

THE HOUSE OF REPRESENTATIVES convened on February 9, 1825, to break the electoral deadlock and decide the final outcome of the presidential election. On the first ballot, by a majority vote, John Quincy Adams was elected as the nation's sixth president.[59] Andrew Jackson swallowed his anger and disappointment temporarily and met with Adams later that evening at a reception held at the President's House. He was, in Adams' words: "altogether placid and courteous," but it was a façade that was soon shattered.[60]

In the election, Jackson had clearly won a plurality of both the popular and electoral vote but had still been denied the presidency by Congress. He was convinced that there had been a covert arrangement, a virtual cabal, between John Quincy Adams and Henry Clay whereby the Speaker would use his influence to lobby mem-

The Electoral ballot from the state of Virginia in the 1824 presidential election. Virginia cast its allotment of 24 electoral votes for William Crawford. None of the four candidates, however, won a majority of electoral votes so the election was sent to the House of Representatives for a final decision. (National Archives) bers of the House to throw the election to Adams. This so-called "corrupt bargain" seemed to be confirmed when Clay was appointed the new Secretary of State, an office that many saw to be the logical stepping stone to the presidency. Jackson bitterly remarked: "I weep for the liberty of my country. The rights of the people have been bartered for promises of office…demagogues barter them as sheep in the shambles for their own views and personal aggrandizement."[61]

As Adams prepared to take the oath of office, his supporters arrived en masse in Washington to celebrate his victory. One critic cynically observed that: "The city is thronged with strangers and *Yankees* swarm like the locusts of Egypt in our houses, our beds, and our kneading troughs!"[62] There would be no "honeymoon period" for the new president, however, as Jackson's supporters were determined to undermine and sabotage the new administration. A popular joke of the day asked: "Why is Adams on shaky ground?" Answer: "Because he stands on slippery Clay." The Tennessee legislature, in a contentious act, boldly re-nominated Jackson for president in October 1825, a full three years before the next scheduled election.[63] The political acrimony and division caused a permanent split within the Democratic-Republican Party and resulted in the creation of a new rival, the Whig party.

The presidential campaign of 1828 was one of the most vicious and unprincipled in American history. With the popular vote becoming increasingly more significant, Jackson used his broad populist appeal to maximum advantage and was easily able to defeat Adams in the election. He carried all of the southern and western states and won in an electoral landslide. It proved to be a landmark election and Jackson's presidency would mark a major turning point in American history, one that was not welcomed by James Madison.

ANDREW JACKSON'S INAUGURAL FESTIVITIES in March, 1829, quickly degenerated into a spectacle as over 20,000 of his supporters arrived in the nation's capital to claim their spoils. There were not enough accommodations available within the city to accommodate the revelers, so many had to seek lodging in nearby Georgetown and Alexandria.[64] After Chief Justice John Marshall administered the oath to Jackson on the east portico of the U.S. Capitol, the new president delivered the traditional, albeit unmemorable, inaugural address. After the formal ceremonies had concluded, the true celebrations began as the hordes marched down Pennsylvania Avenue to converge on the President's House. Wearing their muddy boots, they crowded into the formal rooms where they consumed the food and drank up all of the available

Andrew Jackson, "Old Hickory," the seventh President of the United States. Jackson was a populist hero and a champion of the common man. (Library of Congress)

liquor. Margaret Bayard Smith was dismayed by the anarchy and bedlam, writing: "The Majesty of the People had disappeared, and a rabble, a mob, of boys, negros, women, children, scrambling fighting, romping. What a pity what a pity!...the whole house had been inundated by the rabble mob."[65] Some people stole souvenirs while others cut out pieces of drapery and upholstery for keepsakes. Smith recounted that: "Cut glass and china to the amount of several thousands dollars had been broken in the struggle to get the refreshments, punch and other articles had been carried out in tubs and buckets, but had it been in hogsheads it would have been insufficient, ice-creams, and cake and lemonade…Ladies fainted, men were seen with bloody noses and such a scene of confusion took place as is impossible to describe."[66] The crowd had become so large and unruly that the newly inaugurated president was "nearly pressed to death and almost suffocated and torn to pieces by the people in their eagerness to shake hands with Old Hickory." He was eventually forced to flee and seek sanctuary at John Gadsby's new hotel.[67] Smith lamented: "…it was the People's day, and the People's President and the People would rule. God grant that one day or other, the People, do not put down all rule and rulers. I fear, enlightened Freemen as they are, they will be found, as they have been found in all ages and countries where they get the Power in their hands, that of all tyrants, they are the most ferocious, cruel and despotic."[68]

Crowds of Jackson supporters gather on the lawn in front of the President's House, March 4, 1829. The presidential reception quickly degenerated into chaos and people besieged the mansion in search of food, drink, and souvenirs. (Library of Congress)

THOMAS JEFFERSON HAD QUIETLY celebrated his 83rd birthday in April of 1826 at his mountain-top home. The "sage" of Monticello was frail and ailing, well aware that his own life was rapidly nearing an end. Jefferson wrote nostalgically to his closest friend and confident, James Madison: "To myself you have been a pillar of support through life. Take care of me when dead, and be assured that I shall leave with you my last affections."[69]

In their old age, Thomas Jefferson and John Adams had been finally able to put aside their political differences and renew their friendship. Between 1812 and 1826, the two maintained a remarkable correspondence, exchanging some 158 letters.[70] Adams, who was eight years Jefferson's senior, had lost his beloved Abigail in 1818 and he too was in ill-health and suffering from a variety of age-related ailments. In one of his last letters to Jefferson, he wrote: "I wish your health may continue to the last much better than mine. The little strength of mind and considerable strength of body that I once possessed appear to be all gone."[71] He added somberly: "We shall meet again, so wishes and so believes your friend, but if we are disappointed we shall never know it."[72]

Both of these great patriots were concerned that the current generation of Americans had lost their sense of the past and were ignorant of the perilous times during which the nation had been forged. Indeed, most of the nation's citizens took for granted the rights and liberty that they had inherited and typically failed to cherish what they had not earned. With the fiftieth anniversary of the Declaration of Independence approaching, Jefferson found some solace in reflecting upon the past, with his awareness that his revolutionary document would remain a timeless treatise on human liberty and individual freedom.

The mayor of Washington, D.C., Roger Weightman, hoped that Jefferson would personally attend the capital's scheduled Fourth of July commemorations and he extended a formal invitation to the former president. But Jefferson was far too weak to make the

LETTER from THOMAS JEFFERSON,

To Mr. WEIGHTMAN, late Mayor of Washington.

Monticello, June 24th, 1826.

RESPECTED SIR :

The kind invitation I receive from you, on the part of the citizens of the city of Washington, to be present with them at their celebration on the fiftieth anniversary of American Independence, as one of the surviving signers of an instrument pregnant with our own, and the fate of the world, is most flattering to myself, and heightened by the honorable accompaniment proposed for the comfort of such a journey. It adds sensibly to the sufferings of sickness, to be deprived by it of a personal participation in the rejoicings of that day. But acquiescence is a duty, under circumstances not placed among those we are permitted to control. I should indeed, with peculiar delight, have met and exchanged there congratulations personally with the small band, the remnant of that host of worthies, who joined with us on that day, in the bold and doubtful election we were to make for our country, between submission or the sword; and to have enjoyed with them the consolatory fact, that our fellow citizens, after half a century of experience and prosperity, continue to approve the choice we made. May it be to the world, what I believe it will be, (to some parts sooner, to others later, but finally to all,) the signal of arousing men to burst the chains under which monkish ignorance and superstition had persuaded them to bind themselves, and to assume the blessings and security of self-government. That form which we have substituted, restores the free right to the unbounded exercise of reason and freedom of opinion. All eyes are opened, or opening to the rights of man.— The general spread of the light of science has already laid open to every view the palpable truth, that the mass of mankind has not been born with saddles on their backs, nor a favored few, booted and spurred, ready to ride them legitimately, by the grace of God. These are grounds of hope for others. For ourselves, let the annual return of this day, forever refresh our recollections of these rights, and an undiminished devotion to them.

I will ask permission here to express the pleasure with which I should have met my antient neighbours of the city of Washington and its vicinity, with whom I passed so many years of a pleasing social intercourse ; an intercourse which so much relieved the anxieties of the public cares, and left impressions so deeply engraved in my affections, as never to be forgotten. With my regret that ill health forbids me the gratification of an acceptance, be pleased to receive for yourself, and those for whom you write, the assurance of my highest respect and friendly attachments.

TH: JEFFERSON.

A printed broadside of Thomas Jefferson's Fourth of July message, 1826. He optimistically declared that: "All eyes are opened, or opening to the rights of man."(Library of Congress)

journey and reluctantly declined. In his written regrets,
though, Jefferson proclaimed
that: "All eyes are opened, or
opening to the rights of man.
The general spread of science
has already laid open to every view the palpable truth,
that the mass of mankind has
not been born with saddles
on their backs, nor a favored
few booted and spurred ready
to ride them legitimately,
by the grace of God. These
are grounds of hope for others."[73] He went on to urge the
American people to "Let the
annual return of this day forever refresh our recollections
of these rights [of] man, and
an undiminished devotion to
them."[74]

*Thomas Jefferson's grave at Monticello. Both Jef-
ferson and John Adams died on July 4, 1826--the
fiftieth anniversary of the signing of the Declaration of Independence.* (Library of Congress)

Just a few days later, on July
4, 1826, Thomas Jefferson and John Adams both expired within a
few hours of each other. It was precisely fifty years to the day after
the Continental Congress had adopted the Declaration of Independence.[75] Now, only James Madison survived as the direct link to the
nation's founding era.

MADISON WAS RENOWNED THROUGHOUT Virginia as one
of the Commonwealth's most skilled and capable famers. Always
a studious man and a scholar, he read widely and was anxious to
implement the latest scientific farming principles in an ongoing ef-

fort to maximize crop yields and increase his anemic plantation's productivity. Once, at a dinner party with Thomas Jefferson, John Quincy Adams recorded that: "[Jefferson believed] the person who united with other science the greatest agricultural knowledge of any man he knew was Mr. Madison. He was the best farmer in the world."[76]

But despite his skill, James Madison's Montpelier was like all antebellum plantations, cursed by the weather, Hessian flies, crop infestations, and global market fluctuations.[77] These factors were beyond Madison's control, but nevertheless they continued to frustrate him and caused considerable financial strife. In a private letter to Jefferson, Madison lamented: "Since my return to private life such have been the unkind seasons, and the ravages of insects, that I have made but one tolerable crop of Tobacco, and but one of Wheat." He observed that the price for these meager crops was so low that: "having no resources but in the earth I cultivate, I have been living very much throughout on borrowed means."[78] Indeed, Virginia's tobacco culture, which had its origins over two centuries earlier at Jamestown, was in total collapse. Many younger Virginians simply abandoned their ancestral family farms with their massive acreage of depleted, useless soil to seek their new fortunes on the unspoiled western frontier.[79] Of those who remained, many attempted to make a profit by selling off large numbers of their surplus slaves. Unscrupulous and greedy slave-traders eagerly purchased these hapless people and transported them down to the deep cotton south, a region which was in continual need of labor due to its perpetual growing season. This lucrative practice horrified the old Virginia gentry, and in particular, Madison, who refused to engage in the insidious business even though of his 112 slaves, 40 were unproductive children under the age of fourteen.[80] Madison instead tried to diversify by growing wheat as well as operating a grist mill business, but nothing could generate sufficient revenue to offset his expenses. Compounding his financial woes was Payne Todd's reckless spending and rapidly accumulating debt. In a confidential letter to Edward

Coles, Madison chronicled his stepson's most recent "strange and distressing career." He recorded that Payne owed $1,000 to a creditor in Philadelphia; $700 to another individual in New York; $1,300 in Georgetown; and another $600 to an unnamed source. Madison wearily concluded that: "[Payne's] career must soon be fatal to everything dear to him in life; and you will know how to press on him the misery he is inflicting on his parents."[81]

As much as Madison was ashamed and embarrassed by his stepson's irresponsible behavior, he attempted to conceal the actual scope and gravity of Payne's debts from his wife. In reality, Dolley's mendacious son was little more than a ne'er-do-well and Madison was forced to concede that: "With all the concealments and alleviations I have been able to effect, his mother has known enough to make her wretched the whole time of his strange absence and mysterious silence; and it is no longer possible to keep from her the results now threatened. As it is utterly out of my power to support [him] where he is, his continuance there must bring on him the most woeful and degrading consequences."[82]

In an effort to satisfy some of Payne's increasingly irate creditors, Madison tried to mortgage some of his real estate holdings. But land prices in Virginia were so depressed that "not a single purchaser has been found."[83] He was, however, successful in financing a $4,000 bank note which was to help rescue Payne from immediate financial ruin but to his dismay, this enormous sum of money was quickly squandered.[84] By indulging Payne's uncontrolled behavior, Madison was, in fact, actually perpetuating it. There had never been any serious or lasting consequences for Payne actions, so emboldened, he persisted in his itinerant wanderings traveling from city-to-city, from Richmond to Boston. Payne obstinately refused to seek any honest or gainful employment, but was more than willing to engage in subterfuge and fanciful, impractical commercial schemes in a perpetual quest for an easy fortune. These fruitless ventures would include attempts at developing a gold mine as well as building a new railroad. These endeavors inevitably ended in abject failure and succeeded only in amassing more debt.

Dolley continued to ignore Payne's personal slights and persisted in sending him money. In one doleful letter, she wrote to her son: "I enclose you 30$ instead of 20 which you mentiond. & tho I am sure 'tis insufficient for the j[o]urney, I am unable to add to the sum to day—I recently pd. Holoway $200, on your note, with interest for 2 years—The other small debts in this quarter I settled long ago with funds of yours in my hands."[85] She implored him to come home to Montpelier: "I hope you will write me the moment you get this, that I may know certainly your determinations & make up my own... we might rejoice in your immediate union—provided it brought you spe[e]dily to our arms, who love with inexpressible tenderness & constancy. Your own—Mother."[86]

Her pleas were of no avail and finally Madison, exasperated by Payne's insensitive treatment of his mother, wrote a remarkable and uncharacteristically blunt letter to his stepson: "My dear P. What shall I say to you? It is painful to utter reproaches; yet how can they be avoided? Your last letter to your mother made us confident that we should see you in a few days. Weeks have passed without even a line explaining the disappointment, or soothing the anxieties of the tenderest of mothers, wound up to the highest pitch by this addition to your long and mysterious absence."[87] He urged Payne to return to Virginia regardless of his precarious financial circumstances. "Let the worst be known, that the best may be made of it."[88] He continued: "I must not conclude without imploring and conjuring you to hasten to the embraces of your parents, and to put an end to the uncertainties that afflict them; giving immediate assurance that you will do so by a line to your mother by the first mail after this gets to hand. You cannot be too quick in affording relief to her present feelings."[89]

Dolley was quietly resigned to the fact that her son would never be happy living a quiet, contemplative life on a rural Virginia plantation. Instead, he craved and lusted after the excitements and inducements of city life. Dolley acknowledged as much in a letter to her niece, Mary Cutts: "I sincerely hope to see him soon, though it is impossible for him to prefer Virginia to the North." Montpelier at least was a bucolic sanctuary of happiness and solitude. "Here I find it most agreeable to stay at home," she concluded, "everything around me is so beautiful."[90]

AS THE DECADE APPROACHED an end, the Madisons suffered a series of family crises. "Mother" Madison who was approaching 98 years of age, had enjoyed relatively good health despite her years. In the summer of 1828 on a visit to Montpelier, Margaret Bayard Smith observed that: "[Mrs. Madison] lacks but 3 years of being a hundred years old. When I enquired of how she was, 'I have been a blest woman,' she replied, 'blest all my life, and blest in this my old age. I have no sickness, no pain, excepting my hearing, my senses are but little impaired. I pass my time in reading and knitting."[91] But within a few months, on February 11, 1829, Nelly Conway Madison died and was buried next to her husband in the family cemetery. It was a painful loss for both James and Dolley who were themselves elderly. Madison, whose health had always been fragile, was suffering from numerous age-related ailments, particularly the painful and often debilitating effects of rheumatism and arthritis. That year, he also was sick with a prolonged bout with the flu. Slow to recover, he was bedridden much of the time.[92] To add to their personal woes, word was received that Payne Todd had been confined to a debtor's prison in Philadelphia. It was no longer possible to overlook their son's irresponsible behavior. Dolley was in anguish, writing: "My pride—my sensibility, & every feeling of my Soul is wounded."[93] In a sad letter to sister, Anna, she confided: "I rcd. One [letter] from him in which he tells me that he was Boarding within

Prison bounds! For a d[ebt] of 2—or 300$ he has submitted to this horrid—horrid situation. It almost breaks my heart to think of it."[94] Even more distressing were the observations from one Madison relative who informed the family that he had been stunned by Payne's deteriorating health and physical appearance. He warned ominously that: "unless [Payne] can be forced to leave this place, all hope of reclaiming him will be lost."[95]

ON APRIL 30, 1829, George Washington Adams drowned after falling overboard while sailing on a steamer, *Benjamin Franklin*, en route from Rhode Island to New York. No one knew if it was a tragic accident or an intentional suicide, but the 28-year old lawyer had been drinking heavily and acting strangely before the incident. He claimed to be suffering from severe headaches and was hearing birds talking to him.[96] It was common knowledge that George Adams was an alcoholic, but he was also being secretly blackmailed by his former mistress, Eliza Dolph, who had recently given birth to his illegitimate child.

His father, the former president, John Quincy Adams, was disconsolate and his despair made worse by the fact that his son's body was not recovered for over a month.[97] In his private diary Adams wrote: "Oh! My unhappy Son! What a Paradise of early enjoyment I had figured to myself as awaiting thee and me. It is withered forever."[98]

Another son, John Adams II, was also proving to be a disappointment to the family. His mother, Louisa, once referred to her son as "a hotheaded, noble, rash boy" who was frequently a source of exasperation for his father. [99] Indeed, John Quincy once angrily chastised him: "I have received three Letters from you since I have been here, all grumbling Letters; and all very badly written…You conclude [the letter] by saying that you hope I will forgive anything

rash in my Son; but I shall do no such thing. If my Son be rash he
might take the consequences…Are you so much of a baby that you
must be coaxed to spell your Letters, by sugar plumbs? or are you
such an independent Gentleman, that you can brook no control, and
must have every thing you ask for? If so I desire you not to write
for anything to me." He concluded by signing the letter, "Being always your affection and whenever you deserve it, you[r] indulgent
father."[100]

The Adams' were well aware that their middle son had a propen-
sity to make bad decisions. In May 1823, near the end of his senior
year at Harvard, John foolishly organized and led a student protest
that quickly degenerated into a riot. His boorish behavior resulted
in his expulsion and was yet another family embarrassment for the
Adams'. As an adult, John failed at business and found himself in
constant financial difficulty. He began to experience severe bouts
of depression and found solace in drink; his health rapidly declined
while his gambling debts accumulated. John Adams II was destined
to die prematurely just a few years later while living in Washington,
D.C.[101] His brother, Charles Francis astutely wrote: "vices are hereditary in families…our family has been so severely scourged by
this vice [alcoholism] that every member of it is constantly on his
trial."[102] There seemed to be a curse upon the children of the great
American families and John Payne Todd appeared destined for similar calamity.

Endnotes

Epigraph: A toast given at Orange County Court House in honor of a visit by the Marquis de Lafayette quoted in Virginia Moore (1979), *The Madison's: A Biography*. New York, McGraw-Hill Book Company, p. 400.

1 James Monroe carried all 24 states and received 231 electoral votes.

2 Eliphalet Nott quoted in Early Lee Fox. *The American Colonization Society 1817-1840*. Baltimore, the Johns Hopkins Press, 1919, p. 16.

3 Miller, John Chester (1991). *The Wolf by the Ears: Thomas Jefferson and Slavery*. Charlottesville, The University of Virginia Press, p. 264.

4 *Ibid.*, pp. 265-266.

5 *Ibid.*, p. 235.

6 Maine became the 23rd state on March 15, 1820, while Missouri was admitted as the 24th state on August 10, 1821.

7 Miller, p. 246. There would be 12 slave states and 12 free states in the Senate.

8 Thomas Jefferson letter to Congressman John Holmes, 22 April 1820, available at http://www.loc.gov/exhibits/jefferson/159.html.

9 Virginia Moore (1979). *The Madison's: A Biography*. New York, McGraw-Hill Book Company, p. 385.

10 Phoebe Pemberton Morris letter to Anthony Morris, 4 February 1812, quoted in H.L. Dufour Woolfley (2013). *A Quaker Goes to Spain: The Diplomatic Mission of Anthony Morris, 1813-1816*. Bethlehem, PA., Lehigh University Press.

11 Phoebe Pemberton Morris letter to Dolley Payne Madison, 22 March 1820, quoted in Allan Clark (1914). *The Life and Letters of Dolly Madison*. Washington, DC, W.F. Roberts Company, p. 211.

12 Phoebe Pemberton Morris letter to Dolley Payne Madison, 6 May 1811, quoted in David Mattern and Holley Schulman, eds. (2003). *The Selected Letters of Dolley Payne Madison*. Charlottesville, University of Virginia Press, pp. 139.

13 Anthony Morris letter to Dolley Payne Madison, 14 July 1820, quoted in Mattern. *Selected Letters*, pp. 240-241.

14 Phoebe Pemberton Morris letter to Dolley Payne Madison, 15 July 1820, quoted in Clark, pp. 215-216.

15 Phoebe Pemberton Morris quoted in Moore, p. 386.

16 Phoebe Pemberton Morris quoted in Clark, p. 216.

17 Dufour, p. 153.

18 The Six Buildings were located along Pennsylvania Avenue between 21st and 22nd Streets, NW.

19 Phoebe Pemberton Morris letter to Dolley Payne Madison, 19 January 1824, quoted in Mattern. *Selected Letters*, p. 251.

20 *Ibid.*, p. 251.

21 James Monroe quoted in A. Levasseur (1829). *Lafayette in America in 1824 and 1825; or, Journal of a Voyage to the United States*, Philadelphia, Cary and Lea, p. 10.

22 Lafayette was granted honorary American citizenship by Congress in 2002, one of only seven foreigners ever so recognized. The others were Winston Churchill (1963), Raoul Wallenberg (1981), William and Hannah Penn (1984), Mother Theresa (1996), and Casimir Pulaski (2009).

23 John Adams quoted in David McCullough (2001). *John Adams*. New York, Simon & Schuster, p. 637.

24 James Madison quoted in Ralph Ketcham (1990). *James Madison: A Biography*. Charlottesville, University of Virginia Press, p. 664.

25 Levasseur, p. 181.

26 *Ibid.*, pp. 181-182.

27 The Marquis de Lafayette quoted in Dumas Malone (1981). *Jefferson and His Time: The Sage of Monticello*. Boston, Little, Brown, & Company, p. 405.

28 Madison was actually 73-years old at the time of Lafayette's 1824 visit. Levasseur, p. 221.

29 Jefferson specifically instructed that on the obelisk that would mark his grave would be inscribed only three "testimonials...[for] I wished to be remembered." These were "Author of the Declaration of American Independence of the Statute of Virginia for religious freedom & the Father of the University of Virginia." See: http://www.monticello.org.

30 Hogan, Pendleton (1996). *The Lawn: A Guide to Jefferson's University*. Charlottesville, VA., the University of Virginia Press, p. 2.

31 Levasseur, p. 220.

32 The Lawn at the University of Virginia was declared by UNESCO to be a World Heritage site and is the only college to be so recognized. See http://whc.unesco.org. Also Gary Wills (2002). *Mr. Jefferson's University*. Washington, DC, National Geographic Society, pp. 8-9.

33 Malone, p. 408.

34 Thomas Jefferson quoted in James Morton Smith (1995). *The Republic of Letters: The Correspondence between Thomas Jefferson and James Madison 1776-1826.* New York, W.W. Norton & Company.

35 Ralph Ketcham (2009). *The Madisons at Montpelier: Reflections on the Founding Couple.* Charlottesville, University of Virginia Press, p. 108.

36 Dolley Payne Madison letter to John Payne Todd, 9 April 1823, quoted in Lucie Cutts (1887). *Memoirs and Letters of Dolly Madison: Wife of James Madison, President of the United States.* Boston, Houghton, Mifflin and Company, p. 166.

37 Levasseur, p. 222.

38 Douglas B. Chambers (2005). *Murder at Montpelier: Igbo Africans in Virginia.* Jackson, MI., University Press of Mississippi, p.96. Like most slaves, Milly did not know her exact age; she was born circa 1721. The great abolitionist, Frederick Douglass, wrote in his *Narrative Life* that "I do not remember to have ever met a slave who could tell of his birthday. They seldom come nearer to it than planting-time, harvest-time, cherry-time, spring-time, or fall-time. A want of information concerning my own was a source of unhappiness to me even during childhood. The white children could tell their ages. I could not tell why I ought to be deprived of the same privilege." See Frederick Douglass (1845). *A Narrative Life of Frederick Douglass, An American Slave.* Boston, Anti-Slave Office, p. 1.

39 *Ibid.,* p. 96.

40 Moore, p. 399.

41 Levasseur, p. 222.

42 Levasseur quoted in Moore, p. 399.

43 James Madison quoted in Ketcham, *James Madison: A Biography*, p. 665.

44 Dolley Payne Madison letter to John Payne Todd, 2 December 1824, quoted in Mattern, *Selected Letters*, pp. 257-258.

45 Dolley Payne Madison letter to John Payne Todd, 2 December 1824, quoted in Mattern, Selected Letters, p. 258.

46 Moore, pp. 397, 402.

47 Dolley Payne Madison letter to John Payne Todd, 2 December 1824, quoted in Mattern, Selected Letters, p 258.

48 Goodwin, Maud Wilder (1897). *Dolly Madison: Women of Colonial and Revolutionary Times.* New York, Charles Scribner's Sons, pp. 212-213.

49 A state's electoral vote is determined by its combined representation in the House of Representatives and Senate (# of Congressmen + 2 = Total Electors). Thus, the fewest number of electors a state could have is 3, since all states have at least one Congressman and two Senators. In 1824, New York, the nation's most populous state, had the most electoral votes with 36, while Delaware, Illinois, Missouri, and Mississippi had the fewest, with three each.

50 *Presidential Elections 1789-2004* (2005). Norwalk, CT., Easton Press, pp. 24-25.

51 Delaware, Georgia, Louisiana, New York, South Carolina, and Vermont.

52 James Madison, Federalist #10 quoted in Alexander Hamilton, James Madison, and John Jay (1979). *The Federalist or the New Constitution*. Norwalk, CT., Easton Press. p.59.

53 See James Madison, "Vices of the Political System of the United States," available at: http://press-pubs.uchicago.edu/founders/documents/v1ch5s16.html.

54 John Adams quoted in Buchanan, Patrick J. "Democracy's Era is Over," *Daily News Record*. August 12, 2014, p. A6

55 John Quincy Adams quoted in Stanley Weintraub and Rodelle Weintraub (2000). *Dear Young Friend: The Letters of American Presidents to Children*. Mechanicsburg, PA., Stackpole Books, p. 33.

56 Egbert R. Watson quoted in Harlow Giles Unger, (2012). *John Quincy Adams*. Philadelphia, Da Capo Press, p. 229.

57 John Quincy Adams quoted in Nevins, Allan, ed. (1951). *The Diary of John Quincy Adams, 1794-1845: American Diplomacy, and Political, Social, and Intellectual Life, from Washington to Polk*. New York, Frederick Unger Publishing Company, p. 240.

58 See http://www.gilderlehrman.org/history-by-era/age-jackson/essays/adams-v-jackson-election-1824.

59 Each state delegation in the House was entitled to cast a single vote for president. The final results were 13 states for Adams,7 for Jackson, and 4 for Crawford.

60 John Quincy Adams quoted in Nevins, p. 342.

61 Andrew Jackson quoted in Unger, p. 238.

62 Sarah Seaton quoted in Unger, p. 237.

63 Unger, p. 244.

64 Smith, p. 291.

65 Margaret Bayard Smith letter to Mrs. Kirkpatrick, 11 March 1829 quoted in Smith, p. 295.

66 *Ibid*., pp. 295-296.

67 *Ibid*., p. 295.

68 *Ibid.*, p. 296.

69 Thomas Jefferson quoted in Alan Pell Crawford (2008). *Twilight at Monticello: The Final Years of Thomas Jefferson.* New York, Random House, p. 222.

70 Cappon, p. xxix. John Adams wrote 109 letters to Jefferson during the period from 1812 to 1826, compared to just 49 that Jefferson to him. Jefferson's last letter to Adams was written on March 25, 1826; Adams wrote his final letter to Jefferson on April 17, 1826.

71 John Adams letter to Thomas Jefferson, 25 February 1825, quoted in Cappon, p. 608.

72 *Ibid.*, p. 608.

73 Thomas Jefferson quoted in Malone, p. 497. Also, see The Thomas Jefferson Papers at the Library of Congress available at: http://hdl.loc.gov/loc.mss/mtj.mtjbib024904.

74 Thomas Jefferson quoted in Cappon, Lester J., ed. (1988). *The Adams-Jefferson Letters: The Complete Correspondence between Thomas Jefferson and John Adams.* Williamsburg, VA. The Institute of Early American History and Culture, p. 559.

75 Three American presidents have died on July 4—Thomas Jefferson (d. 1826), John Adams (d. 1826), and James Monroe (d. 1831). Only one American president was born on the 4th—Calvin Coolidge (b. 1872).

76 John Quincy Adams diary entry for Nov. 3, 1807 quoted in Allan Nevins, Ed. (1969). *The Diary of John Quincy Adams 1794-1845: American Diplomacy, and Political, Social, and Intellectual Life from Washington to Polk.* New York, Frederick Ungar Publishing Co, p. 47.

77 Hessian flies attack primarily wheat and other cereal crops. It was widely believed that the flies were imported to America during the Revolution by German soldiers fighting for the British.

78 James Madison to Thomas Jefferson quoted in Ketcham, *The Madisons at Montpelier*, pp 37-38.

79 Edward Coles, one of Dolley Madison's cousins and James Madison's secretary while president, left Virginia in 1819 and moved to Illinois. There he manumitted his slaves believing that the entire system was corrupt and immoral.

80 The slave statistics were listed in the 1820 census.

81 James Madison letter to Edward Coles, 23 February 1827, quoted in Ethel Stephens Arnett (1972). *Mrs. James Madison: The Incomparable Dolley.* Greensboro, Piedmont Press.p. 285.

82 *Ibid.*, p. 285.

83 *Ibid.*, p. 285.

84 Mattern, *Selected Letters*, p. 220.

85 Dolley Payne Madison letter to John Payne Todd, 2 December 1824, quoted in Mattern, *Selected Letters*, p. 258.

86 Dolley Payne Madison letter to John Payne Todd, 2 December 1824, quoted in Mattern, *Selected Letters*, pp. 257-258.

87 James Madison letter to John Payne Todd, 13 February 1825, quoted in Moore, p. 409.

88 James Madison quoted in Moore, p. 409.

89 James Madison quoted in Moore, p. 409.

90 Dolley Payne Madison letter to Mary Cutts, 30 July 1826, quoted in Cutts, p. 176.

91 Margaret Bayard Smith, 17 August 1828, quoted in Clark, p 232.

92 Ketcham, *The Madisons at Montpelier*, p. 58.

93 Dolley Payne Madison quoted in Catherine Allgor (2006). *A Perfect Union: Dolley Madison and the Creation of the American Nation*. New York, Henry Holt and Company, p. 352.

94 Dolley Payne Madison letter to Anna Cutts, 6 June 1829, quoted in Mattern, *Selected Letters*, p. 279.

95 Mattern, *Selected Letters*, p. 220.

96 Paul C. Nagel (1983). *Descent from Glory: Four Generations of the John Adams Family*. New York, Oxford University Press, p. 159.

97 Harlow Giles Unger (2012). *John Quincy Adams*. Philadelphia, Da Capo Press, p. 256.

98 John Quincy Adams quoted in Nagel, p. 159.

99 Louisa Adams quoted in Nagel, p. 138.

100 John Quincy Adams letter to John Adams II, 17 November 1817, quoted in Stanley Weintraub and Rodelle Weintraub (2000). *Dear Young Friend: The Letters of American Presidents to Children*. Mechanicsburg, PA., Stackpole Books.

101 Nagel, p. 272.

102 Charles Francis Adams quoted in Nagel, p. 174.

Chapter V

1830-1839

"Having outlived so many of my contemporaries...I may be thought to have outlived myself."

James Madison

As the nation began its sixth decade of independence, growing sectional tensions threatened to disrupt the nation's unity. An increasingly vocal group of radical abolitionists demanded an immediate end to slavery—there could be no further compromises, no gradualism, no accommodations regardless of the potential social or economic consequences for the south. In their view, the entire system of slavery was evil and morally corrupt, contaminating all who were associated with it.

On New Year's Day, 1831, William Lloyd Garrison began the publication of his abolitionist newspaper, The Liberator. In its opening editorial, he proclaimed: "I will be as harsh as truth, and as uncompromising as justice. On this subject, I do not wish to think, or speak, or write, with moderation. No! no! Tell a man whose house is on fire to give a moderate alarm; tell him to moderately rescue his wife from the hands of the ravisher; tell the mother to gradually extricate her babe from the fire into

William Lloyd Garrison.
(Library of Congress)

169

"The Horrid Massacre Broadside." In 1831, Nat Turner led an unsuccessful but bloody slave rebellion in southern Virginia. The incident terrified Southerners who blamed radical abolitionists for inciting the uprising. (Library of Congress)

which it has fallen;--but urge me not to use moderation in a cause like the present. I am in earnest—I will not equivocate—I will not excuse—I will not retreat a single inch—AND I WILL BE HEARD."[1] Garrison openly denounced the United States Constitution with its de facto *recognition of the right to own slaves, calling it "a covenant with Death." Before long, abolitionists ritually burned copies of the document at their rallies.[2]*

Southerners felt betrayed by the north and became increasing defensive about their so-called "peculiar institution." They believed that the radicals were inciting the slave population, and their fears seemed to be confirmed just a few months later when a charismatic slave named Nat Turner led a group of slaves on a bloody rampage through Southampton, Virginia. His renegade band indiscriminately slaughtered sixty-one men, women, and children on eleven different farms. The slave rebellion was widely reported throughout the nation and reinforced plantation owners' fear about a potential uprising among their own slaves. Even more alarming was the fact that the horrors perpetrated by Nat Turner and his followers were committed by slaves who lived in close proximity to their owners rather than on large plantations.[3] They knew their victims yet showed no mercy. The myth of a tranquil, passive, loyal slave population had been forever shattered. The viciousness of the murders terrified whites, especially in regions (including Madison's own home district of Orange County) where slaves outnumbered the white population.[4] The "bloody butchery," as the Richmond Enquirer *reported, was widespread. "[The rebellious slaves] were mounted to the number of 40 or 50; and with knives and axes—knocking on the head, or cutting the throat of their victims…Not a white person escaped, at all of the houses they visited, except two!"[5]*

The rebellion was swiftly and brutally suppressed as vigilantes searched for and eventually apprehended Turner and all of his cohorts. They were tried and convicted of rebellion with sixteen of Turner's followers promptly executed. Turner himself was hung on November 11. His dead body was skinned, while his decapitated head was put on public display as a warning to all potential insurrectionists. In a letter to her niece, Mary Cutts, Dolley somberly wrote: "I hope the bustle and alarm of Insurrections are over in the city—tho' I hope all will be on guard after this. I am quiet, knowing little about it and that I cannot help myself if I am in danger. I believe there is none at present."[6]

Another great national crisis occurred a few months later after the federal government passed a new and controversial tariff law. Intended to raise revenue while simultaneously protecting infant northern industries from foreign competition, the 1832 tax was met with outrage throughout the south. Plantation holders claimed that the federal government was becoming despotic, since the adverse fiscal consequences of the tariff legislation fell disproportionately upon the region's rural farmers. Vice President John C. Calhoun resigned his office in order to lead the opposition to the law, and his native South Carolina declared the federal law unconstitutional and void in a provocative nullification resolution.

The nullifiers falsely claimed that James Madison supported their position, citing his previous opposition to the Alien and Sedition Acts of 1798. In truth, Madison was alarmed by the overt and in-

tentional distortion of his earlier, principled position. Moreover, he was dismayed by the current generation's historical amnesia. The abrogation of federal law seriously threatened the very existence of the Constitution and would mean a return to the chaos and uncertainty of the Confederation period. Madison remained steadfast and consistent in his interpretation of the Constitution and in the supremacy of federal law. When he reluctantly made his opinions public, the supporters of nullification quickly denounced the aged Madison, claiming that "the weakness and decrepitude of old age" had adversely impacted his thinking.[7] Historian Drew McCoy maintains that: "[Madison] continued to worry that self-promoting politicians would indulge their ambition by recklessly inflaming the public mind on false issues."[8]

President Andrew Jackson was incensed and determined to assert federal authority even if it meant using military force to enforce the hated legislation. The ominous specter of civil war loomed and finally brought federal legislators to their senses. They were able to formulate a legislative compromise which quelled the opposition. Open conflict had been temporarily averted but sectional divisions continued to widen as the philosophical debate concerning the issue of states' rights versus federal authority still festered.

There was, however, a general national consensus over the issue of Texas and continued westward expansion. For years, pioneers and settlers had flocked into the regions north of the Rio Grande, an area controlled by Mexico. The Americans brought with them their culture, language, and slaves, ignoring with impunity the proclamations and laws of the sovereign Mexican government. In 1836, after trying to reassert Mexican authority over the province, the military dictator, Santa Anna led an invading army into Texas to subdue the insurgence. At a small, fortified Catholic mission known as the Alamo, Santa Anna, and his army waged a thirteen day siege before finally overrunning the small garrison of defenders. All of the Americans were killed, including the famed pioneer and folk hero, Davy Crockett. One of James Madison's nephews, James Madison Rose, also died during the fighting.[9] Dolley Madison wrote: "What terrible massacre is stated to have been committed upon our people in Texas. The papers are filled with distressing news of the war that is going on there and at the south with the Indians. We wish it could all be terminated without further slaying."[10]

Santa Anna's victory was short-lived, as the Texans mobilized and rallied under the leadership of Sam Houston. Within just a few weeks of his Alamo victory, Santa Anna's forces were decisively defeated at the battle of San Jacinto and he was forced to recognize the establishment of the independent state of Texas, the so-called Lone Star Republic. Just six weeks later, James Madison, the last of the Founding Fathers, would be dead.

PAYNE TODD'S INITIAL IMPRISONMENT was mercifully brief after his parents once again came to his financial rescue. The Madison's fully expected him to be chastened by the traumatic

The Walnut Street Jail in Philadelphia. John Payne Todd was imprisioned twice for failutre to pay his debts. By some estimates, his stepfather paid over $60,000 during his lifetime to bail Payne out of financial trouble.. (Library of Congress)

experience and to return home to Montpelier, but, typically, Payne ignored their pleas. He soon returned to his old, bad spending habits and within a matter of just a few months, he was again confined to a debtor's cell in Philadelphia. The Walnut Street Jail had been established during the colonial period in 1773 and was located between Sixth and Prune Streets adjacent to State House (Independence) Square.[11] By the time of Payne's incarceration, though, the structure was close to sixty years old and dilapidated. Disease was rampant among the inmate population and mortality was high due to serious overcrowding. One contemporary report concluded bluntly that the jail was "the 'most extensive and corrupt' institution in the country."[12]

Fortunately for Payne and his fellow debtors, they were generally segregated from the more dangerous criminals. They were also allowed special privileges and benefits, which included the right to receive visitors, as well as gifts of food and other amenities to help make their incarceration a bit more palatable.[13] There were a series of rules, however, which included a strict proscription against all "kinds of wines, spirituous liquors, porter, strong beer [and] cider."[14]

Anthony Morris, Dolley's oldest and most loyal friend, was aware of Payne's imprisonment and attempted to intercede on his behalf. Morris knew that Payne's irresponsible behavior was a source of embarrassment for the Madisons so he diplomatically wrote to Dolley's sister, Anna Cutts, about Todd's current unfortunate circumstances. Morris explained that Payne was finally willing to return home but: "…to do this, $200 in cash, and an assumption of $400 [payable] at any convenient future day are said to be require[ed]."[15] It was a considerable sum of money and Morris needed further instructions on how he was to proceed. He continued: "Whether any circumstances Exist in his most unfortunate situation, which would make it inexpedient to communicate his wishes to Mr. and Mrs. Madison, I am entirely ignorant; but it could not resist my desire to know this you, whether anything I can do by attempting a compromise with his Creditors, or otherwise would conduce to the attainment of Mrs. Madison's object what it may is, on her son's acct."[16]

Payne's economic misfortunes were actually quite prevalent in antebellum America, but debtors' prisons were far more common in the nation's cities than in the rural south.[17] Most large plantation holders were similarly in debt, but without a national hard currency, it was difficult to accurately gauge the actual extent and scope of their indebtedness. Daily financial transactions involved complex interpersonal relationships and were frequently recorded only in a set of ledger books. These accounts were never balanced or totaled until the death of an owner finally necessitated that the books be closed and audited so that outstanding obligations could be settled. Slaves were considered to be an important part of an estate's assets and they could be legally seized or sold by creditors. Indeed, according to Alan Taylor: "property rights trumped all, no indebted master could legally manumit without the consent of his creditors."[18] Decedents and heirs were frequently stunned to see their anticipated inheritance quickly disappear to pay off decades of accumulated debt. In the case of Thomas Jefferson, within six months of his death, his relatives were forced to hold a public auction which advertised the sale of "130 VALUABLE NEGROES, stock, crops, &c Household and Kitchen Furniture."[19] In 1828, Jefferson's grandson, Francis Epps, had to sell off the former president's beloved Bedford County retreat, Poplar Forest, and just three years later the Monticello homestead itself was sold.[20] Dolley Madison would likewise be fated to sell off her beloved Montpelier within a few years after the death of her husband, due to her own dire financial circumstances.

But Payne Todd's business debts and grandiose schemes were far easier to track. His creditors were not deceived by the Byzantine bookkeeping practices of the plantation south and were unsympathetic to his economic difficulties or pitiful excuses. They demanded prompt repayment of their loans and used all legal recourse available to collect. By having the sheriff confine Payne to jail, it was hoped that his incarceration would compel him to reveal any and all hidden assets. Moreover, it had the added benefit of lawfully holding him hostage to extract a virtual ransom from his tormented parents, who were willing to pay to obtain their son's freedom.[21] Anthony Morris' timely intercession ultimately helped satisfy Payne's financial obligations and he was released from jail, appropriately, on July 4, 1830.[22] By some estimates, James Madison would spend in excess of $60,000 over the years to cover his stepson's financial liabilities but the actual amount probably exceeded even that princely sum.[23]

This time, Payne did retreat temporarily to the sanctuary of Montpelier, suitably penitent although unreformed. Everyone was stunned by the stark deterioration in his physical appearance. At 38-years of age, his profligate lifestyle had taken a toll. According to author Maud Wilder Goodwin: "As a result of his free indulgence, his face became bloated, and his figure shapeless, and so completely did his aspect change that few would have recognized in his sodden features and heavy form the alert, graceful, laughing-eyed lad who had entered manhood as 'the Prince' with brighter prospects than any youth in America."[24] Similarly, biographer Virginia Moore concluded simply that Payne was "gross of body."[25]

TWO GREAT PROJECTS CONSUMED James Madison during the waning years of his life. One was the continuation of Jefferson's efforts to develop and expand the University of Virginia. The other was to edit and compile his voluminous collection of papers for eventual publication. These invaluable materials included his own personal notes which he had taken while serving as a Virginia delegate during the Constitutional Convention of 1787. Madison had been the sole person to attend all of the critical sessions and deliberations in Philadelphia. Since the delegates had agreed to meet in strict secrecy, few details were publically known about what had occurred within the chambers or what negotiations and concessions had led to the final composition of the document. Madison's private papers were thus a unique and detailed record of the daily proceedings and an invaluable historical resource.[26] In a personal letter to Edward Everett, Madison confided that his notes were "the best history of our country," and the eventual publication of these

A portrait of James Madison circa 1833 shortly before his death. Madison suffered from severe rheumatism and a variety of ailments that made it difficult for him to read and write. Harriet Martineau observed during a visit in 1835: "[Madison] complained of one ear being deaf, and his sight, which had never been perfect, pevented him reading much." (Library of Congress)

documents would be important for all Americans to learn about "the cause of true liberty."[27]

   Madison made the conscious decision to delay the final publication of his papers until after his death, convinced that these primary source materials were worth in the excess of $100,000. This enormous sum would ensure Dolley's financial well-being for the remainder of her life. In reality, though, Madison grossly overestimated the actual worth of his papers. No American publisher was willing to invest such money without the certainty of a financial profit.

   The organizing of Madison's papers and archives was a Herculean task and time was of an essence. The increasingly enfeebled Madison enlisted the help of his neighbor and brother-in-law, John Coles Payne, in the endeavor while Dolley and even sometimes Payne served as his scribes.[28] The ravages of age and ill-health both plagued and frustrated Madison. In a letter to Margaret Bayard Smith, he somberly divulged: "I am very thankful, my kind friend, for the interest you take in my health. It is not good, and at my age, nature can afford little of the medical aid she exerts on younger patients. I have indeed got through the most painful stages of my principal malady, a diffusive and obstinate Rheumatism, but I feel its crippling effects on my limbs, particularly my hands and fingers, as this little effort of the pen will shew."[29] Madison's hands were so crippled from arthritis that his servants had to be enlisted to cut his food for him.[30] Of greater concern, though, was Madison growing inability to write. In another letter, he somberly acknowledged: "[My malady] disables my pen, & my hand from holding a Book or handling my papers."[31] Dolley confirmed her husband's condition, writing: "His hands and fingers are still so swelled and sore as to be nearly used, but I lend him mine."[32] Despite these infirmities, Madison remained lucid and, in Henry Clay's words: "Mr. Madison is feeble in health, but his mind and memory are perfectly sound."[33]

──────────────

MADISON WAS WELL AWARE of his impending death. He decided to update his last will and testament on April 19, 1835 and he also recorded his final wishes for the nation. Madison wrote: "As this advice, if it ever see the light will not do it till I am no more it may be considered as issuing from the tomb when the truth alone can be respected, and the happiness of man alone consulted. It will be entitled therefore to whatever weight, can be derived from good intentions, and from the experience of one, who has served his Country in various stations through a period of forty years, who espoused in his youth and adhered through his life to the cause of its liberty and who has borne a part in most of the transactions which will constitute epochs of its destiny." He continued, "The advice nearest to my heart and deepest in my convictions is that the Union of States be cherished and perpetuated. Let the open enemy to it be regarded as a Pandora with her box opened; and the disguised one, as the Serpent creeping with his deadly wiles into Paradise."[34]

His chronic rheumatism made it difficult for him to walk and Madison was slowly becoming an invalid, confined to a first floor room at Montpelier located immediately adjacent to the formal dining room. He still continued to enjoy visitors and robust conversation from his bedchamber, but his physical deterioration was rapid. On the morning of June 28, 1838, Madison was attended by his niece, Nelly Conway Madison Willis and two of his slaves (Paul Jennings and Sukey).[35] According to Jennings's firsthand account: "Sukey brought him his breakfast, as usual. He could not swallow. His niece, Mrs. Wil[l]is, said, 'What is the matter, Uncle James.' 'Nothing more than a change of *mind*, my dear.' His head instantly dropped, and he ceased breathing as quickly as the snuff of a candle goes out."[36] James Madison was 85 years old; he and Dolley had been married for almost 42 years.

Madison was buried near his parents in the family cemetery just a short distance from the original Mount Pleasant homestead that had been founded by his grandfather. Dolley was so aggrieved that she was unable to attend the committal services.[37] Montpelier's slave community, though, did assemble at the gravesite, conscious that with Madison's death, their own individual circumstances were in serious peril.

The news of Madison's death, although not unexpected, still shocked the nation. President Andrew Jackson graciously sent his condolences to Dolley, calling Madison one of the nation's "most valued citizens." He added: "Be assured, madam, that there is not one of your countrymen who feels more poignantly the blow which has fallen upon you, or who will cherish with a more enduring constancy the memory of the virtues, the services, and the purity of the illustrious man whose glorious and patriotic life has just been terminated by a tranquil death."[38]

MADISON WAS DETERMINED in death to prevent his stepson from ever exerting any claim to the Montpelier estate. In his will, he stipulated that Dolley would inherit the property but also obligated her to pay over $9,000 in behest within three years to some 31 family members.[39] The former president also left generous sums to the University of Virginia ($1,500), Princeton ($1,000), and the College at Uniontown ($1,000), as well as an additional grant of $2,000 to the American Colonization Society.[40]

Madison purposefully left no money to Payne Todd. He did bequeath to his troublesome stepson, though, a case of medals from Washington Irving as well as a "walking staff made from a timber of the frigate *Constitution*."[41] Payne's paltry inheritance seemed to be an insulting and vindictive act, but Madison believed that in life he had already financially provided for Payne, and that his stepson had squandered all future financial entitlements. Payne deserved nothing more and as proof, Madison secretly entrusted to his brother-in-law, John Coles Payne, dozens of receipts and vouchers that documented and chronicled his numerous financial expenditures over the years on his stepson's behalf.[42]

Ex President Madison – The death of Ex-President Madison, though an event not unexpected, has produced a sensation in the public mind corresponding with the distinguished talents and exalted character of the deceased. He was born March 16, 1751; was a member of the Legislature of Virginia, 1775; one of the Council of the same state, 1776; member of Congress of the Revolution, and of the Convention which formed the Constitution of the United States; one of the principal contributors to the celebrated work 'The Federalist;' was elected a member of the first Congress, in which body he remained many years; was made secretary of state under Jefferson, March 5th 1801; was inaugurated President of the United States, March 4th, 1809, in which office he continued, by re-election, eight years; died Jun 28th, 1836, in the 86th year of his age, six days added to his life would have carried him to the 4th of July, on which memorable days all his predecessors in office died, with the exception of Washington. The proud but melancholy list, now stands as follows:

George Washington	10th Dec. 1799	68
John Adams	4th July 1826	91
Thomas Jefferson	4th July 1826	84
James Monroe	4th July 1831	73
James Madison	28 June 1836	86

The average age of the five is 80 years and a fraction. John Quincy Adams is the only Ex-President who survives.

DEATH OF MR. MADISON – It does not appear that Mr. Madison suffered from illness, it was a gradual prostration of the vial powers, - his mind at times was more than ordinarily clear and luminous, and when roused by the conversation of friends, was cheerful in an extraordinary degree. That excellent and exalted woman, Mrs. Madison, never left him for a moment, but cheered him to the last with those friendly attends for which she has ever been remarkable. His remains were interred at the family vault at Montpelier, on the 30th June, amid the tears of an affectionate family, and sorrowing neighborhood.

A facimile of a newpaper account of James Madison's death on June 28, 1836. Madison was actually 85 years of age. He was buried in the family cemetery at Montpelier.

Surprisingly, the normally astute Madison had unwittingly placed his widow in a perilous financial situation. To honor the liberal terms of husband's will, Dolley needed to liquidate some of her assets quickly and this necessarily included the selling of slaves. Madison had expressed his desire that Montpelier's slaves "should [not] be sold without his or her consent," but this was now unrealistic.[43] In 1830, the census showed that there were 103 slaves living on the plantation—56 males and 47 females. Of these, 40% were unproductive children under the age of ten while nine were elderly and two listed as blind.[44] Despite his avowed aversion to the domestic slave trade, Madison's own financial difficulties had compelled him to sell sixteen of his slaves in 1834 to a relative living in Louisiana and yet another twelve just a few months later. Madison was fully aware that in doing so, he was compromising his professed values but his accumulating debt was quickly becoming insurmountable.[45] Dolley was now placed into a similar moral quandary. Her cousin, Edward

Annie Payne, Dolley Madison's beloved niece. She became her aunt's closest companion and a surrogate daughter. (Greensboro Historical Museum)

Coles, noted: "Mr. Madison…has left so many more [slaves] than can be judiciously employed on his estate that his poor Widow is compelled, it is said, to sell many of them. Thus he has imposed on his widow a most painful task, one which he ought to have performed himself."[46] Once again, financial needs trumped all espoused principles and Dolley sold some of Montpelier's slaves by the end of the summer of 1836.[47] It was an odious business as Edward Coles noted: "Reports has gotten abroad that [Mrs. Madison] wished to sell many of [her slaves] & every day or two…a Negro trader would make his appearance, & was permitted to examine the Negroes. It was like a hawk among the pigeons. The poor creatures w[oul]d run to the house and protest ag[ains]t being sold."[48] Three years later apparently through Payne Todd's intercession, a Louisiana planter named George Augustus Waggaman, inquired if Dolley would be willing to sell more of her slaves. He wrote to her that he "thought it probable, in order to rid yourself of the trouble of the management, you would be willing to dispose of the negroes on your Estate, in

Virginia."[49] In her quick response, Dolley informed Waggaman that she "had not at any period intended to part with more than half about fifty, owing to their reluctance to leave this place or its neighbourhood, added to which the Manager at Montpellier is now finishing a large and tedious crop of Tobacco and preparing for a similar one of wheat, Tobacco, &c. which seems to require them all except the children of which there is a full proportion."[50]

In the immediate aftermath of her husband's death, Dolley was emotionally devastated and overwhelmed. She found it impossible to effectively run a complex plantation operation and even the hired overseers could do little to improve the productivity of the farm operations or generate sufficient revenue. In a candid letter to Payne Todd, Dolley once lamented: "Our last tobacco was a failure; it sold at seven when seventeen was expected; so it goes with planters."[51]

Further complicating Dolley's precarious situation was her own physical infirmities. The most troublesome was a recurring and painful inflammation of the eyes which made it difficult for her to see let alone read or write. The malady caused excruciating headaches which incapacitated Dolley for extended periods of time. She had to spend much of the day confined to her bedroom with the curtains tightly drawn to prevent any light from penetrating the area. Fortunately, her dutiful niece, Anna (the daughter of John Coles Payne), had moved in with her at Montpelier and proved to be a loyal caregiver and constant companion.[52] Dolley confided to her friend, Henry Clay: "The continued and very severe affection of my eyes not permitting but with much difficulty even the signature of my name, has deferred, dear friend, the acknowledgments due for your very kind and acceptable letter…the failure of my general health combining equal, and sometimes greater suffering, rendered dictation very painful."[53]

She periodically traveled to both Warm and White Sulphur Springs to seek a remedy for her eyes. There she would relax and drink "moderately of the waters, and bathing my poor eyes a dozen times a day. The effect was excellent…and my eyes grew white again;

but in my drive home of six days in the dust they took the fancy to relapse a little."[54] But she had little success with her attending physicians who applied "leeches and blisters" but could provide little by way of relief.[55] Dolley complained that "[I] cannot say much of their present opinions" and, in a letter to Edward Coles, she explained that her eyelids were constantly inflamed and that she suffered from "heat and itching" that could be relieved "only by the application of milk and water or cream, and sometimes fresh butter."[56] This painful eye condition would never be fully cured and would intermittently torment her throughout the remainder of her life.

AFTER JAMES MADISON'S DEATH, there was no one left to deter or restrain Payne Todd's impulses or actions. His mother continued to overlook his many faults and readily excused all of his poor conduct and impaired judgment. In her desperate need of money, Dolley foolishly entrusted Payne with the responsibility of finding a printer for her husband's notes on the Constitutional Convention. Within weeks of his stepfather's death, sensing an easy profit, Payne was in New York City actively lobbying and meeting with potential buyers and book publishers. Few showed any interest in the project and most were quickly alienated by Payne's aggressive, arrogant, and unethical behavior. According to Edward Coles, Payne cunningly attempted "to get proposals of one Bookseller & then going to another & seeing if a Better Bargain could be got out of him."[57] This was unscrupulous and unprofessional and seemed to confirm James Kirke Paulding's blunt assessment that John Payne Todd was "the last man in the world to compass such a business."[58]

After failing to find a buyer, Payne returned to Washington, D.C., where he reverted to his old habits. William Cabell Rives recorded that: "[Dolley Madison's son] Todd is here [in Washington] playing the fool in high style…the man is deranged if he ever had any sense."[59] He accused Payne of associating with "the Blacklegs and Gamblers of Washington. Their Gigs and Flasks stand at his door, and he appears to be in their hands."[60]

Since no reputable American publisher was interested in her husband's papers, Dolley resorted to seeking relief through the intercession of the federal government. She hoped that Congress would purchase her husband's three volumes of records of the Constitutional Convention for the good of posterity. In a letter to Henry Clay, Dolley wrote: "My Son went in July as far as New-York and remained there for the purpose of negotiating with the most eminent publishers, and I have had communication with those in other Cities; but no offer has been made by any entitled to confidence, which would free me from heavy and inconvenient pecuniary advances and the risk of impositions and eventual loss."[61]

There was a great deal of sympathy and affection in the nation's capital for Dolley Madison. She was a beloved and treasured figure. Andrew Jackson, now a lame duck president, urged in December 1836 that Congress appropriate the requested funds to purchase Mr. Madison's papers. He rationalized that "it would educate subsequent generations on how their government was formed."[62] But there was significant and principled opposition to such a proposal. Senator John C. Calhoun, a strict constructionist, argued persuasively that the United States Constitution did not grant the federal government the authority to purchase private papers no matter what their origin. Moreover, he believed that this would have been the opinion of James Madison, himself, as a defender and advocate of limited and enumerated federal power.[63]

Calhoun was opposed in the contentious debates by both Henry Clay and Daniel Webster who rationalized that they did not see any "constitutional objections to the purchase of these manuscripts."[64] Finally, a rider "for the purchase of the manuscripts of the late Mr. Madison" was inserted in a larger omnibus appropriation bill which successfully passed on the final day of the twenty-fourth Congress (March 3, 1837) by a 25 to 12 vote.[65] The legislation granted to Dolley Madison the sum of $30,000 for her husband's work, but this amount was far less than anticipated. The infusion of money did allow for her to fund the many obligations incurred by Madison's will, but Dolley remained personally financially destitute. With her beloved Montpelier neglected and falling slowly and steadily into disrepair, she decided to abandon her isolated, lonely existence to return to Washington, D.C. There, she and niece Anna took up residence at the former home of her sister, Anna Cutts, on the corner of Lafayette Square and H Street.[66] Her distinguished neighbors included Mrs. Alexander Hamilton, Mrs. Stephan Decatur, and Mrs. Tobias Lear. "Her return to Washington was hailed by all" and the home soon became the focal point of Washington society despite Dolley's considerable financial difficulties.[67] As her grandniece, Lucie Cutts remembered: "As the time of mourning passed, her house again became filled with friends, and she was gladly welcomed back, receiving almost as much attention as she had done before. On the 1st of January, the Fourth of July, and every other gala day, her house was thrown open, and the throng of visitors was equal to that which assembled at the White House. Friends and strangers of all grades came."[68] The newly inaugurated president, Martin Van Buren, himself a widower, frequently enlisted Dolley's assistance in hosting and entertaining at the President's House.[69]

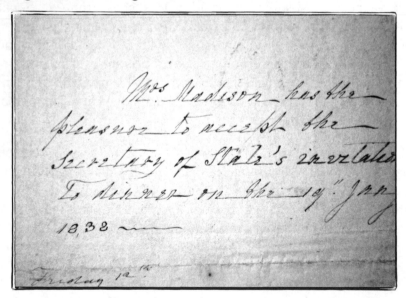

A card from Dolley Madison accepting a dinner invitation from Secretary of State John Forsyth. The former first lady returned temporarily to Washington in 1838. (Greensboro Historical Museum)

During this interlude in D.C., John Quincy Adams had the opportunity to visit Dolley Madison. He had not seen the former first lady since 1809. "The succeeding twenty years she has passed in retirement," he wrote. "She intended to have removed to this place last autumn, but was prevented by an inflammatory disease in her eyes, from which she has almost wholly recovered. There is no trace of it in her appearance now."[70] Indeed, Adams was struck by Dolley's pleasing appearance. Approaching 70, he observed that: "The depredations of time are not so perceptible in her personal appearance as might be expected. She is a woman of placid, equable temperament, and less susceptible of laceration by the scourges of the world abroad than most others."[71]

DOLLEY WOULD PERIODICALLY RETURN to Montpelier over the next few years and would often stay for extended periods of time. Payne Todd likewise returned to Orange County, ostensibly to help oversee his mother's faltering plantation operations, but he also took advantage of the time to begin the development of his own property at Toddsberth.[72] He "appropriated" several of Montpelier's slaves to begin the construction of his own house as well as to start operations on a new marble quarry located on the premises.[73] This removal of labor further exacerbated Montpelier's financial insolvency.

It was becoming increasingly apparent that Dolley would have to sell Montpelier to pay her burdensome debts, and Payne eagerly began assessing the estate's valuable artwork, mementos, sculptures, library, furnishings, and other household inventory for eventual sale. Todd's thirst for money remained unquenchable and despite his renewed efforts to improve his Toddsberth property, by the end of the decade, it was still assessed at a meager $84.22 in value. As John Payne Todd formulated his future plans, only silence emanated from the Montpelier cemetery where his stepfather's grave remained unmarked.

Endnotes

Epigraph: James Madison letter to Jared Sparks, 1 June 1831, quoted in David Mattern, Ed. (1997). *James Madison's "Advice to My Country."* Charlottesville, University Press of Virginia, p. 72.

1 John Jay Chapman (1921). *William Lloyd Garrison.* Boston, The Atlantic Monthly Press, p. 39.

2 William Lloyd Garrison quoted in Chapman, p. 172.

3 Kenneth S. Greenberg, ed., T*he Confessions of Nat Turner and Related Documents.* Boston, Bedford Books of St. Martin's Press, pp. 3-6.

4 The 1830 Census places the slave population in Orange County at 7,983 (55%) compared to 6,456 whites. See http://fisher.libvirginia.edu/collections/stats/histcensus.

5 *Richmond Enquirer,* 4 October 1831.

6 Dolley Payne Madison letter to Mary E.E. Cutts, 16 September 1831, quoted in David Mattern and Holly C. Shulman, eds. (2003). *The Selected Letters of Dolley Payne Madison.* Charlottesville, University of Virginia Press, p 293.

7 Drew R. McCoy (1989). *The Last of the Fathers: James Madison & the Republican Legacy.* New York, Cambridge University Press, p. 154.

8 *Ibid.,* p. 152.

9 James Madison Rose was the youngest son of Frances Taylor Madison Rose. She was Madison's youngest sister and had relocated with her family to Alabama in 1822. She died there in 1823. See Holly Shulman (2011). "Madison v. Madison: Dolley Payne Madison and Her Inheritance of the Montpelier Estate 1836-1838." *Virginia Magazine of History and Biography* 119 (4): p. 393.

10 Dolley P. Madison letter to Mary Cutts, 18 April 1836, quoted in the Cutts family collection of James Madison and Dolley Madison papers 1794-1845, Library of Congress, Microfilm 14, 326-1P.

11 Prune Street is today known as Locus Street. See Megley K. Teeters (1955). *The Cradle of the Penitentiary: The Walnut Street Jail at Philadelphia, 1773-1835.* Philadelphia, Pennsylvania Prison Society, p. 17.

12 *Ibid.,* p. 121.

13 The poor were treated differently than people of Payne Todd's caste. They were confined together in poorly ventilated basement rooms and were considered to be misfits and vagrants.

14 "Set of Rules for Debtors' Apartment" quoted in Teeters, p. 140.

15 Letter from Anthony Morris to Anna Payne Cutts, May 19, 1830, quoted in Allan Clark (1914). *The Life and Letters of Dolly Madison.* Washington, DC, W.F. Roberts Company, pp. 239-240.

16 *Ibid.*

17 Federal imprisonment for debt was eliminated in 1833 while most states eliminated the practice by 1850.

18 Alan Taylor (2013). *The Internal Enemy: Slavery and War in Virginia 1772-1832*. New York, W.W. Norton and Company, p. 39.

19 Advertisement quoted in Alan Pell Crawford (2008). *Twilight at Monticello: The Final Years of Thomas Jefferson*. New York, Random House, pp. 247-248.

20 *Ibid.*, p. 253.

21 Woody Holton, review *Republic of Debtors: Bankruptcy in the Age of American Independence*, by Bruce H. Mann, *New England Quarterly*, Vol. 77, No. 4 (December 2004), p. 656.

22 H.L. Dufour Woolfley (2013). *A Quaker Goes to Spain: The Diplomatic Mission of Anthony Morris, 1813-1816*. Bethlehem, PA., Lehigh University Press, p. 156.

23 Bruce Chadwick (2014). *James & Dolley Madison: America's First Power Couple*. New York: Prometheus Books, p. 323.

24 Maud Wilder Goodwin (1896). *Dolly Madison*. New York, Charles Scribner's Sons, pp. 268-269.

25 Virginia Moore (1979). *The Madison's: A Biography*. New York, McGraw-Hill Book Company, p. 437.

26 Holly Schulman (2010). "A Constant Attention': Dolley Madison and the Publication of the Papers of James Madison, 1836-1837." *Virginia Magazine of History and Biography* 118 (1), p. 42.

27 James Madison letter to Edward Everett quoted in Schulman: "A Constant Attention," p. 42.

28 Dolley's only surviving brother had recovered from his earlier bouts with alcoholism and had settled with his family at a nearby plantation in Orange County. His daughter, Anna, was a frequent visitor to Montpelier and became Dolley's closest companion and confidant. See Schulman: constant attention, p. 41.

29 James Madison letter to Margaret Bayard Smith, circa 17 January 1835, quoted in Gary Hunt, Ed. (1906). *The First Forty Years of Washington Society Portrayed by the Family of Letters by Mrs. Samuel (Margaret Bayard) Harrison Smith*. New York, Charles Scribner & Sons, p.358.

30 Elizabeth Dowling Taylor (2012). *A Slave in the White House: Paul Jennings and the Madisons*. New York: Palgrave/McMillan Books, pp. 117-118.

31 James Madison quoted in Taylor, p. 118.

32 Dolley Madison quoted in Taylor, p. 118.

33 Henry Clay letter to Robert S. Rose, 10 September 1832, quoted in Robert Seager II, ed. *The Papers of Henry Clay, Vol. 8 5 March 1829 – 31 December 1836,* Lexington, University Press of Kentucky, p. 574.

34 James Madison quoted in Arnett, p. 276. See also Mattern, Advice to My Country, pp. 104-105.

35 Nelly Conway Madison Willis (b. December 29, 1780 – d. November 4, 1862) was the daughter of Madison's brother, Ambrose. She married Dr. John Willis and lived nearby at Woodley Plantation. She was widowed in 1811.

36 Jennings, p. 18.

37 Taylor, p. 131-132.

38 Andrew Jackson letter to Dolley Payne Madison, 9 July 1836, quoted in Goodwin, p. 249.

39 Holly Schulman (2011). "Madison v. Madison: Dolley Payne Madison and Her Inheritance of the Montpelier Estate 1836-1838." *Virginia Magazine of History and Biography* 119 (4): p. 351.

40 James Madison's Will, 19 April 1835 available at http:/www.newrivernotes.com/topical_books_ xxxx_history_of_organge_county.html.

41 L.G. Moffatt and J. M. Carrière. "A Frenchman Visits Norfolk, Fredericksburg and Orange County, 1816," *The Virginia Magazine of History and Biography*. Vol. 53, No. 3, July 1945, p. 199 n. 10.

42 Ethel Stephens Arnett (1972). *Mrs. James Madison: The Incomparable Dolley*. Greensboro, Piedmont Press, p. 286.

43 James Madison's Will.

44 The Madison census date appears on p. 320 of the Census of 1830 records for Orange County, Virginia. This material is readily available from a variety of resources online. The demographic breakdown for the enslaved population at Montpelier was as follows: 23 males/18 females under the age of 10; 14 males/12 females aged 10 to 24; 5 males/7 females between 24 and 36 years of age; 9 males/6 females aged 36 to 55; and 5 males/4 females over the age of 55. The other three residents at Montpelier in 1830 were James and Dolley Madison as well as Payne Todd.

45 Taylor, pp. 124-125, 127.

46 Edward Coles quoted in Taylor, p. 147.

47 *Ibid.*, p. 132.

48 Edward Coles letter to Sally Coles Stevenson, 12 November 1836, quoted in Taylor, p. 133.

49 George Augustus Waggaman letter to Dolley Payne Madison, 6 October 1839, available at http:// rotunda.upress.virginia.edu:8080/dmde/bio-intro.xqy#widowhood.

50 Dolley Payne Madison letter to George Augustus Waggaman, 10 October 1839, available at http:// rotunda.upress.virginia.edu:8080/dmde/bio-intro.xqy#widowhood.

51 Dolley Payne Todd letter to John Payne Todd, 20 July 1834, quoted in Lucie Cutts (1887). *Memoirs and Letters of Dolly Madison: Wife of James Madison, President of the United States*. Boston, Houghton, Mifflin and Company, p 191.

52 Alice Curtis Desmond (1950). *Glamorous Dolly Madison*. New York, Dodd, Mead & Company, p. 246.

53 Dolley Payne Todd letter to Henry Clay, 8 November 1836, quoted in Seager, p. 868.

54 Dolley Payne Madison quoted in Desmond, p. 247.

55 Dolley Payne Madison letter to Ann Murry, 9 October 1836, quoted in Mattern, *Selected Letters*, p. 335.

56 Dolley Payne Madison letter to Edward Coles, 7 January 1837, quoted in Mattern, *Selected Letters,* pp. 342-343.

57 Edward Coles quoted in Schulmann, "Madison v. Madison," p. 47.

58 James Kirke Paulding quoted in David W. Houpt (2010). "Securing a Legacy: The Publication of James Madison's Notes from the Constitutional Convention." *Virginia Magazine of History and Biography* 118 (1): p. 13.

59 William Cabell Rives quoted in Schulman, "A Constant Attention," p. 48.

60 William Cabel Rives quoted in Schulman, "Madison v. Madison," p. 366.

61 Dolley Payne Madison letter to Henry Clay, 8 November 1836 quoted in Robert Seager II, ed. (1984). The Papers of Henry Clay, Vol. 8 5 March 1829 – 31 December 1836, Lexington, University Press of Kentucky, p. 868.

62 Andrew Jackson quoted in Houpt, p. 24.

63 Houpt, p. 27.

64 Daniel Webster quoted in Houpt, p. 28.

65 Public Statutes at Large of the United States of America for the Twenty-fourth Congress available online at http://www.loc.gov.

66 Elizabeth Lippincott Dean (1928). *Dolly Madison: The Nation's Hostess*. Boston, Lothrop, Lee & Shepard Co., p. 203.

67 *Ibid.*, p. 205; Mary Cutts quoted in Arnett, p. 329. Interestingly, both Hamilton and Decatur had been killed in duels.

68 Lucie Cutts, p 329.

69 Desmond, p. 204.

70 John Quincy Adams diary entry for October 24, 1837 quoted in Allan Nevins, Ed. (1969). *The Diary of John Quincy Adams 1794-1845: American Diplomacy, and Political, Social, and Intellectual Life from Washington to Polk*. New York, Frederick Ungar Publishing Co, p. 487.

71 *Ibid.*, p. 486.

72 Ralph Ketcham (2009). *The Madisons at Montpelier: Reflections on the Founding Couple*. Charlottesville, University of Virginia Press, p. 178.

73 There were nine Montpelier slaves reportedly working at the Marble Quarry while others were engaged in construction. See Matthew G. Hyland (2007). *Montpelier and the Madisons: House*. Home and American Heritage. Charleston, SC, History Press Hyland, p. 92.

74 *Ibid.*, p. 92.

Chapter Six

1840-1849

"I have promised to make them suffer and I will redeem my pledge."

John Payne Todd

I n 1840, the newly formed Whig party nominated William Henry Harrison as its candidate to run against the incumbent Democratic president, Martin Van Buren. The 67-year old Harrison had been born in 1773 just prior to the American Revolution and had become a popular hero, widely known for his military prowess and his reputation as a fierce Indian fighter. His victory at the battle of Tippecanoe was legendary, as was his defeat of the Shawnee Indian chief, Tecumseh, during the War of 1812. As Harrison's running-mate, the Whigs selected former Virginia governor and ex-U.S. Senator, John Tyler.

The so-called "Log Cabin and Hard Cider Campaign," featured few serious debates or any substantive discussion of issues. Instead, political surrogates delivered campaign promises that were freely adjusted and adapted to reflect sectional realities. Political rallies were popular, highly attended entertainment and often featured dazzling torch-light parades along with the requisite copious amounts of alcohol. The Whig presidential ticket distinguished itself by a memorable and clever campaign slogan, "Tippecanoe and Tyler, Too," which their opponents ineffectively mocked claiming that "There was rhyme but no reason in it."[1]

The 1840 presidential "Log Cabin and Hard Cider" campaign. William Henry Harrison and John Tyler's memorable campaign slogan was "Tippecanoe and Tyler, Too!" (Library of Congress)

In the general election, Harrison successfully defeated Van Buren and was inaugurated in March 1841 as the nation's ninth President. On a cold winter day in Washington, Harrison delivered an endless, rambling two hour address, pledging to curb executive powers and abuses by promising to serve only a single term of office. He also vowed to accede to the will of Congress on virtually all important policy matters. The following day after the inaugural festivities had concluded, absent of any official responsibilities, Vice President John Tyler quietly returned to the sanctuary of his home in Williamsburg.[2]

Just three weeks later, the elderly Harrison developed a serious illness that left him bedridden. His doctors were perplexed and attempted every known remedy and cure while the new president was "bled, blistered, cupped, leeched, massaged, poked, and otherwise battered."[3] Within just a few days, the new president was dead, and, according to biographer Robert Seager, "What the armies of Tecumseh...had failed to accomplish in a dozen campaigns, the medical profession had managed in one short week."[4] Informed of Harrison's demise, John Tyler returned to Washington to assume the duties of the president.

It was a unique period in American history where in the span of just nine years, the nation would have five different presidents. In

1846, the country engaged in its second constitutionally declared war, this time against neighboring Mexico. The conflict was mercifully short, lasting less than two years and ended in 1848 with the signing of the Treaty of Guadalupe Hidalgo. The Rio Grande River was officially recognized as the boundary between the United States and Mexico, confirming the admission of Texas to the union as the nation's 28th state. Mexico was also forced to cede large tracts of land in the southwest, including California. America's manifest destiny was finally fulfilled.

For Dolley Madison, this would be the last decade of her life, and it was destined to be a time of poignant contrasts. As the sole link back to the founding era, she would receive a triumphal welcome back to Washington, D.C. in December 1843. There, her social prominence, grace, and personal dignity would successfully disguise her extremely frugal living circumstances. The money she had once received from the Congressional appropriation for her husband's notes on the Constitutional Convention had long since disappeared and had done little to alieve her precarious situation. Dolley Madison was, in reality, financially destitute and the ominous specter of debt would embarrass and haunt her until her dying days.

A FTER JAMES MADISON'S DEATH in 1836, Payne Todd was freed from any lingering guilt that may have been associated with his stepfather's disapproval of his reckless behavior. He now began to spend increasing longer periods of time in Orange County, where he finally initiated plans to develop his property at Toddsberth. The estate, located just four miles east of Montpelier, was adjacent to an important stage line to Gordonsville. Payne's modest landholdings had been recently increased by a 50-acre grant deeded to him by Dolley in 1838.[5]

By now, it was becoming painfully apparent that his mother would not be able to maintain or effectively run Montpelier. Her unending financial woes would eventually force her to sell the Madison's ancestral estate to raise revenue. In the meantime, Payne encouraged Dolley to begin transferring much of the plantation's valuable furniture, heirlooms, books, artwork, and artifacts to Toddsberth. It was yet another one of his cunning schemes to thwart nervous creditors, and he knew that once he was in possession of these items, he could surreptitiously sell them for a considerable profit as authentic Madison souvenirs and relics.[6]

Despite his nefarious intentions, Payne Todd genuinely loved his mother, and hoped to provide for her during her old age and widowhood.[7] As Lucie Cutts noted: "[Payne] intended his mother to pass the remaining years of her life [at Toddsberth]; spending much money in carrying out his eccentric ideas for her comfort."[8] But Todd had never been a careful planner nor was he a trained architect.

John Payne Todd's distinctive signature. (Library of Congress)

As a result, the various structures that he had haphazardly erected around the Toddsberth compound proved to be an eclectic array of undistinguished buildings. Lucie Cutts observed: "we looked [at] those buildings with sadness, for ridiculous in the eyes of a stranger."[9]

The central feature of Payne's estate was a conspicuous, 30-foot diameter "Round House" with a cedar shingle roof.[10] This circular, two-story building housed a ballroom on the upper floor which could be used for entertaining, dancing, and dining. The room's walls were plastered and lined with floor-to-ceiling bookshelves to house the estate's phantom library. The basement of the structure contained a wine cellar as well as an ice house.[11] Historian Catherine Allgor speculates that: "this fantastical edifice stood as the most obvious sign of his mental deterioration."[12]

Nearby, Payne built several log cabins for the estate's enslaved population, as well as numerous outbuildings and small cottages. One house was specifically designed for his mother's use. It was a single story dwelling that featured a bizarre window-door combination to accommodate Dolley's growing frailties by allowing her to enter via the dining room in order to avoid "the fatigue of a staircase."[13] By 1844, though, Dolley was residing exclusively in Washington and was reluctant to leave her many friends and intimate social circle. In a letter to his mother, Payne pleaded with her to move to Toddsberth: "as the country air is likely to be invigorating. Independent of seeing you, it is of great importance that I should impress upon you the relation you bear to [the] property which alone can [a]ffect the success of measures I have taken in your favor."[14] It was one of the few requests from her wayward son that Dolley would refuse to honor.

During this time period, Payne was engaged in his latest business venture, the development of a marble quarry on the Toddsberth property. Chartered by an act of the Virginia state legislature in 1840, the so-called Montpelier Marble Company listed Todd as its sole proprietor and investor, with the

A contemporary photograph of one of the ravines from the marble quarry at Toddsberth. The quarry was abandoned by Payne Todd after due to a flaw in the marble. (Philip Bigler)

professed mission to "quarry marble, porphyry agate, flagstones for paving and slate for roofing homes in the County of Orange."[15] Typically, Dolley was encouraged by Payne's renewed initiative, confidently writing that: "Payne is...improving his knowledge of geology."[16] She later reported to Eliza Collins Lee that: "Payne left me for Richmond to have sawed & polished there some specimens of fine marble of which he has a quarry."[17]

But like all of Payne Todd's entrepreneurial efforts, this latest endeavor eventually failed. Although he was able to successfully mine and sell a small amount of white and colored stone to neighbors for fireplace mantles and other small projects, the bulk of the Toddsberth marble was contaminated by "a small streak of quarts... [which] prevented its utilization on an extensive scale."[18] Indeed, this flaw in the stone made it virtually impossible to cut and "ruined every tool used."[19] The quarry was soon abandoned, leaving behind only the scarred earth from the excavations while Payne suffered yet another ruinous financial disaster.

Compounding Payne's misfortunes was a major fire that occurred at Toddsberth in March 1841. Payne's personal home was completely destroyed although most of the adjacent outbuildings were spared. In a letter to Elizabeth Coles, Dolley recounted the tragic event: "Having heard on Saturday that my son had lost his pleasant establishment at Todd's Birth, by fire—he was absent in Richmond when it occurred, from the chamber of an inmate. Payne's favorite occupation had long been to improve and embellish his house, and grounds so that I feel the more sorrow at the disappointment which awaits his return—that of finding only, ashes—but the wind was tempered it appears, as all his out-houses which were very near, escaped—and his furniture was saved."[20]

IN FEBRUARY 1841, AT age 73, Dolley Payne Madison composed her last will and testament. It was a generous if somewhat curious document that left the Montpelier manor house to Payne Todd. "I

A free franked envelope from Dolley Payne Madison to her son, John Payne Todd. Dolley wrote her son regularly during this period but was often frustrated by her son's lack of response. (Greensboro Historical Museum)

give and bequeath to my Son John P. Todd," Dolley wrote, "my house and lots in the City of Washington with the lands appertaining to the Montp[e]llier estate..." She also provided additional enticements to encourage her son to marry, oblivious to the reality that such prospects had long since vanished for the 49-year old bachelor. An additional $500 was allotted to Payne "for the purpose of erecting a plain monument of White Marble over the remains of my dear Husband," along with her explicit instructions that "it is my desire and request to be laid by his side."[21]

Dolley was careful to include her favorite niece, Annie, in her will in recognition of her constant loyalty and companionship. She wrote: "I give to my niece Anna Payne, three thousand dollars, with my negro Woman and her children one third of my wearing apparel, my forte piano and the furniture of my chamber" along with one hundred books and "a likeness of Mr Madison and Myself." Furthermore, she specifically instructed Anna to have "my private papers...burn[ed]."[22]

This initial last will and testament was an act of sheer fantasy since its terms would be impossible to fulfill. Indeed, Dolley's financial problems rendered the document moot from its inception and it would eventually have to be seriously revised and altered to accommodate her fiscal realities. In the interim, Dolley again enlisted her son to help sell an additional four volumes of her husband's voluminous papers. Her efforts to have them published in New York by Harper and Brothers had failed, and President John Tyler urged her to once again seek Congressional relief in yet another appropriations bill.[23]

Payne was once again of little help, and in early 1844, Dolley plaintively wrote to her son: "If you love me, my dear son, write to me—tell me when you will come to offer the papers to Congress, and to do something with the 4th: volume—we are without funds and those we owe are impatient—the time has arrived now when if lost or neglected will never return to us!...Oh, my son! I am too unhappy not to have you with me, and not to have even your opinion and directions, what to do myself or what individuals to engage and at what time! Do not let this often repeated request offend or hurt you my son—but reflect on the miseries of your mother, when she sees that nothing but a happy and early result of this duty will give her bread or continue to her what is better a respectable standing before the world—but I will say little more—as it is not good for me to write."[24]

Dolley's immediate recourse was to sell off her treasured Montpelier estate. She entered into negotiations with a Richmond merchant, Henry W. Moncure, during the summer of 1843, and permanently relocated that December to her home on Lafayette Square in Washington, D.C. Once again, she empowered Payne to serve as her personal emissary in her business transactions.

The next spring, in an effort to shield some of her dwindling assets, Dolley transferred the ownership of several Montpelier slaves to Payne Todd: "I Dolley P. Madison late resident of the County of Orange and State of Virginia and now residing in the City of Washington District of Columbia...do grant bargain and sell and confirm unto John P. Todd a certain number of negro Slaves named Tydal of 65 yrs of age, Willoughby about 60 yrs do, John abt 40 yrs, Jerry abt 32 yrs. Matthew abt 45 yrs, Winny abt 45 yrs, Milly abt 40 yrs Sarah abt 50 yrs Caty and young children about 22 Charlotte abt 20 Raif Junr about 33 yrs, Joshua abt 22, Nicholas 36 yrs, Nicholas Junr abt 13 yrs, Gabriel abt 50 yrs and Charles abt 30 yrs with Sylvia and four children she abt 33 yrs old."[25] Many of the remaining slaves, though, were seized as capital and held in jail by the local Orange County sheriff. He threatened to sell these people off to raise funds to satisfy creditors. One of Dolley's loyal servants, Sarah, appealed to her mistress in a letter for help. She explained the precarious situation of the Montpelier slaves, writing: "My Mistress: I don't like to send you bad news but the condition of all of us your servants is very bad…we are afraid we shall be bought by what are called Negro buyers and sent away from our husbands and wives. If we are obliged to be sold perhaps you could get neighbors to buy us that have husbands and wives, so as to save us some misery."[26]

Payne openly disliked Henry Moncure and this personal animosity often made their business dealings contentious.[27] Adding to their widening personal rift was an incident where Payne attempted to remove a large, expensive threshing machine from the Montpelier property even though it was to have been conveyed in the sale of the estate. His actions led to a civil lawsuit where Payne was accused in court documents of "carrying the same away a wheat machine which was a [fixture] to the barn, and was only [prevented] from [removing] the same by the arrival of this defendant on the premis[e]s just at the moment when the [removal] was about to be [effected]."[28] Moncure's complaint continued that: "It was then left so injured as to have been of no use since."[29]

The final sale of Montpelier was concluded in August 1844 and included the transfer of 750 acres of land.[30] Dolley confided in a personal letter to Henry Moncure: "No one, I think, can appreciate my feelings of grief and dismay at the necessity of transferring to another a beloved home."[31] Moncure was sympathetic to Dolley's predicament and graciously offered to cancel the transaction if she received her anticipated financial windfall from Congress and her circumstances changed but Dolley realized that this was impossible. She thanked Moncure for his kindness but concluded: "I have received dear Friend your generous and considerate proposals, and I thank you for them—I will not however take such latitude in the advantage you offer me, as to annul the arrangements you concluded with my son—I had made up my mind to them, when I sent the Deed."[32] Payne, though, remained rancorous over losing his expected inheritance and wrote to his mother: "The sale to H.W. Moncure, I consider a most unfortunate one and I would certainly wish it done away for he is the source of more difficulty than could have be apprehended; but more anon—I write by a small end of a Candle at 2 Oclock this morng—12 Sepr' 44. Which is burning out."[33] He continued undeterred in his looting of Montpelier and its valuables, informing Dolley that: "Your papers were brought to Toddsberthe in the wooden desk or chest flat in the Waggon all safe & untouched in the same position & put away equally safe for you to open in the Spring-The waggon will be loaded after they all come here—All the books are at Toddsberthe safely placed on Shelves Upstairs & cellar all cleared one new house finished & another in progress so therefore plenty of room & some perhaps for private entertainment."[34] Over the ensuing years, Payne regularly disposed of President Madison's cherished library, selling hundreds of volumes. Many were sold to stage travelers and other visitors at bargain prices, including to a Methodist minister who bought several books "with Madison's name on the fly leaves, at ten cents a volume."[35]

WITH THE SALE OF Montpelier completed and the Toddsberth marble quarry in virtual bankruptcy, Payne Todd was coming to the stark realization that his prime years were now behind him. Most of his life had been squandered by his endless pursuit of personal

An entry from Payne Todd's Memorandum Book, August 1845. He notes: "Chewed tobacco a little which after this seemed to taste well. I am afraid of the Chocolate giving a fever." (Library of Congress)

gain, debauchery, and pleasure, while his numerous public failings became emblematic of his failure to achieve his parents' hopes and dreams. His many faults and shortcomings were never just private family matters but always subject to public scrutiny and innuendo, easily attributed to the lack of character of "the" Dolley Madison's spoiled, indolent, and disreputable son. This had become an increasingly burdensome cross for Payne to bear.

Payne still never hesitated to use his distinguished lineage in his efforts to advance his own personal fortune. In one last desperate attempt to achieve some professional recognition and success, Payne sought through the intercession of his mother with President John Tyler, a political appointment as the American counsel in Liverpool. After a few weeks, Payne was dismayed when he learned that his application had been summarily rejected by the State Department, with one administration official dismissing him with the terse statement: "Mr. Todd is not fitted for the office."[36]

Dejected and discouraged, Payne retreated to his unfinished Toddsberth compound. There, he maintained a personal memorandum book for four years, from 1844 through 1848. Most of the volume was devoted to routine matters and general business correspondence but some of his entries contained revealing personal reflections. These personal writings, though, were irregular and unpredictable and frequently degenerated into incoherent ramblings. His handwriting simultaneously deteriorated into an indecipherable scrawl.

Payne attempted to chronicle some of his efforts at reform, in hopes of "a changed character if it can be affected."[37] He tried to improve his personal hygiene by regularly brushing his teeth, and simultaneously attempted to cure himself of a wide array of physical ailments through self-medication and a series of bizarre home remedies.[38] For his painful rheumatism, Payne experimented with drinking "several tumblers of brown sugar & water."[39] In another entry, he penned: "I felt very much inflamed by excessive coffing, a pain in the side which abated with the coff & inflammation by taking bark sugar & 12 ½ ch of Paregoric sent for. Better to day."[40] These fabricated tonics did little to improve his overall health which continued to deteriorate throughout the decade. Payne was frequently

Payne scrawled this entry from the Aeneid *on a single page of his Memorandum book. It was often used to justify a retirement from public life.* (Library of Congress)

sick suffering from fever, nausea, diarrhea, and a variety of stomach ailments. These illnesses were most likely symptomatic of his chronic alcoholism and profligate lifestyle.

At times, Payne tried to abstain from drinking. To reduce his cravings for alcohol, he tried drinking large amounts of ice water and milk while regularly chewing tobacco. In February 1845, he recorded: "Eat Breakfast of Ham & drank two tumblers of milk & 7 or 8 of pure water. Tea & Coffee at night & no tobacco but a smoke. I drank nothing spirituous which however was followed by a heart burn during the night & rather a nausea arising the following day."[41] Payne's efforts at rehabilitation were feeble and he inevitably relapsed. "On Saturday last," he noted in his journal, "I lost or misplaced or was robbed of my watch & very improperly getting inebriated."[42]

In December 1845, John Payne Todd mysteriously scrawled in a single page of his memorandum book, the Latin phrase: "*Non Tali auxilio egemus, nec defensoribus istis.*"[43] The axiom was well-known during the 19th century among the literate class and it originates from Book Two of Virgil's *Aeneid*. It translates literally as: "Not such aid nor such defenders does this time require."[44] In the context of the Roman epic, Aeneas provides a graphic description of the final destruction of the city of Troy to Queen Dido.[45] According to Aeneas, the elderly Trojan king, Priam, was attempting to don his armor in order to join the fight against the invading Greeks when he is interrupted by his wife, Hecuba. She informs her husband that the situation is hopeless—there is nothing that the king could do to save his city from destruction. At this climatic moment, Hecuba makes her famous proclamation (*Non Tali auxilio...*)—in essence, whatever fighting there was left to be done in the defense of Troy, it was now the obligation of younger, more virile warriors. Soon, Priam and Hecuba witness the brutal slaying of their son, Polites. The king, himself, is then killed by Neoptolemus, the son of the legendary Greek warrior, Achilles.

Why Payne Todd would record this particular quotation in his own private journal is unknowable but most educated Americans were all well-versed in Greek and Roman literature. They frequently punctuated their writings with classical allegories and Hecuba's famous phrase was often used to justify a retirement and withdrawal from political life. Thomas Jefferson, for instance, wrote to his friend, John Adams, during the War of 1812: "But our machines have now been running for 70. or 80. years, and we must expect that, worn as they are, here a pivot, there a wheel, now a pinion, next a spring, will be giving way: and however we may tinker them up for awhile, all will at length surcease motion. Our watches, with works of brass and steel, wear out within that period." The crisis facing the nation was no longer their concern. Jefferson continued: "…With this however you and I shall have nothing to do; our being truly the case wherein '*Non Tali auxilio egemus, nec defensoribus istis.*'"[46] Jefferson later would use the same quotation from the Aeneid in a letter to C.W. Glooch in 1826: "I am not the champion called for by our present danger, *Non tali auxilio, nec defensoribus istis, tempus eget.* A waning body, a waning mind, and waning memory, with habitual ill health warn me to withdraw and relinquish the arena to younger and abler athletes."[47]

Perhaps Payne's inclusion of the Latin verse was merely indicative of his weary and depressed state of mind or of his desire to reduce the turmoil in his life. In a less cryptic and more honest entry in his memorandum book, Payne describes himself simply as "sick and unhappy."[48]

AS DOLLEY CONTINUED HER quest for a buyer for her husband's supplemental papers, she was reduced to living a frugal existence while in Washington. Her former slave, Paul Jennings, recalled that: "In the last days of her life…she was in a state of absolute poverty, and I think sometimes suffered for the necessaries in life."[49] In a remarkable role reversal, Jennings took pity upon his former mistress and "occasionally gave her small sums from my own pocket," while Senator Daniel Webster frequently sent her caches of food and other provisions in order to live.[50]

Despite her financial poverty, Dolley successfully retained her personal dignity and was still a celebrity in Washington. She received constant requests from admirers for her autograph and had so many social invitations that they were "[more] that I can perform."[51] Although by now her clothing, gowns, and turbans had long ceased to be fashionable, she was nevertheless an esteemed guest at the various fetes, galas, and commemorations that were regularly held

The explosion on the Princeton. *President John Tyler had invited Dolley Madison to be one of the guests on the vessel on February 28, 1844. The ship's massive new gun exploded killing the Secretary of State and several others.* (Library of Congress)

throughout the nation's capital. In late February 1844, Dolley was invited by then President, John Tyler, to join him as a guest onboard the American frigate, *Princeton*. The warship had been converted for the occasion into a floating party where over 200 dignitaries and guests were to witness the spectacle of the test firing of what was purported to be the world's largest naval gun, the 12-inch "Peacemaker."[52]

On an unseasonably warm winter's day, the ship departed on schedule from the port of Alexandria to great fanfare. A few miles downriver near Fort Washington, the massive cannon was test-fired for the first time, to the delight of the spectators and politicians. The gun was again discharged a few minutes later as the *Princeton* continued to sail southward on the Potomac River. Afterwards, the majority of guests adjourned to below deck to drink champagne and to feast upon various hors d'oeuvres, where purportedly "wit and mirth, and every circumstance pervaded."[53] On the return trip to Alexandria, as the vessel was passing by George Washington's Mount Vernon home, Captain Robert Stockton ordered the firing of the "Peacemaker" one last time in a traditional naval salute to the first president and the father of the country. In doing so, the gun suddenly exploded, sending deadly shrapnel across the deck and instantly killing the Secretary of State, Abel P. Upshur, the Secretary of the Navy, Thomas W. Gilmer, along with four others. Captain Stockton himself was seriously wounded in the incident, as were Senator Thomas Hart Benton and nine other sailors. Fortuitously, President Tyler and Dolley Madison had been safely below deck when the explosion occurred, but they emerged to witness the incredible scene of carnage and destruction. Dolley heroically began to attend to the injured and the wounded as the *Princeton* limped slowly back to port. According to Lucie Cutts, Dolley: "With great presence of mind she went about doing her best to soothe and assist in caring for the wounded, until forced to go home."[54]

Dolley was intrigued by the latest technological innovations and inventions that were sweeping the United States at the advent of

An extraordinary daguerreotype showing President James Polk and others on the South Portico of the Executive Mansion. Dolley Madison is pictured second from right. She moved during the long exposure, blurring her image. (Courtesy of George Eastman House, International Museum of Film)

its industrial age. In March 1844, she was invited to attend the first demonstration of Samuel Morris' "Electro-Magnetic Telegraph" at the United States Capitol. In the basement Supreme Court chambers, a special telegraph terminal was set up and connected by wire to a railroad depot located some 50 miles away in Baltimore. At precisely 8:45 AM, the first message ever sent electronically was transmitted by Morris to the astonishment of the onlookers. It read simply: "What hath God wrought?" Morse then honored Dolley Madison by inviting her to be the first private citizen to send her own telegraphic message.[55] The newspapers universally lauded the event, prophesizing that this new, marvelous technology was, in essence, "the an-

Quarter plate daguerrotype of Anna Payne and Dolley Madison taken by Mathew Brady, 1848. Dolley Madison was the first presidential spouse to have ever been photographed. (© The National Portrait Gallery. Image source: Art Resource, NY)

nihilation of space."[56] Within a year, telegraph wires were strung throughout the east coast, linking the nation's largest cities and forever changing communications within the United States.

During her Washington residency, Dolley earned the distinction of becoming the first presidential wife to have ever been photographed. On July 17, 1847, she and Anna were invited to the Executive Mansion by the new president, James K. Polk. There, a group daguerreotype image was made on the South Portico. The remarkable picture showed President Polk, his wife—Sarah, Secretary of State and future president, James Buchanan, Anna Payne, and several others. Unfortunately, Dolley moved slightly during the required long photographic exposure, blurring her image. Fortunately, the next year she would sit for studio portraits at the request of photographer Mathew Brady and some of these images were pristine as well as astonishing.[57]

During the 19th century, sessions of United States Congress were high entertainment in Washington, D.C. and often featured intense debates and dramatic political confrontations. Dolley was a frequent visitor in the gallery and her presence was always noted by members. In an unprecedented action, the House of Representative honored Dolley by providing her a seat on the floor of the chamber. The formal invitation sent to her noted that whenever she desired to attend sessions of Congress: "she be requested to take a seat within the Hall."[58]

In 1848, Dolley narrowly escaped being killed in a fire at her home. While she and Anna were asleep upstairs, a neighbor noticed flames coming from the residence and promptly alerted servants to the danger. According to her grandniece: "As the flames began to ascend towards her room in the early morning, a neighbor aroused the servants…[Ralph] rushing towards his mistress' room, broke down the door and found her quietly sleeping in the midst of dense clouds of smoke."[59] After being awoken, Dolley instructed that a trunk with her husband's valuable papers be rescued before escaping barefoot into the garden clad in only a "black velvet gown and nightcap."[60] Neighbors rallied to her aid and used dozens of buckets of water to extinguish the flames, saving the house from destruction. Dolley informed Payne Todd about the harrowing events in a letter on May 21, 1848: "You have seen by the Gazettes, my dear son, that we had an alarm of fire in our house…our neighbors (just awakened) came to our assistance, and soon separated the fire from the window frame in which it had made great progress…the watch is nightly around the City."[61]

THROUGHOUT HER LIFE, DOLLEY maintained her strong religious convictions even though she had been expelled from the Society of Friends after her marriage to the Protestant James Madison. She became a devout Episcopalian and while in Washington, Dolley and her niece, Annie, were regular parishioners at St. John's Church on Lafayette Square. On July 15, 1845, Dolley received her "long-wished for confirmation" although she had yet to be baptized since the Quakers rejected such sacramental rituals.[62]

Dolley's strong religious beliefs were evidenced in one of her responses to a letter from Payne requesting money. She responded: "I am too sensible to all the troubles you encounter but I trust in Our Heavenly Father, who has in His Mercy supported us to this day." She urged him to "let your Faith be in Him, with Prayers for His continued goodness to us, who are nothing without Him."[63]

Payne was ostensibly working to help Dolley secure the much needed Congressional appropriation to purchase her husband's remaining papers. Once again, though, Payne neglected his responsibilities.[64] For whatever reasons, Payne's correspondence with his mother became increasing erratic and capricious. Dolley's was constantly concerned about his silence and in June 1845, wrote: "What has been the matter with you and [where] have you been my beloved? It has been long since you wrote me, or acknowledged the receiving of one of my several letters."[65] In another letter, she asked: "It has been too long since I was cheered with a line from you—what are you about, that prevents your communicating with your Mother?" She signed the letter: "Anxious! Mother." [66]

Payne was, typically, broke and being harassed by his many creditors. To help quench his insatiable appetite for money, he began to sell off the family's slaves despite his mother's avowed disdain for the practice. On three separate occasions, Payne reportedly netted payments of $2,075, $1,925, and $3,000 for his human transactions.[67]

By the winter of 1848, Dolley's health was failing and she took increasing solace in remembering the past. She informed her son: "I am not well."[68] That February, though, she received welcomed news that Congress had finally agreed in principle to purchase her cache of Madison papers for $25,000, but the legislative process once again proved to be agonizingly slow.[69] In a letter to Payne, she wrote: "Nothing has yet been done in Congress—when it is, I'll let you know immediately."[70] But just two weeks later, coincidentally on her 80th birthday, the legislation was finally passed. Her grand-nephew, J. Madison Cutts, delivered the exciting news to Dolley, thrilled that: "Thus did Congress and a grateful country relieve her distress."[71] This was only partially true. Fearing that Payne would somehow find a way to extort Dolley's money, Congress specified that $20,000 of the appropriated funds be held in trust. Placed under the able administration of James Buchanan, John Mason, and Richard Smith, the interest derived from these savings was expected to provide a steady income for Dolley for the remainder of her life, and came with the stipulation that she could dispense of the trust funds as she wished upon her death.[72] This financial arrangement protected Dolley's capital but it infuriated Payne, who threated to sue the newly appointed trustees. The threat of legal action embarrassed and appalled Dolley. She urged Payne to cease his legal maneuvering and wrote to him: "At this moment I am much distressed at the conversations you held…[I request] you abandon the idea."[73] He reluctantly, if sullenly, complied.

IN THE SUMER OF 1849, Dolley was again in ill health. Payne Todd was well aware of his 81-year old mother's deteriorating condition and he journeyed to Washington in June to visit her. At that time, he insisted that she prepare a new will, one which would reflect her current financial situation. In the new document, Dolley named Payne as the sole executor of her estate and the heir to all of her possessions and money.[74] How much of this was a matter of coercion is unclear, but Payne was clearly the chief beneficiary of the new legal document.[75]

The next month, Dolley's illness had progressed to the point where she was confined to bed. She remained aware but was semi-conscious. Her doctors attempted to make her comfortable by prescribing small doses of opium. As Elizabeth Collins Lee later recalled: "I was with her every day during her illness—Tho greatly prostrate from the first she lay quiet, with her eyes shut and when not disturbed by the frequent attacks of her disease appeared to suffer no pain and conscious when spoken to tho she spoke but very faintly."[76]

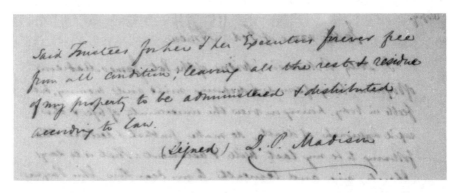

Dolley Madison's signature on her July 9, 1849 will. This was prepared just three days prior to her death and divided the Congressional appropriation of $20,000 equally between her son and niece, Annie. Payne Todd was furious and contested the will after Dolley's death. (Library of Congress)

Throughout this trying ordeal, the ever loyal Anna Payne maintained a constant vigil, rarely leaving her beloved aunt's bedside.

On July 9, just three days before her death, James Madison Cutts encouraged Dolley to draft yet another will. He was apparently unaware that she had already done so at the insistence of Payne Todd and this would become a source of bitter contention within the family. Cutts encouraged Dolley to acknowledge Annie for her years of loyalty and companionship. The death-bed document which Dolley signed was short and succinct. It began: "In the name of God, Amen." She continued that with "the rapid approach of death" she desired to leave $10,000 of the Congressional trust to her son, Payne, while the remaining $10,000 should go "to my adopted daughter Annie Payne."[77]

Over the next three days, family members and friends gathered and often read Bible passages to Dolley, including many of her favorite verses from the Gospel of Saint John.[78] During this time, Dolley lapsed in and out of consciousness, but she was aware that Payne had arrived to be with her during her last hours. In a quiet voice, she was heard to mumble the words: "My poor boy."[79]

Dolley Payne Madison died peacefully on the evening of July 12, 1849 at her home on Lafayette Square. She had known every American president since the nation's founding and was "said to be.... the most popular person in the United States."[80] President Zachary Taylor eulogized: "she was truly our First Lady for a half-century."[81]

––––––––––––––

DOLLEY'S BODY LAY INSTATE for three days at her home to allow time for her many well-wishers to pay their final respects. As the news of her death spread across the nation, she was mourned and eulogized everywhere. Kentucky Governor, John J. Crittenden, wrote: "She was the bright example in which was combined the grace, the dignity and virtue of her sex," while Congressman Alexander Stephens lauded: "No woman in this country and few in any other ever filled a larger sphere in their day than Mrs. Madison did in hers."[82] The *Daily National Intelligencer* reported: "Beloved by all…universally respected…whenever she appeared, every one became conscious of the presence of the spirit of benignity and gentleness."[83] In the Virginia state capital, Richmond women were urged to show their respect by wearing black mourning bows on the left sleeve of their dresses for thirty days.[84]

On July 16, Dolley's body was removed to nearby St. John's Church for religious services. Afterwards, a large funeral possession consisting of family members, clergy, the President, members of the cabinet, Supreme Court Justices, Congressmen, foreign dignitaries, as well as hundreds of private citizens escorted the body to Congressional Cemetery where Dolley's body was to lie in temporary repose in the Public Vault until Payne Todd could make final arrangements to return the remains to Montpelier for final burial.[85]

AN INVENTORY OF DOLLEY Madison's possessions was compiled just four weeks after her death on August 14. Among her personal possessions were a necklace with double headed eagle, 24 silver forks, two gravy spoons, a comb, a cameo, and a mosaic necklace. She also had a pair of "miniature bracelets of Mr. Madison and Mr. Todd," a pair of silver knee buckles owned by Thomas Jefferson as well as a pair owned by James Madison.[86] Payne was hardly concerned with these trinkets or small family heirlooms, but he was incensed to learn that Dolley had altered her will to include his cousin, Annie. He vowed to contest the document in court and demanded all of the $20,000 in Congressional appropriations.

Payne's litigious nature disgusted his family and many of their friends. After Dolley's death, they felt emboldened to denounce openly Payne's disgraceful behavior. Virginia Trist bitterly noted: "Her son, Payne Todd, was a notoriously bad character. His misconduct was the sorrow of his mother's life. Mr. Madison, during his lifetime, bore with him like a father and paid many of his debts, but he was an incorrigible spendthrift. His heartless, unprincipled conduct embittered the last years of his mother's life, and no doubt shortened it."[87] An intimate family member ominously acknowledged: "As for my cousin [Payne Todd]…His manners were perfectly Grandisonian, but I was a little afraid of him. Do not ask me why."[88]

J. Madison Cutts who had assisted Dolley in the preparation of her final will sent a enigmatic letter forewarning Annie of the trouble to follow. He wrote: "Before the death of our venerated Aunt, I foresaw what might take place, I took many effectual measures for your benefits. Immediately after her death, I came to you, I said that , as you know your Aunt and father confided in me…God knows, if I can serve you I will…I see that you are misled and from the contents of your note and other information can scarce hope to remedy the evil. I never meant to enter into any misunderstand or wrangle with strangers about the family matters."[89] It was an all too accurate prophecy of events to come.

Endnotes

Epigraph: John Payne Todd letter to Dolley Payne Madison, 26 November 1844, quoted in quoted in David Mattern and Holly Schulman eds., (2003). *The Selected Letters of Dolley Payne Madison*. Charlottesville, University of Virginia Press, p. 324.

1 Robert Seager (1963). *And Tyler, Too*. Norwalk, CT., Easton Press, pp. 135-136.

2 *Ibid*., pp. 154-155.

3 *Ibid*., pp. 145-146.

4 *Ibid*., p. 146.

5 "Story of 'Todd's Berth' Recalled by Old Photo," *The Free Lance-Star*, January 28, 1937, p. 6.

6 Frank S. Walker (2004). *Remembering: A History of Orange County Virginia*. Orange, VA., Orange County Historical Society, p. 130. Lucie Cutts noted, "Most of the precious souvenirs were re-moved to 'Toddsbirth,' the residence of her son, Payne Todd." See Lucie Cutts (1887). *Memoirs and Letters of Dolly Madison: Wife of James Madison, President of the United States*. Boston, Houghton, Mifflin and Company.

7 Catherine Allgor, (2006). *A Perfect Union: Dolley Madison and the Creation of the American Nation*. New York, Henry Holt and Company, p. 381

8 Cutts, pp. 206-207.

9 Lucie Cutts quoted in Ethel Stephens Arnett (1972). *Mrs. James Madison: The Incomparable Dolley*. Greensboro, Piedmont Press, p. 349.

10 Mabel Hicks Gipson, (1962). Letter to the Editor, *Orange Review*.

11 Arnett, pp. 348-349 and W. W. Scott, (1907). *A History of Orange County: From its Formation in 1734 (O.S.) to the end of Reconstruction 1870 compiled mainly from Original Records*. Richmond, Everett Waddey Company, p. 7.

12 Allgor, p. 381.

13 Cutts, p. 206.

14 John Payne Todd quoted in Arnett, pp. 270-271.

15 *The Free-Lance Star*, p. 6. Todd's business endeavor was described by a contemporary as follows: "The Montpellier Marble Quarry is situated on the road upon which the Southeastern mail passed to Nashville & New Orleans from Washington at the Seat of Madison's old Mill on Todd's line…& called 5 ½ miles from Gordonsville Depot the western extremity of a rail road to Richmond about 70 miles and to Potomac Landing of the Southern Boat 95 miles. By land the mouth of Potomac Creek about 45 miles descending and about 18 miles from James River navigation on the Rivanna…The Quarry is partially developed has been uncovered to display…It has a fall of water passing by it which turned a grist mill during the warm seasons."

16 Dolley Payne Madison quoted in Virginia Moore (1979). *The Madison's: A Biography*. New York, McGraw-Hill Book Company, p. 456.

17 Dolley Payne Madison letter to Eliza Collins Lee, 19 February 1840, quoted in David Matter and Holly C. Shulman, eds. (2003). *The Selected Letters of Dolley Payne Madison*. Charlottesville, University of Virginia Press, p. 351.

18 *Ibid.*, p. 6.

19 Scott, p. 7.

20 Dolley Payne Madison letter to Elizabeth Coles, 8 March 1841 quoted in David Mattern and Holly Schulman eds., (2003). *The Selected Letters of Dolley Payne Madison*. Charlottesville, University of Virginia Press, p. 358.

21 Will of Dolley Madison quoted in Mattern, *Selected Letters*, pp. 355-356. This document is readily available online.

22 *Ibid.*, pp. 355-356.

23 Mattern, *Selected Letters*, p. 322.

24 Dolley Payne Madison letter to John Payne Todd, 22 January 1844, quoted in Mattern, *Selected Letters*, p. 369.

25 Deed to John Payne Todd, 16 June 1844, quoted in Mattern, *Selected Letters*, p. 372.

26 Sarah letter to Dolley Payne Madison, 5 July 1844, quoted in Allan Clark (1914). *The Life and Letters of Dolly Madison*. Washington, DC, W.F. Roberts Company, p. 342.

27 Elizabeth Dowling Taylor (2012). *A Slave in the White House: Paul Jennings and the Madisons*. New York: Palgrave/McMillan Books, pp. 152.

28 Court case quoted in Matt Reeves. *Threshing Machine Feature—2012 Excavations*, retrieved November 20, 2014, http://www.montpelier.org.

29 *Ibid.*

30 Mattern, *Selected Letters*, p. 373.

31 Dolley Payne Madison letter to Henry W. Moncure, 12 August 1844, quoted in Clark, p. 342.

32 Dolley Payne Todd letter to William H. Moncure, 3 September 1844, quoted in Clark, pp. 343-344.

33 John Payne Todd letter to Dolley Payne Madison, 12 September 1844, quoted in Mattern, *Selected Letters*, p. 377.

34 John Payne Todd letter to Dolley Payne Madison, October 1844, quoted in Mattern, *Selected Letters*, p. 378.

35 Scott, p. 8.

36 Arnett, pp. 357-358.

37 "Memorandum Book of John Payne Todd, 1844-1848," *The Papers and Collection of Peter Force*. Library of Congress Archival Manuscript Material, Microfilm 17,137 (reel 68) mm 82043026. Journal entry August 1845 from "The Memorandum Book."

38 Allgor, Catherine (2006). *A Perfect Union: Dolley Madison and the Creation of the American Nation*. New York, Henry Holt and Company, p. 381.

39 Journal entry for February 18, 1846 from the "Memorandum Book."

40 Journal entry for March 15, 1847 from the "Memorandum Book."

41 Journal entry for February 9, 1845 from the "Memorandum Book."

42 Journal entry for November 1845 from the "Memorandum Book."

43 "Memorandum Book of John Payne Todd, 1844-1848," *The Papers and Collection of Peter Force*. Library of Congress Archival Manuscript Material, Microfilm 17,137 (reel 68) mm 82043026.

44 See Book II, Line 506 in the *Aeneid*.

45 Interestingly, one of the slaves implicated in the murder of James Madison's grandfather, Ambrose, was named Dido after the legendary queen of Carthage. Planters often named their slaves after heroic characters in antiquity, an irony given their status as chattels.

46 Thomas Jefferson letter to John Adams, July 5, 1814 available at http://www.let.rug.nl/usa/presidents/thomas-jefferson/letters-of-thomas-jefferson/jefl231.php.

47 Thomas Jefferson letter to C.W. Glooch, 1826.

48 Journal entry in July 1844 from the "Memorandum Book."

49 Paul Jennings quoted in Clark, p. 390.

50 Jennings quoted in Clark, p. 390.

51 Dolley Payne Madison quoted in Mattern, *Selected Letters*, p. 320.

52 Seager, p. 204.

53 *Ibid.*, p. 204.

54 Lucie Cutts (1887). *Memoirs and Letters of Dolly Madison: Wife of James Madison, President of the United States*. Boston, Houghton, Mifflin and Company, p. 205.

55 Catherine Allgor, Ed. (2012). *The Queen of America: Mary Cutts's Life of Dolley Madison*. Charlottesville, University of Virginia Press, p. 12.

56 Clark, pp. 339-340.

57 The famous image of Dolley Madison with President Polk *et al.* is available from the George Eastman house of International Museum of Photography and Film.

58 Mattern, *Selected Letters*, p. 347.

59 Lucie Cutts quoted in Clark, p. 419.

60 Cutts, p. 208.

61 Dolley Payne Madison letter to John Payne Todd, 21 May 1848, quoted in Clark, pp. 419-420.

62 Cutts, p. 207. Dolley was baptized after her confirmation on June 2, 1846. Arnett, p. 366.

63 Dolley Payne Madison letter to John Payne Todd, 24 September 1847 quoted in Allgor, *The Queen of America*, p. 385.

64 Allgor, p. 187.

65 Dolley Payne Madison letter to John Payne Todd, 14 June 1845, quoted in Allgor, p. 379.

66 Dolley Payne Madison letter to John Payne Todd, 23 April 1846, quoted in Allgor, p. 383.

67 Arnett, p. 375.

68 Dolley Payne Madison letter to John Payne Todd available at the Library of Congress, http://hdl. loc.gov/loc.mss/mjm.24_1108_1109.

69 *Ibid.*, p. 375.

70 Dolley Payne Todd letter to John Payne Todd, 9 May 1848, quoted in Arnett, p. 376.

71 J. Madison Cutts quoted in Arnett, p. 378.

72 Buchanan was the Secretary of State, Mason was the Secretary of the Navy, and Sith had worked for the Bank of Metropolis. See Arnett, p. 378.

73 Dolley Payne Madison quoted in Arnett, p. 379.

74 Mattern, *Selected Letters*, p. 325.

75 The will Payne had his mother sign was dated June 11, 1849. See Clark, p. 454.

76 Elizabeth Collins Lee to Zaccheus Collins Lee quoted in Mattern, *Selected Letters*, p. 390.

77 Dolley Madison's last will was composed on July 9, 1849. See Clark, p. 503.

78 Cutts, pp. 209-210.

79 Richard N. Cote (2005). *Strength and Honor: The Life of Dolley Madison*. Mount Pleasant, SC, Corinthian Books, p. 357.

80 Mrs. Trist quoted in Clark, p. 458.

81 This was the first time that the title "First Lady" had ever been used to refer to a presidential spouse. It would become an honorific for every subsequent presidential wife. Zachary Taylor quoted in Philip Bigler and Annie Lorsbach (2009). *Liberty & Learning: The Essential James Madison*. Harrisonburg, VA., The James Madison Center, p. 139.

82 John J. Crittenden and Alexander Stephens quoted in Clark, pp. 456-457.

83 *National Daily Intelligencer* quoted in Bigler, p. 139.

84 Clark, p. 452.

85 Arnett, p. 392.

86 Inventory of Dolley Madison's Possessions compiled on 14 August 1849 from the collections of the Greensboro Historical Museum.

87 Virginia "Jenny" Trist quoted in Clark, p. 458.

88 Clark, p. 484.

89 J. Madison Cutts letter to Anna Payne, 24 August 1849, in the Collections of the Greensboro Historical Museum.

Chapter Seven

1850 - 1852

"He drank to excess; he ate in excess; His letters on business indicate he was querulous and suspicious."

Allan Clark

Z achary Taylor, *"Old Rough and Ready,"* became the nation's 12th president without having ever served in any public or elective office. The elderly, 65-year old Kentucky plantation holder had spent his entire adult life in the military and had emerged from the recent Mexican-American conflict as one of the nation's greatest heroes. It was this fame that had propelled Taylor into the presidency, but the general was a political novice and was used to having his orders obeyed without question or discussion. He came to Washington, D.C. ill-equipped to govern by the requisite subtlety, negotiation, concession, and conciliation. The new president had little of the political skill required to lead the country during a time of increasing sectional turmoil and political strife. [1]

The recent acquisition of vast new territories from the Mexican War had once again resurrected the issue of the expansion of slavery into newly acquired lands. In January 1850, Senators Henry Clay and Daniel Webster, both members of President Taylor's own Whig Party, attempted to assuage the growing political passions by proposing a series of dramatic legislation which soon became known collectively as the *"Compromise of 1850."* The bills were intended

An election poster for the Whig candidate, Zachary Taylor, during the 1850 presidential campaign. Taylor had spent his entire life in the military and had no political experience. He vowed to veto the Compromise of 1850 should it be passed by Congress. (Library of Congress)

to mollify and appease both northerners and southerners by providing important concessions to each section.

The discovery of gold in California the previous year had resulted in a massive, international migration into the region. The proposed legislation called for bypassing the traditional territorial status and immediately admitting California to the union as a free state. This would knowingly disrupt the delicate sectional balance between slave and free states which had existed for over thirty years in the United States Senate. To placate southerners for ceding this important political power, a strong fugitive slave law would be simultaneously enacted and, more importantly, enforced. All runaways, even those who had successfully reached the "sanctuary" of northern "free soil," would be required to be returned to their previous owners. The bill also included provisions for the settlement of an ongo-

ing boundary dispute between New Mexico and Texas as well as a prohibition on the selling of slaves within the boundaries of the District of Columbia. The right to engage in the robust domestic slave trade throughout the remainder of the south, though, was re-affirmed.[2]

As with most political compromises, few people approved of all of the provisions. A strong and vocal opposition to the legislation quickly developed in Congress. Many were troubled by the fact that the proposed law would effectively negate the three decades old Missouri Compromise and open lands north of the 36°30' line to the importation of slavery. Proponents countered that the original law was archaic and outdated, noting accurately that Congress had the fundamental right to repeal or replace any legislation that it had previously passed. President Taylor entered into the fray by openly declaring his opposition to any future expansion of slavery into the nation's territories and threatened to veto the Clay/Webster bills should they pass both houses of Congress. Joining the President in his opposition were the abolitionists led by the formidable Massachusetts senator, Charles Sumner. The legislation was likewise opposed, albeit for vastly different reasons, by numerous pro-slavery Congressmen, including John C. Calhoun of South Carolina who called the bill: "radically wrong...[a] surrender of the exercise of judgment and conscience."[3]

On the floor of the United States Senate, Daniel Webster made an impassioned and eloquent plea to his colleagues to pass the compromise for the good of the nation and to avert the very real specter of an armed sectional conflict. He began his address by appealing to his fellow representatives' patriotism: "I wish to speak to-day, not as a Massachusetts man, nor as a Northern man, but as an American."[4] The new Whig Vice President, Millard Fillmore, as President of the Senate, actively opposed the President's position and claimed that he would cast a decisive vote in favor of the legislation should the vote end in a tie.

The legislative impasse continued throughout the early summer. Then, on July 9, 1850, shocking news was received that President Taylor had died after a short illness from cholera. A grand funeral procession was held in his honor a few days later. The caisson carrying the remains of the deceased President was pulled by eight elegant white horses, followed closely behind with Taylor's own mount, Old Whitey, who served as a caparisoned horse symbolizing a fallen leader. The President's body was conveyed to Congressional Cemetery where it was placed in temporary repose in the Public Vault next to the coffin of the former First Lady, Dolley Madison. Taylor's body would be returned to Louisville, Kentucky later that October for final burial.[5]

Vice President Millard Fillmore was sworn in as the new president the day after Taylor's death. It was a somber occasion conducted within the House chambers. With the inauguration of a new president and after nine months of contentious debates, the Compromise of 1850 was finally passed and signed into law that September.[6] The immediate crisis had been averted. But, it was still a perilous time when skilled political leadership was desperately needed and tragically, the nation's three greatest Congressmen—John C. Calhoun, Henry Clay, and Daniel Webster—all died within a short two year span.[7] The Congress was now completely dominated by rabid partisans and they were in no mood for further compromise or legislative concessions. The growing bitterness and anger erupted into physical violence in 1856 when South Carolina Congressman, Preston Brooks, openly confronted the abolitionist, Charles Sumner, on the Senate floor for a perceived slander he had made against one of Brook's relatives in an earlier speech. Brooks brutally cane-whipped Sumner into unconsciousness before finally being restrained. It would take three years before Sumner had recovered sufficiently from his injuries to reclaim his conspicuously empty Senate seat.[8] Brooks was quickly censured by the House of Representatives and resigned from Congress but the Congressman offered no apologies and showed no remorse for his actions. His South Carolina constituents instead lauded him as a southern hero and promptly sent

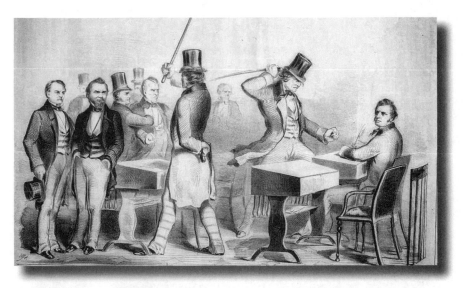

A lithograph entitled an "Argument of the Chivalry," It shows Congressman Preston Brooks con-fronting abolitionist Senator Charles Sumner on the Senate floor. Brooks cane-whipped Sumner into unconsciousness over remarks he had made during a previous speech. The caption for the print reads: "The symbol of the North is the pen; the symbol of the South is the bludgeon." (Library of Congress)

Brooks dozens of replacement canes. They then reelected him to his vacated seat in the House of Representatives, prompting many members of the United States Congress to carry side arms to the Capitol for their own personal protection.[9]

Further causing the deterioration in the nation's political discourse was the complete void in capable leadership in the executive branch. During a remarkable twenty year span from 1840 through 1860, the United States endured an unprecedented eight single term presidents (Martin Van Buren, William Henry Harrison, John Tyler, James K. Polk, Zachary Taylor, Milliard Fillmore, Franklin Pierce, and James Buchanan). These administrations were collectively un-distinguished and the men were intellectual mediocrities, especially when compared to those titans who had been elected to the presi-dency (George Washington, John Adams, Thomas Jefferson, James Madison, James Monroe, and John Quincy Adams), during the first four decades of the republic.[10]

Franklin Pierce was elected president in 1852, proclaiming in his inaugural address: "I believe that involuntary servitude, as it exists in different States of this Confederacy, is recognized by the Constitution. I believe that it stands like any other admitted right, and that the States where it exists are entitled to efficient remedies to enforce the constitutional provisions. I hold that the laws of 1850, commonly called the 'compromise measures,' are strictly constitutional and to be unhesitatingly carried into effect. I believe that the constituted authorities of this Republic are bound to regard the rights of the South in this respect as they would view any other legal and constitutional right, and that the laws to enforce them should be respected and obeyed, not with a reluctance encouraged by abstract opinions as to their propriety in a different state of society, but cheerfully and according to the decisions of the tribunal to which their exposition belongs."[11] Pierce ended his speech by earnestly evoking the ghosts of Thomas Jefferson and George Washington but his remarks lacked eloquence and subtly, memorable only for his affirmation of the constitutional right to own slaves.

Harriet Beech Stowe, *the author of* Uncle Tom's Cabin. (National Archives)

By contrast, Harriet Beecher Stowe published Uncle Tom's Cabin *in 1852. Ostensibly a work of fiction, it was a powerful indictment of slavery, but Stowe claimed that her work was based upon fact and "the separate incidents that compose the narrative are, to a very great extent, authentic."[12] She skillfully humanized slaves for the first time and her major characters—Uncle Tom, Eliza, and little Eva--were sympathetic and admirable, a stark counterpoint to the wicked Simon Legree, whose character soon became an archetype of an evil slave owner.* Uncle Tom's Cabin *sold an astonishing 300,000 copies during its first year of publication and was lauded throughout the north, while the south denounced the book as nothing more than abolitionist propaganda. The nation was further polarized and the American republic once envisioned by James Madison at the Constitutional Convention in Philadelphia in 1787 was on the brink of catastrophe.*

IT WASN'T LONG AFTER his mother's death that Payne Todd chose to contest her final will in court. He felt personally betrayed, abused, and fully entitled to all of what remained of Dolley's wealth. He certainly had no intention of sharing any of the $20,000 Congressional appropriation with his cousin, Annie.

Payne's attorneys quickly maneuvered to negate Dolley's final testament, arguing that the court should recognize her previous June will as valid by declaring Todd to be his mother's chief executor and sole beneficiary. This legal haggling by Payne was selfish and contemptible and would result only in lasting ill-will and bitterness among family members and friends.

In truth, Anna had more than earned a portion of Dolley's inheritance. Ever since Madison's death in 1836, she had been her aunt's closest companion. For over thirteen years, she had served as a noble and selfless caretaker. As Harriett Taylor Upton observed: "[Annie] was one of the few purely unselfish persons whom one may meet in life."[13] Dolley frequently acknowledged Annie as her *de facto* adoptive daughter.

Dolley's death had been a traumatic event for Annie and she openly grieved over the loss of her beloved aunt. Payne's litigation only added to her emotional distress. During this sad time, Anna was also forced to abandon the Lafayette Square home that she had shared with her Aunt Dolley and moved to the E Street home of her distant relatives, Dr. and Mrs. James Miller.[14] This relocation even-

Dr. James H. Causten, Jr. He married Annie Payne, Dolley Madison's niece, in 1850 and became her greatest advocate during her legal struggles with Payne Todd. (Greensboro Historical Museum)

tually proved to be a fortuitous, since there Annie was introduced to a handsome, 34-year old physician named James H. Causten, Jr. Causten was a friend and protégée of Dr. Miller's and had already distinguished himself as both a diplomat and linguist. The couple fell deeply in love and after a whirlwind romance, they were married in April 9, 1850, just nine months after Dolley Madison's death.[15] Everyone was delighted with the marriage and Causten's sister, Henrietta "Netty" Shriver, wrote approvingly: "My dear brother, must I tell you how sincerely I am rejoiced to hear of your happiness. May God grant you a long life and a happy one with this new found treasure."[16] Mrs. Richard Smith presented the newlyweds with a purple velvet Bible while John Quincy Adams's widow, Louisa, gave them a fan as a wedding gift. Other bridal presents including pearl rings, a silver basket, linens, a pair of knit slippers, and a turquoise broach. Causten's father presented the couple with a new, stylish, mahogany drafting table.[17]

Annie's new husband became her staunchest advocate during her legal troubles with Payne Todd. Causten was not intimidated nor cowed by Payne's brutish tactics and erratic behavior. He was determined that his wife receive the inheritance that was due to her in accordance with the terms of Dolley's final will.

THE COURTS RULED ON Payne Todd's case in February 1851, upholding the legality of Dolley's final July 9th will and forever dashing his hopes for financial salvation. Annie was finally vindicated and Payne chose not to appeal the ruling. The entire lawsuit, though, had been a costly and foolish endeavor. Dr. Causten noted that the resulting attorney fees had totaled in excess of five thousand dollars, complaining bitterly that: "Annie will derive no immediate benefit from the bequest at all. If we add to the costs already known, the fees paid by Mr. Todd and to be repaid by Annie for counsel, the aggregate will be somewhere about five thousand dollars—or 25% of the numerical capital: actually thrown away in consequence of Mr. Todd's unfilial conduct, as neither he nor Annie have had the slightest benefit of it."[18]

What funds that Payne eventually received from the released Congressional appropriation did little to help him retire his seemingly endless debts. In March 1851, he sanctioned a public auction of Madison memorabilia in Washington, D.C. in yet another effort to raise money. Annie and her husband were appalled that Payne would permit, let alone authorize, such a humiliating public spectacle. They were further dismayed to learn that included in the inventory for sale was a cherished portrait of Dolley Madison painted by Gilbert Stuart. The artist had completed the portrait in 1804, and for years it had been a focal point in the drawing room at Montpelier. Dolley would later bring the cherished painting to her home on Lafayette Square for display. The idea that such a priceless heirloom would be callously disposed of at public auction without regard for its historic merit or sentimental value was simply intolerable. Fortunately, Dr. Causten and Annie were able to successfully bid on the Stuart painting to prevent it from disappearing forever into private hands. It would ultimately be donated to the White House where it is today on permanent display.[19] It was now painfully obvious to Annie that she rather than Payne was to be the true custodian of the Madison legacy.

WITH THE LEGAL CASE resolved, Anna and James were able to refocus on their marriage, and in 1851 welcomed the birth of their daughter, Mary. That same year, Payne Todd sustained a serious injury from a fall and sought additional medical treatment in Boston. His overall health had been deteriorating for years and in his weakened condition, he contracted typhoid fever. He managed to return to Washington, D.C. in hopes of a recovery, and rented an apartment on Pennsylvania Avenue just a short distance from the Willard Hotel.

Despite their onerous legal quarrels with Payne, Annie and her husband still visited him regularly during this last illness.[20] They urged Payne to seek religious counsel and he finally consented to meet with the Reverend French. He confided that he was a Quaker, purportedly confessing that: "I have always believed in the Quaker doctrine. I believe the work of reconciliation is between the Creator and created alone."[21] Payne seemed to be at last reflecting upon his

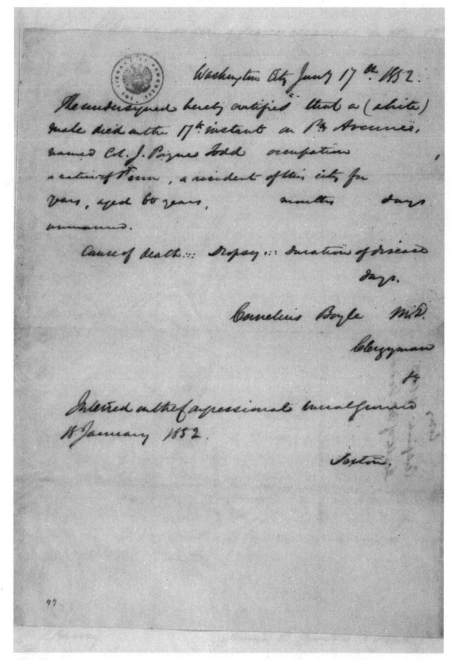

The official death certificate for John Payne Todd signed by Dr. Cornelius Boyle. The listed cause of death was "dropsy." (Library of Congress)

life. "I forgive my enemies if I have any," Payne mumbled. "I have never willfully injured anyone—but myself—I have been my own worst enemy."[22]

John Payne Todd died on Saturday, January 17, 1852 at the age of 59 and "full of grief for a wasted life."[23] Dr. Cornelius Boyle listed the official cause of death as "dropsy," a ghastly condition typified by fluid retention and painful swelling in the legs and limbs which eventually causes cardiac arrest.[24] The disease is often symptomatic of chronic alcoholism and cirrhosis of the liver.

There would be no grand funeral or eloquent eulogies for Payne Todd. Indeed, few noted his passing and his death was acknowledged only days later in a terse statement in the *Daily National Intelligencer*:

> *In this city, on the morning of the 17th instant, John Payne Todd, Esq., in the 61st year (sic) of the age.*"[25]

As one of Payne's closest living relatives, Annie felt obligated to attend her cousin's committal services at Congressional Cemetery the next day. It was a further testament to her innate good nature; she was once again willing to overlook Payne's many trespasses and personal slights. But the weather that Sunday was abominable as James Causten noted: "[it was] a stormy, snowy day, perhaps the very worst day of this hard winter."[26] Consequently, he dissuaded Annie from going, later recalling that: "the weather becoming so dreadful that the idea was abandoned."[27] Dr. Causten personally represented the family at the gravesite but there were no mourners, just a few spectators and isolated curiosity-seekers. Payne's mortal remains were committed to the earth just a few hundred yards south of the Public Vault were Dolley Madison was entombed. Mother and son were reunited in death, at least temporarily.

After Payne's burial, Dr. Causten sardonically noted: "The effects and personal property left by him, which is known, are too trifling to produce enough to pay his funeral expenses."[28]

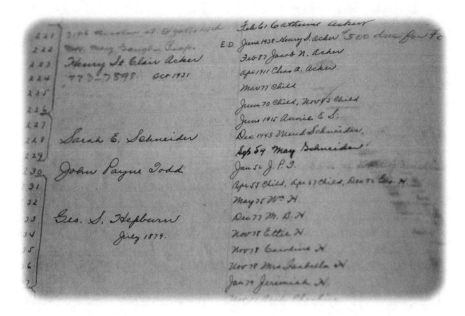

The burial register containing John Payne Todd's name. In pencil is written: "Son of Dolly Madison." Payne Todd was interred at Congressional on a bitterly cold, winter's day, January 18, 1852. Dr. James Cauten was one of the few people who attended the funeral. (Congressional Cemetery)

AT THE TIME OF his death, Payne Todd still owned eleven slaves who were in residence at his Toddsberth home. They were all elderly, ranging in age from 50 through 78, with the average age being 62. In an effort at post-mortem munificence, Payne manumitted his slaves and ordered that each person be given an imbursement of $200. The remainder of his estate was willed to the American Colonization Society.

In reality, the numerous claims that would be made against Payne's estate meant that virtually all of his possessions would have to be sold in order to satisfy creditors. This included ownership of his slaves who were most likely doomed to a lifetime of servitude. In disgust, James Causten dismissed Payne's will as just another fable, claiming: "It proves the cranky character of the man to the last."[29]

Endnotes

Epigraph: Allan Clark (1914). The Life and Letters of Dolly Madison. Washington, DC, W.F. Roberts Company, p. 484.

1 Paul Finkelman (2011). *Millard Fillmore*. New York, Time Books, p. 1.

2 *Ibid.*, p. 65.

3 John C. Calhoun quoted in Finkelman, p. 70.

4 Daniel Webster quoted in Finkelman, p. 69.

5 Zachary Taylor's body was returned to Louisville on October 24, 1850 and was buried in the family plot at his plantation, Springfield. His remains were later removed to a newly constructed mausoleum. Many speculated that Taylor had been poisoned and in 1991, his remains were exhumed and examined. No evidence of any foul play was found and the cause of death was determined to be cholera morbus or acute gastroenteritis. Johnson, Abby Arthur and Ronald Maberry Johnson (2012). *In the Shadow of the United States Capitol: Congressional Cemetery and the Memory of the Nation.* Washington, DC, New Academia Publishing, p. 89.

6 Green, Constance McLaughlin (1962). *Washington: Village and Capital, 1800-1878.* Princeton, Princeton University Press, p. 178-179.

7 John C. Calhoun died on March 31, 1850; Henry Clay died June 29, 1852; Daniel Webster's death was on October 24, 1852.

8 Kenneth M. Stampp (1990). *America in 1857: A Nation on the Brink.* New York, Oxford University Press, p. 11. During his three year absence, Sumner's seat remained conspicuously vacant, a silent testament to the atrocity committed against him.

9 *Ibid.*, p. 17. Although reelected and returned to Congress, Preston Brooks died on January 27, 1857 shortly after returning to Washington from a respiratory ailment. His remains were stored temporarily in the Public Vault at Congressional Cemetery.

10 In the first 48 years of the nation's history under the Constitution (1789 through 1837), there were just seven American presidents—George Washington, John Adams, Thomas Jefferson, James Madison, James Monroe, John Quincy Adams, and Andrew Jackson. All were elected to two terms, with the exception of John Adams and his son, John Quincy.

11 Franklin Pierce quoted in *Inaugural Addresses of the Presidents of the United States from George Washington 1780 to George Bush 1989* (1989). Washington, D.C., Government Printing Office, p. 122.

12 Harriett Beecher Stowe (1852). *Uncle Tom's Cabin, or, Life Among the Lowly.* Boston, John P. Jewett & Company, p. 310.

13 Harriett Taylor Upton quoted in Clark, p. 485.

14 Ethel Stephens Arnett (1972). *Mrs. James Madison: The Incomparable Dolley.* Greensboro, Piedmont Press, 396.

15 *Ibid.*, p. 397.

16 Letter to James H. Causten, 28 February 1850 from the collections of the Greensboro Historical Museum.

17 "List of Bridal Presents," 9 April 1850, from the collections of the Greensboro Historical Museum.

18 James H. Causten letter to John C. Payne quoted in Arnett, p. 398.

19 According to the White House Historical Association, the painting was inherited by Anna's daughter, Mary Causten Kunkel who sold it in 1899. It was on display at the Pennsylvania Academy of Fine Arts until it was loaned to the White House in 1970. It was made a part of the permanent collections in 1994. See the White House Historical Society's website at http://www.whitehousehistory.org/whha_about/whitehouse_collection.

20 Arnett, p. 399.

21 Arnett, p. 400.

22 John Payne Todd quoted in Arnett, p. 400.

23 Lucie Cutts (1887). *Memoirs and Letters of Dolly Madison: Wife of James Madison, President of the United States*. Boston, Houghton, Mifflin and Company, p. 210. As with many things associated with John Payne Todd, there is some confusion concerning his actual death date. Dr. James Causten in a letter to Annie's father, wrote: Mr. Payne Todd finally paid the debt to nature on the 16th of January, and was buried on the 17th." See Arnett, p. 400. The *Daily National Intelligencer* and the actual death certificate list January 17 as Payne's death date. Dr. Boyle also wrote on the death certificate: Interred at the Congressional burial ground, 18 January 1852. The records at Congressional Cemetery confirm the interment taking place on Sunday, January 18. For this book, I have chosen to use January 17 as Payne Todd's death date.

24 "Dropsy" is more commonly known today as edema. John Payne Todd's death certificate is available at the Library of Congress. See http://www.loc.gov.

25 Clark, p. 485.

26 James Causten quoted in Arnett, p. 400.

27 *Ibid.*, p. 400.

28 *Ibid.*, p. 400.

29 *Ibid.*, p. 400.

Epilogue

"No studies seem so well calculated to give a proper expansion to the mind as...history."

James Madison

The drama surrounding Dolley Madison's meager estate and possessions did not end with Payne Todd's death. Within just days of his interment at Congressional Cemetery, Anna Payne Causten asserted her legal claims to whatever family items and heirlooms that were in Todd's possession at the time of his death. Her husband addressed a formal letter "To the trustees of the Dolley Madison estate" claiming that everything in question now "becomes the property of my wife, Annie Payne Causten, late Annie Payne."[1]

There was, in truth, very little left of any real monetary value but still Payne's last landlord confiscated all of his household goods and property in a concerted effort to collect on delinquent rent,. These items were quickly disposed of in an unseemly liquidation sale where Annie's husband was able to buy back some of Dolley's clothing and personal articles that held sentimental value. The entire episode was yet another humiliating spectacle and in utter disgust, Causten wrote to Dolley's surviving brother, John Coles Payne: "Twas the last shame Payne Todd could extend to her even by accident."[2]

Shortly before her death, Dolley Madison had carefully instructed Annie to collect all of her surviving personal correspondence and then to determine "what she thought essential for her own use... the rest," she ordered, "should be destroyed."[3] Despite the irreparable loss to the historical record, the practice of purging and destroying private correspondence was quite common during the antebellum period. Yet this intentional destruction of certain, select documents was miniscule when compared to the losses incurred by Payne's reckless storage and handling of much of the remaining Madison family papers. On a trip to Montpelier in 1851, Causten first stopped by Toddsberth. There he was horrified to discover that dozens of significant letters and documents were scattered about the property. He wrote: "The whole lawn was strewn with papers which of course I examined." Most of the materials represented personal correspondence from the time of Payne's incarceration for debt in Philadelphia. "I gathered them all up," Causten explained to his wife, "and put them in the carriage, that is all of Yr Aunts letters that were legible."[4]

To satisfy Payne's ever-present creditors, his Orange County estate had to be audited in order to assess its proper value, while an inventory had to be compiled of all of the household goods, farm implements, and livestock. A report entitled: "An inventory and appraisement of the goods & chattels taken at Todds Berth on the 28th of September 1852 belonging to the late John P. Todd"[5] was issued and it catalogued a wide variety of items, including: "[a] Walnut Table with a drawer, 3 Curtain Rods, Box Containing a shocking machine with tubes, Copper heater, Lead pot, Picture Frame." There were also "4 busts, 2 candle sticks, 1 Gilt frame, Todd's likeness, Medicine Box, Looking glass," as well as a model of the "Frigate Constitution in Glass base." From the Rotunda (Round House) were "1 Portable Desk large, French Bedstead, Shelves, Ladder." The livestock included "1 Black cow, 1 Red cow" and there was still an unsold "Crop of corn."[6] Numerous tools came from the blacksmith shop as well as various pots, pans, and utensils from the kitchen and meal house and farm implements such as plows, hoes, picks,

Am't Brought forward

	2 Candle Sticks	.25
	Sand Box Map Picture frame	.12
	1 Gilt Frame	.25
	Todds likeness	.03
	Pr Brass Andirons & Fender	3.00
	Hand Bellows	.01
	Buggy Box	.06
	Medicine Box	.06
	Looking Glass	2.00
	Frigate Constitution in Glass Box	2.00
	2 Busts covered with Glass	2.00
	Mantle Looking Glass gilt frame	2.00
	Brass Andirons Fender & Shovel	3.00
	7 Dishes	3.50
	Tureen	1.00
	2 Sauce Bowls	.25
	Decanter Stand & Tumblers	1.50
	2 Sets of Castors 14 plates & Sand	1.00
	Waiter 2 Saucers 2 Cups	.06
	1/2 Dozen Dutch Silver forks	.25
	1 Dozen Common Spoons	.50
	1 Silver Ladle	3.00
	Snuffers, Waiter, Brush, Paper Holder	.25
	Egg Stand, Coffee Pot, Bottle Stand, Tea Pot,	.50
	Spy Glass Rangeone	5.00
	Water Stand	.50
	2 Busts	2.00
	Walnut Press	1.50
	Round Table (Mahogany)	1.00
	Pine Table	.50
	2 Knife Boxes	2.00
	Walnut Candle Stand	.25

carried forward

"An inventory and appraisement of the goods & chattels taken at Todds Berth on the 28th of September 1852." All of Payne Todd's possessions and property were carefully audited after his death. The Toddsberth estate was sold in 1853. (Library of Congress)

and wagons. These items represented the total sum of Payne Todd's assets.

Later that fall, another public auction was held and Todd's possessions were sold off to the highest bidder as were various papers, books, artwork, paintings, and Madison-era memorabilia. The Toddsberth property itself was disposed of the following year.[7]

Broadside advertising the sale of books from James Madison's private library. Much of the Madison family papers, artworks, and hierlooms had to be sold after John Payne Todd's death to satisfy creditors. (Library of Congress)

FOR SOME INEXPLICABLE REASON, Payne Todd had never made any effort to have his mother's body returned to Montpelier for proper burial despite her explicit wishes to be laid to rest next to her beloved husband. Moreover, for over twenty-five years, Payne had neglected to purchase an appropriate tombstone for James Madison's grave which remained unmarked in the family cemetery. One newspaper article noted that President Madison's grave was "undistinguished by monument of any kind. Only tradition pointed out the mound of earth which marked the last resting place of the great statesman."[8] John Coles Payne, concluded that Payne's thoughtlessness had proved once again that: "[Dolley] had been deceived by her son."[9]

Twenty months after her death, Dolley Madison's body remained at Congressional Cemetery unceremoniously stored in the communal Public Vault. This utilitarian mausoleum was intended for short-term use to allow bereaved family members adequate time to make more suitable funeral arrangements. But Dolley's situation remained indefinite and this was humiliating and intolerable to her niece, Annie. Her husband concluded bluntly that: "nothing that Payne Todd ever had anything to do with seems to be improved by his meddling."[10] On February 10, 1852, acting on his own initiative, Dr. James Causten arranged to have Dolley's remains removed from the Public Vault and transferred the short distance to his family's private mausoleum at Congressional.[11] He wrote: "I have removed Mrs. Madison's remains from the Public Vault to my father's Private Vault, until I can determine what else is to be done."[12]

Tragically, just seven months later, the ever loyal Annie died prematurely. She was survived by her husband and a fifteen month old daughter.[13] Causten's sister, Henrietta, tried to console her grieving brother: "Your telegraphic dispatch informing us of our dear Annie's departure is just received—words are inadequate my dear brother to express the deep sympathy I feel for you...May the good God who tempers the wind to the shorn lamb give you strength and fortitude to bear this affliction."[14] Causten somberly reported back that: "my first melancholy duty was to attend to the deposit of her remains in my family vault by the side of her aunt, Mrs. D. P. Madison."[15]

The Causten Vault a Congressional Cemetery. Dolley Madison's remains were interred here for six years. Both Anna (1852) and James Causten (1856) would be buried here as well. (Philip Bigler)

Dolley Madison's body remained in the Causten mausoleum for another six years, until finally arrangements were made to return her body to Montpelier on January 12, 1858 for proper burial. By now, several concerned local citizens had raised sufficient funds and erected a proper, 22-foot granite obelisk over her husband's grave.

MADISON'S ORANGE COUNTY, WITH its centralized location and critical rail junction, became the center stage for much of the American Civil War. The region was a strategic crossroads for both the Union and Confederate armies, with the major battles of Chancellorsville, the Wilderness, and Spotsylvania Court House were all fought in the immediate vicinity. During the winter months of 1863-1864, troops from Confederate General James Longstreet's First Corps and A.P. Hill's Third Corps bivouacked in the area. In close proximity, just across the Rapidan River, was the entire Army of the Potomac, still flush from its gallant victory at Gettysburg the previous July.

In the previous campaign, Lee's Army of Northern Virginia had suffered thousands of irreplaceable casualties and the army had been reduced in strength to around 63,000 troops. These remaining men, although unbroken, were ill-equipped, hungry, and mostly barefoot. William Mahone, a Confederate officer and graduate of the Virginia

Military Institute, commandeered the Zion Church and converted it into a makeshift factory to produce much needed shoes for the troops.[16] The church had been established in 1813 near Madison Run, but was relocated in 1858 to its new site directly opposite the deteriorating ruins of Payne's old Toddsberth plantation.[17]

As one of the nation's Founding Fathers, James Madison was revered by both sides during the war. The Federals claimed to be fighting to preserve the union which Madison helped forge in Philadelphia in 1787, while the Confederates asserted that they were the champions of state's rights and the true principles of federalism. Montpelier was, thus, a sacrosanct place that was spared destruction. Indeed, many soldiers visited the site during lulls in the fighting although by this time, the mansion had been neglected and was rundown. The Madison family graveyard was a particular place of pilgrimage and there, the graves of James and Dolley Madison were now well-preserved and marked by separate, white obelisks.[18]

Few soldiers, though, had any interest in the history of nearby Toddsberth. An exception was Lt. John Hampden Chamberlayne, a Confederate artillery officer who served with the Army of Northern Virginia and was encamped nearby in August 1862.[19] He wrote: "Our camp here is a pleasant place, where Payne Todd lived...he spent all the property Mr. Madison owned & most that Mrs. Madison got from the Government. The marks of the poor spend thrift are still to be seen, walks that he began, never to finish, an attempted ice house turned into a stately pleasure dome, like Kubla Kahn's' quarries opened for marble which was not there."[20] He continued "wise heads of the neighborhoods still shake sadly smile & shake over his mad pranks...time crumbles away his house of feasting, nature with green leafy hand sweeps gently over his walks, screens beautifully his quarries, and the very memory of the prodigal perishes..."[21]

After the war was over, *The Native Virginian* newspaper described Toddsberth simply as "a dilapidated hamlet near Madison Run."[22] Over the ensuing years, fire, scavengers, and time would destroy much of what remained of John Payne Todd's eccentric compound. The Round House or Rotunda, which had once been the prominent feature on the property, did survive in ruin into the twentieth century but by the time of the Great Depression, the structure's walls and roof had collapsed so that only the stone foundation and brick cellar remained.[23] Mary Agnes Gipson Harlow who lived on an adjacent farm as a little girl, remembers that the neighborhood children enjoyed playing in the debris.[24] To their further delight, Randolph Scott, the famed Hollywood movie star and husband of heiress Mary duPont, would frequently ride by on his horse.[25]

The Toddsberth property was far too rocky and hilly to farm efficiently. Subsequent owners constructed a new, utilitarian house on

The Round House or Rotunda at Toddsberth in ruins circa 1920. This structure was the only building to survive into the twentieth century and its foundation became a playground for area children. (Bernadette Fitzgerald)

The Toddsberth property as it appears today. All of Payne Todd's original buildings and structures have long since disappeared, although there are many steep ravines created from mining the old marble quarry. (Philip Bigler)

the land and converted the surrounding acreage into an operating turkey farm. Electricity was unavailable to the residents of Madison Run until near the end of World War II when the Rural Electrification Administration finally wired the area.[26] Todd's nearby marble quarry remained abandoned and had left a gaping hole in the earth which gradually filled with rain and spring water. At a depth of over 100 feet, it became a popular summer swimming spot for area teenagers, but after several drownings, the site was fenced off and closed to all public access.[27] This, however, did not prevent an enterprising bootlegger from covertly operating an illegal whiskey still on the property for years.[28]

The old Toddsberth property was purchased at a foreclosure sale in 1987 by William G. Crum. Over the years, the property had been reduced in size to a 15.5 acre tract which Mr. Crum later subdivided into three sections for family members. Today, the property remains under private ownership and there are no visible signs of any of the original buildings. Moreover, there are no roadside markers or monuments to acknowledge Payne Todd's old homestead. Each day, thousands of motorists speed by on Route 15 completely unaware of its existence or history.

MONTPELIER WAS SOLD SEVERAL times after the Civil War. Each new owner freely modified and modernized the mansion so with each subsequent renovation, the original Madison home quickly disappeared. In 1901, the house along with over 5,000 acres was purchased by the rich chemical tycoon, William duPont of Delaware. He converted and enlarged the manor house into a massive, Georgian-style mansion with 55 rooms.[29] Other than a single portrait of James Madison painted by William Dunlap which hung in the main hall, there was little to identify the property with the James and Dolley Madison. DuPont's daughter, Marion, candidly acknowledged that: "The Madisons probably would recognize the Montpelier gardens today but I don't know if they'd know the house."[30]

The brick exterior of the main house had been covered with stucco and was painted a garish pink while a special train depot opened in 1910 to accommodate the considerable needs of the wealthy duPont family. During this era, over 100 outbuildings, paddocks, and stables were erected throughout the property, including several distinctive Sears and Roebuck catalog barns. There was an outdoor swimming pool, as well as a long, narrow rectangular building which housed the family's private one lane bowling alley. Nearby, was a brick carriage house which contained an octagon cockfighting pit.[31]

Marion duPont (Scott) inherited the property after her father's death in 1927.[32] An avid horsewoman, the old tobacco fields were replaced by horse tracks and thoroughbred exercising facilities. Mrs. Scott regularly sponsored horse races on the property including the prestigious Montpelier Steeple Chase Races which continue to this day.[33] Her favorite racehorses—Battleship, Annapolis, and Accra— were buried in a prominent location on the property immediately adjacent to the mansion.[34] Marion duPont Scott also enjoyed hosting

Montpelier during the duPont era. The mansion was modified and modernized by each of its subsequent owners. At the time of Marion duPont Scott's death in 1983, the house consisted of fifty-five rooms and all traces of the Madison-era home had disappeared. (Library of Congress)

The Red Room at Montpelier. This room was a favorite of Mrs. Scott and featured dozens of trophies and photographs of her prized race horses. The floors were covered with linoleum while a large compass weather vane on the ceiling indicated the direction of the wind for fox hunts. (Library of Congress)

regular fox hunts and she proudly raised purebred border terriers for such occasions.[35]

Mrs. Scott would be the last private owner of Montpelier. After her death in 1983, she bequeathed the estate to the National Trust for Historic Preservation. She indicated in her will her preference that the property be restored to honor James and Dolley Madison in "such manner as to conform as nearly as possible with the architectural pattern which existed when said property was owned and occupied by President Madison."[36]

Although much historical research was conducted on the site to determine the architectural integrity of the house, it was not until 2001 that a grant from the Save America's Treasures program funded the first serious effort to restore the home to its antebellum appearance. Augmented by additional funding from the National Trust and the Mellon Foundation, extensive preservation efforts discovered that much of the original woodwork, fireplace mantles, doors, and windows had been recycled by the duPonts during their earlier expansions, and that these Madison-era artifacts could, indeed, be restored to their original locations. One of the more interesting archaeological finds was the discovery of a small mouse nest inside one of the mansion's interior walls. When removed and analyzed, it was discovered that the mouse had nibbled off some of the Madison's' original wallpaper and in so doing, had preserved it for posterity. Also discovered in this valuable mouse nest were a scrap from a Fredericksburg newspaper and a fragment of a letter written in Madison's own hand.

To return Montpelier to Madison's original design, though, required the destruction of all of the duPont's modern additions. According to the History Channel: "Restorers then tore down two wings, dismantled 14 bathrooms, rebuilt two staircases, and overall reduced the size of the mansion by more than half."[37] The entire process took seven years to complete and the restored and resurrected Montpelier was finally unveiled to the public on Constitution Day 2008.

FOR TODAY'S TIME-CHALLENGED visitors to Virginia, it is necessary to become somewhat of a historical voyeur when visiting the state. Most tourists actually begin their journey in the nation's capital, where they hurriedly visit the various government buildings, monuments, museums, and memorials before making a requisite sightseeing stop at George Washington's Mount Vernon home on the Potomac River. Then, it is just a short three hour drive down Interstates 95 and 64 to the old colonial capital of Williamsburg, where visitors can experience a virtual historical Disneyland. On Duke of Gloucester Street (aka DOG Street), families interact with costumed interpreters and reenactors while engaging in the great debates of the revolutionary era without any fear of repercussions or consequences. In the evening, there is usually time to relax at one of the historic district's many restored taverns, where diners can, in air-conditioned comfort, sip on colonial punch while listening to roving troubadours singing bawdy ballads. It is a highly idealized and sanitized version of the past—there are no unpleasant odors from barnyard animals or from poor sanitation; no fear of disease or premature death. Moreover, no one has to confront the human degradation of slavery or think too deeply.

After spending time immersed in an imaginary world of history, families can, for a price, enjoy some more electrifying entertainment at one of Tidewater Virginia's various amusement and theme parks. Close by is the Great Wolf Lodge, which features indoor swimming pools along with such attractions as the Raccoon Lagoon and the Howlin' Tornado waterslide. There is also Busch Gardens to visit where the children can experience an array of ethnic Potemkin villages (Germany, France, Ireland, Scotland, England, Italy, et al.) before riding Apollo's Chariot and the Lock Ness Monster roller coasters. With such entertainment options, it is easy to become unmindful of Virginia's rich historical past. Too few will venture on to the nearby National Historical Parks at Jamestown and Yorktown, where American history began and the Revolution was won.

There are, however, those determined tourists who will make the effort to drive three hours west to Charlottesville and the Virginia Piedmont. There, these exhausted sightseers will brave massive crowds and hours-long summer waits for a brief, forty minute tour of Thomas Jefferson's Monticello. Unfortunately, most are then unwilling to continue and make the short detour to Montpelier to see James Madison's home despite its recent magnificent restoration. It seems that a scholar-president whose voluminous writings are often nuanced and erudite has little appeal to America's increasingly distracted, self-absorbed society.

Yet James Madison's family story deserves to be studied and remembered. Indeed, Madison keenly understood that despite the many advancements of civilization, human behavior remains essentially unchanged. The tragic story of John Payne Todd, James and Dolley Madison's troublesome son, could easily have been a topic of a Greek epic written by Euripides, Aeschylus, or Sophocles. It is the all too common tale of a promising life destroyed by excess, avarice, and narcissism—a powerful parable about the dark side of the American Dream, from rags-to-riches-to-rags in three generations.

Endnotes

Epigraph: James Madison letter to Reynolds Chapman, 25 January 1821, quoted in David Mattern, Ed. (1997). *James Madison's "Advice to My Country."* Charlottesville, University Press of Virginia.

1 James Causten, Letter to Trustees dated January 1852, from the collections of the Greensboro Historical Museum.

2 James Causten letter to John Coles Payne quoted in Ethel Stephens Arnett (1972). *Mrs. James Madison: The Incomparable Dolley.* Greensboro, Piedmont Press, p. 403.

3 Dolley Payne Madison quoted in Catherine Allgor (2006). *A Perfect Union: Dolley Madison and the Creation of the American Nation.* New York, Henry Holt and Company, p. 402.

4 James Causten letter to Annie Payne Causten quoted in Arnett, p. 404.

5 "An inventory and appraisement of the goods & chattels taken at Todds Berth on the 28th of September 1852 belonging to the late John P. Todd" available at http://www.loc.gov.

6 *Ibid.*

7 Arnett, p. 404.

8 *Frank Leslie's Illustrated*, 30 January 1858 quoted in Philip Bigler and Annie Lorsbach (2008), Liberty & Learning: The Essential James Madison, Harrisonburg, VA., The James Madison Center, p. 140.

9 John Coles Payne quoted in Arnett, p. 402.

10 James Causten quoted in Arnett, p. 401.

11 A few months later, another First Lady, Louisa Adams, was also interred in the Causten Vault. Her remains were returned to Quincy, Massachusetts just a few months later for burial alongside her husband, the late John Quincy Adams.

12 Causten quoted in Arnett, p. 401.

13 Mary Carvello Causten was born on August 8, 1851.

14 Henrietta Causten Shriver letter to James Causten, 10 November 1852, from the collections of the Greensboro Historical Museum.

15 James Causten quoted in Arnett, 406.

16 The Zion Baptist Church is located at 15316 Old Gordonsville Road in Orange.

17 Walker, Frank S., Jr. (2004). *Remembering: A History of Orange County, Virginia.* Orange, Orange County Historical Society, pp. 206-207.

18 Matthew G. Hyland (2007). *Montpelier and the Madisons: House, Home and American Heritage.* Charleston, SC, History Press, p. 102.

19 Lt. John Hampden Chamberlayne was serving with Purcell's Battery of Artillery in August 1862 under the command of Major General A.P. Hill as part of Stonewall Jackson's Second Corps. Chamberlayne would see action at Second Manassas and take part in the Antietam campaign. He was captured on June 28, 1863 at Chambersburg, Pennsylvania just three days before the battle of Gettysburg. Chamberlayne would be confined to a Union prisoner of war camp until he was paroled in March 1864. He returned to the army and fought at the Wilderness, Spotsylvania Court House, Cold Harbor, and Petersburg.

20 J.H. Chamberlayne letter to Lucy Park Chamberlayne, 15 August 1862, quoted in Chamberlayne, C.G. ed. (1992). *Ham Chamberlayne—Virginian: Letters and Papers of an Artillery Officer in the War for Southern Independence 1861-1865*. Wilmington, NC, Broadfoot Publishing Company.

21 *Ibid.*, p. 93.

22 *The Native Virginian*, April 17, 1868, p. 1.

23 Only one photograph of the Round House is known to exist. It is of poor quality and available only on microfilm. See: "Story of 'Todd's Berth' Recalled by Old Photo," *The Free Lance-Star*, 28 January 1837, p. 6.

24 Mary Agnes Gipson Harlow, interview by Philip Bigler, December 22, 2014, Orange, Virginia.

25 Randolph Scott (January 23, 1898 – March 2, 1987) and Mary DuPont were married for only three years (1936 – 1939). Scott was primarily known for his starring roles in westerns.

26 Harlow interview.

27 *Ibid.*

28 *Ibid.*

29 Green, Bryan Clark, Ann L. Miller, and Conover Hunt (2007). *Building a President's House: The Construction of Montpelier*. Orange, Virginia, The Montpelier Foundation, p. 31.

30 Marion duPont quoted in Gerald Strine, ed. (1976). *Montpelier: The Recollections of Marion du-Pont Scott*. New York, Charles Scribner's Sons, p. 34.

31 Strine, p. 67.

32 Marion duPont Scott (May 3, 1894-September 4, 1983).

33 See: http://www.montpelierraces.org/about/history-of-montpelier-races/.

34 Battleship (1927-1958), Annapolis (1926-1957), and Accra (1941-1966). Battleship was sired by the famed racehorse, Man o' War.

35 Strine, p. 57.

36 Hillary Back, *The Restoration of Montpelier*, Harrisonburg, VA., James Madison University, p. 4.

37 Brad Spychalski, "James Madison's Montpelier Restored," *The History Channel Magazine* (2009), p. 36.

Appendix A

Congressional Cemetery

Established in 1807, Congressional Cemetery is the final resting place for over 55,000 people, including many prominent Washingtonians and notable political figures. Located on 35 acres in the southeastern quadrant of the District of Columbia, the cemetery is renowned for its distinguished funeral architecture and sculptures which include numerous elaborate monuments depicting grieving angels, amoretti, and cherubs as well as obelisks and other symbols of mourning. The most recent public memorial to be erected at Congressional is a massive native-American totem which honors those killed during the September 11, 2001 terrorist attack on the Pentagon.

The Lummi tribe totem honoring those killed at the Pentagon on 9-11. Created, designed, and carved by Jewell Praying Wolf James, the healing pole is 34-feet across and is located in the southwest portion of Congressional Cemetery. (Library of Congress)

The Latrobe Cenotaphs

One of the most recognizable features at Congressional Cemetery are the rows of the 171 identical Aquia sandstone cubical markers. Designed by the architect of the United States Capitol, Benjamin Latrobe, these monuments were initially erected to honor a member of Congress who died while in office. Intended to serve as headstones, each marker cost the federal government an average of $115 but critics quickly lampooned and denounced the memorials as drab and ugly. Today, the vast majority of the Latrobe cubes are actually cenotaphs with the physical remains of the honored Congressmen buried elsewhere. The practice of erecting such monuments mercifully ceased in 1877, but the custom was resurrected one last time in 1971 to jointly honor Louisiana Congressman Hale Boggs and Alaska Congressman Nicholas Begich. The two had been killed in a plane crash while campaigning in Alaska and their remains were never recovered.

The Latrobe Cenotaphs. Widely disparaged for their insipid design, there are 171 such monuments at Congressional Cemetery. Only 59 Congressmen, however, are actually buried under the markers. (Library of Congress)

The Public Vault

In order to accommodate the increased need for temporary storage of remains, Congressional Cemetery constructed the Public Vault in 1835 at a cost of $5,000. According to a report from Senate Committee on the District of Columbia: "[The Public Vault] use for receiving the remains of members of Congress was of course declared to be free, a charge of $5 being made to others desiring to place bodies therein." Over 4,000 people would be held in the Public Vault including Vice President John C. Calhoun, three American Presidents, and First Lady Dolley Madison. The above ground mausoleum became obsolete during the Great Depression. Unused and abandoned, it fell into serious disrepair. According to a 2003 report Association

The restored Public Vault at Congressional Cemetery. The mausoleum was used as a place of temporary interment while family members made formal burial arrangements. (Philip Bigler)

for the Preservation of Historic Congressional Cemetery: "Our venerable old Public Vault is in sad shape, its doors hanging on by a thinning strip of a wrought iron hinge...the Public Vault is now just a shadow of its former grandeur." (Johnson, 347). The structure was restored as a historic artifact two years later.

Notables held in the Public Vault:

William Henry Harrison
April 7, 1841 – June 26, 1841

———

John Quincy Adams
February 26, 1848 – March 6, 1848

———

Zachary Taylor
July 13, 1850 – October 25, 1850

———

Dolley Madison
July 16, 1849 – February 10, 1852
Remains transferred to the Causten Vault
Feb. 10, 1852 – January 12, 1858

———

The official interment record for Dolley Madison. It reads: "July 16 - 1849 Mrs. Dolly (sic) Madison Est. to opening and Use of Public Vault for Mrs. Madison $5.00." (Congressional Cemetery)

Famous Interments at Congressional Cemetery

Arsenal Monument: *21 Women killed in the 1864 explosion at the Washington Arsenal* R97/S142

Mathew Brady: *Civil War Photographer* R72/S120

Elbridge Gerry: *Vice President, Signer of the Declaration of Independence* R29/S9

David Herold: *Lincoln Conspirator* R46/S44 (Family grave, his individual grave is unmarked)

J. Edgar Hoover: *FBI Director* R20/S125

Gen. Alexander Macomb: *War of 1812 hero* R55/147

Robert Mills: *Designer of the Washington Monument* R35/111

John Philip Sousa: *Marine Band Director* R77/S163

Tazah: *Apache Chief* R2/S125

William Thorton: *Architect/Designer of the US Capitol* R33/S39

John Payne Todd: *Dolley Madison's son* R41/S230

William Wood: *First Director of the Secret Service* R65/248

The Arsenal Monument at Congressional Cemetery. It marks the grave of 21 women killed while assembling cartridges for the Union Army. (Library of Congress)

Appendix B
Census Data 1790-1850

US Population 1790

> **Total: 3,893,635**
> Slaves: 694,280

Number of States: 13

Largest Cities	*Largest States*
Philadelphia: 28,522	Virginia: 747,610
New York: 49,401	Pennsylvania: 434,373
Boston: 18,320	North Carolina: 393,751
Charleston: 16,359	Massachusetts: 378,787
Baltimore: 13,503	New York: 340,120
	Maryland: 319,728

Mean Center of the United States
Kent County, Maryland

US Population 1800

Total: 5,308,483
Slaves: 893,605

Number of States: 16

Largest Cities	*Largest States*
New York: 60,515	Virginia: 807,557
Philadelphia: 41,220	Pennsylvania: 602,365
Baltimore: 26,514	North Carolina: 478,103
Boston: 24,937	New York: 589,051
Charleston: 18,824	Massachusetts: 422,845
	South Carolina: 345,591

Mean Center of the United States
Howard County, Maryland

Percentage Population Increase
35.1%

States Admitted to the Union
Vermont (1791)
Kentucky (1792)
Tennessee (1796)

US Population 1810

> **Total: 7,239,881**
> Slaves: 1,130,781

Number of States: 17

Largest Cities	*Largest States*
New York: 96,373	New York: 959,049
Philadelphia: 53,722	Virginia: 877,683
Baltimore: 46,555	Pennsylvania: 810,091
Boston: 33,787	North Carolina: 555,500
Charleston: 24,711	Massachusetts: 472,040
	South Carolina: 415,115

Mean Center of the United States
Loudoun County, Virginia

Percentage Population Increase
36.4%

States Admitted to the Union
Ohio (1803)

US Population 1820

> **Total: 9,638,453**
> Slaves: 1,538,038

Number of States: 23

Largest Cities	*Largest States*
New York: 123,706	New York: 1,372,812
Philadelphia: 63,802	Pennsylvania: 1,049,458
Baltimore: 62,738	Virginia: 938,261
Boston: 43,296	North Carolina: 638,829
New Orleans: 27,176	Ohio: 581,434
	Kentucky: 564,317

Mean Center of the United States
Hardy County, (West) Virginia

Percentage Population Increase
33.1%

States Admitted to the Union
Louisiana (1812)
Indiana (1816)
Mississippi (1817)
Illinois (1818)
Alabama (1819)
Maine (1820)

US Population 1830

Total: 12,866,020
Slaves: 2,009,050

Number of States: 24

Largest Cities	*Largest States*
New York: 202,589	New York: 1,918,608
Baltimore: 80,620	Pennsylvania: 1,348,233
Philadelphia: 80,462	Virginia: 1,044,054
Boston: 61,392	Ohio: 937,903
New Orleans: 46,082	North Carolina: 737,987
	Kentucky: 687,917

Mean Center of the United States
Grand County, (West) Virginia

Percentage Population Increase
36.4%

States Admitted to the Union
Missouri (1821)

US Population 1840

Total: 17,069,453
Slaves: 2,487,455

Number of States: 26

Largest Cities	*Largest States*
New York: 312,710	New York: 2,428,921
Baltimore: 102,313	Pennsylvania: 1,724,033
New Orleans: 102,193	Ohio: 1,519,467
Philadelphia: 93,665	Virginia: 1,025,227
Boston: 93,383	Tennessee: 829,210
Cincinnati: 46,338	Kentucky: 779,828

Mean Center of the United States
Upshur County (West) Virginia

Percentage Population Increase
32.7%

States Admitted to the Union
Arkansas (1836)
Michigan (1837)

US Population 1850

> **Total: 23,191,876**
> Slaves: 3,204,313

Number of States: 31

Largest Cities	Largest States
New York: 515,547	New York: 3,097,394
Baltimore: 169,054	Pennsylvania: 2,311,786
Boston: 136,181	Ohio: 1,980,329
Philadelphia: 121,376	Virginia: 1,119,348
New Orleans: 116,375	Tennessee: 1,002,717
Cincinnati: 115,435	Massachusetts: 994,514
	Indiana: 988,416

Mean Center of the United States
Wirt County (West) Virginia

Percentage Population Increase
35.9%

States Admitted to the Union
Florida (1845)
Texas (1845)
Iowa (1846)
Wisconsin (1848)
California (1850)

Facts and Figures

- In 1790, the mean population center of the United States was located in Kent County, Maryland, some 23 miles east of Baltimore on the western shore of the Chesapeake Bay.
- Baltimore, Maryland was one of the most important ports in the nation throughout the antebellum period.
- Virginia had the largest population in the union until Thomas Jefferson's second term as president.
- Four of the first five presidents were from Virginia, leading many to fear the establishment of a "Virginia dynasty."
- Until 1850, in order to maintain the political balance in the Senate, for every free state admitted, a slave state was also admitted to the union. This ended with the admission of California in 1850.
- The cultivation of tobacco destroyed the fertile lands of Virginia and other tidewater regions so that the population of the south shifted towards the cotton producing regions.
- In Orange County, Virginia, the home of James Madison, the slave population represented almost 50% of the inhabitants. In 1790, there were 4,421 slaves living in Orange compared to a freed population of 4,500.
- Virginia's slave population almost doubled from 1790 through 1860 from 292,627 to 490,864, while South Carolina's slave population quadrupled from 107,094 to 402,406.
- In 1850, Virginia, despite the collapse of the tobacco economy, still had the largest slave population in the south--472,528 followed by South Carolina (384,984), Georgia (381,862), Alabama (342,844), and Mississippi (309,878).
- In 1790, there were still 21,193 slaves in New York state.

- In 1860, Mississippi had the largest number of slaves as percentage of the overall population (55%); it also had the largest number of percentage of slave owning families (49%). Slaves constituted 31% of the population in Virginia.
- The life expectancy for a typical woman in the 1790s was just 41 years of age due primarily to the dangers associated with child birth; for men, life expectancy was 44. Infant mortality was common, with most American families experiencing the loss of at least one child.

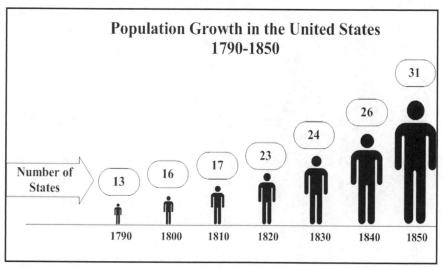

**Population Growth in the United States
1790-1850**

Number of States

| 13 | 16 | 17 | 23 | 24 | 26 | 31 |

| 1790 | 1800 | 1810 | 1820 | 1830 | 1840 | 1850 |

The Louisiana Purchase doubled the size of the United States and made the expansion of slavery a central issue in American politics until the Civil War. For every free state admitted to the Union, a slave state was also added, which balanced the Senate equally between slave and free states. The Compromise of 1850 ended this delicate balance with the admission of California as a free state. (Philip Bigler)

Philip Bigler

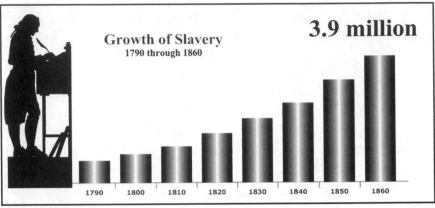

(Philip Bigler)

(Library of Congress)

Slavery in the United States
1790 - 1860

		President
1790:	694,280	Washington
1800:	893,605	Adams
1810:	1,131,781	Madison
1820:	1,538,038	Monroe
1830:	2,009,050	Jackson
1840:	2,487,455	Van Buren
1850:	3,204,313	Taylor/Fillmore
1860:	3,953,761	Buchanan

Appendix C

Payne Family Tree

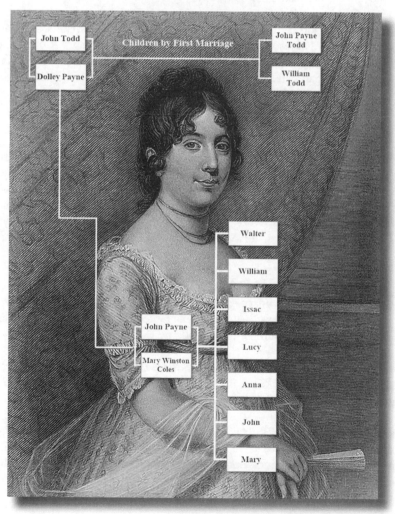

John Todd

Dolley Payne

Children by First Marriage

John Payne Todd

William Todd

John Payne

Mary Winston Coles

Walter

William

Issac

Lucy

Anna

John

Mary

Key Relationships

Anna Payne Cutts (*Dolley Madison's younger sister*): Anna lived with Dolley during her first marriage to John Todd. She also lived with her after Dolley's marriage to James Madison. Their close relationship was more that of a mother-daughter than that of siblings. Anna married Richard Cutts in 1804.

- **Mary Estelle Elizabeth Cutts** (*Anna's daughter/Dolley's niece*): Born on September 16, 1814, Mary Cutts becomes one of Dolley Madison's earliest biographers. Her memoir represents one of the most important contemporary accounts of her aunt's life.

- **James Madison Cutts** (*Dolley Madison's nephew*): J. Madison Cutts was the eldest son of Dolley's sister, Anna Payne, and her husband, Richard Cutts. J. Madison Cutts studied law under William Wirt and later worked in the Treasury Department. He assisted Dolley in the preparation of her final will on July 9, 1849 and would also help his cousin, Annie Payne Causten, settle Dolley's estate.

John Coles Payne (*Dolley Madison's younger brother*): John suffered from alcoholism and periodic bouts of mental illness. In 1806, Madison sent him to Tripoli as part of an American diplomatic mission in an effort to help his sobriety. Payne eventually settled in Orange near Montpelier and often assisted James Madison in organizing and transcribing his voluminous papers. Near his death, Madison entrusted Payne with evidence of Payne Todd's extravagances, but this information was never shared with his sister. After Madison's death, John Coles Payne moved west, relapsed into alcoholism, and died.

- **Annie Payne Causten** (*John Coles Payne's daughter/Dolley's niece*): Annie served as Dolley's primary caretaker during the last years of her aunt's life. She married Dr. James Causten and was forced to battle Payne Todd over the small inheritance left to her in gratitude by Dolley.

Isaac Payne (*Dolley Madison's older brother*): He was an alcoholic and reprobate. Isaac was shot and killed in Norfolk, Virginia in early 1795 after he "offended a man...who sometime afterward shot him with a pistol."

William Temple Payne (*Dolley Madison's older brother*): Temple joined the infant United States Navy as an ensign, for which he was expelled by his Philadelphia Quaker congregation for violation of its pacifist beliefs. He died from illness in early 1795 while living with his brother, Isaac.

Pheobe Morris (*Daughter of Anthony Morris*): Anthony Morris was one of Dolley's closest friends from her early days in Philadelphia and from her relationship with her first husband, John Todd. His daughter, Pheobe, became a surrogate daughter to Dolley and resided with the Madison's in the White House during the winter of 1812. She was an attactive young woman who Dolley hoped would someday marry her son, Payne, and bring some stability and order to his life. Although Payne did seemingly court Pheobe, the relationship never developed romantically and she died unmarried in 1825. She was buried on the family estate, the ancestral home of the Pemberton family, Bolton, in Pennsylvania.

Sally Catlett Madison Macon (*Dolley's sister-in-law*): Sally was James Madison's younger sister. Born in 1764, she was 13 years his junior. She married Thomas Macon at Montpelier in 1790. She died on October 17, 1843 and was buried in the Madison family cemetery.

- **Lucy Hartwell Macon** (*James Madison's niece*): Lucy was born in 1794, the third of nine children. She married Reuben Conway on July 25, 1811. Conway suffered from alcoholism and was the topic of a plaintive letter written to Dolley Madison in 1812.

Elizabeth "Betsy" Patterson Bonaparte (*Family friend*): Betsy Patterson married Napoleon's youngest brother, Jerome, in 1803. The couple had one child, Jerome Napoleon Bonaparte. Napoleon refused to acknowledge the marriage, and Jerome and Betsy were eventually divorced. Betsy became somewhat notorious for her scandalous dress, became a close friend of the Madison's, and help supervise Payne Todd while he was in school at St. Mary's College in Baltimore.

Margaret Bayard Smith (*Family friend*): Margaret Bayard married Samuel Harrison Smith who founded the newspaper, the Washington *National Daily Intelligencer*. Mrs. Smith was an astute observer of Washington society and her many letters and writtngs remain an outstanding primary source for information about the society and politics of the day.

Madison Family Tree

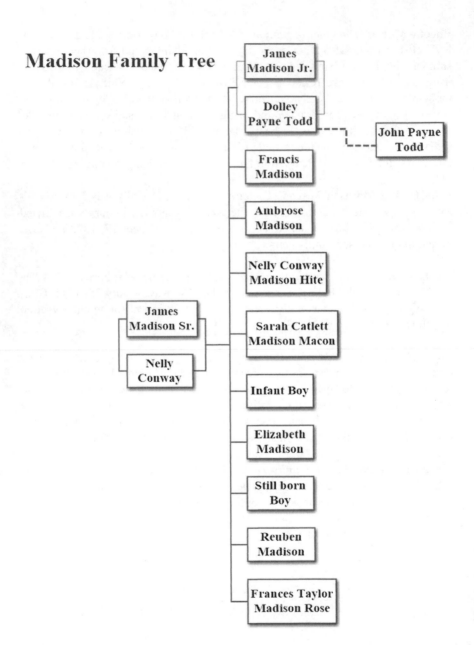

Appendix D

Joseph Wood, Artist

On July 6, 1778, Joseph Wood was born in Rockland County, New York, at a time when fighting in the American Revolution was reaching its peak. Although the patriot cause had been bolstered by the recently negotiated French alliance, significant military aid and additional troops had not yet arrived. Just a few days earlier, General George Washington's Continental army had engaged the British at Monmouth, New Jersey, but the battle proved inconclusive and New York City remained firmly under British occupation. It would take five more years before the last of the Redcoats would evacuate the port. They left behind a city in virtual ruin.

Wood's childhood in New York was tumultuous, tainted not only by the war but also by a strict and authoritarian father. The boy chaffed under his harsh discipline and left home at age 15 to seek his fortune in New York City.[1] There he was apprenticed to a local silversmith but was also able to earn some additional income freelancing as a fiddler.[2]

In 1801, after Wood had completed his voluntary indentureship, he was free to enter into a partnership with an aspiring artist, John Wesley Jarvis. The two young men set up shop at No. 31 Chatham-row and advertised their services in the local newspaper, offering to "execute likenesses for two shillings each." They guaranteed the quality of their work by offering a full refund, claiming "no likeness, no pay."[3]

A self portrait done by Joseph Wood circa 1810. (Image copyright © The Metropolitan Museum of Art. Image source: Art Resource, NY)

With the young republic's growing sense of patriotism, pride and prosperity, the artists successfully painted dozens of miniatures of many of New York's leading citizens. Wood showed considerable artistic talent and his small, detailed portraits were quite coveted and his professional reputation correspondingly blossomed. As one contemporary noted, Wood was "…exercising his talents in New York without rival."[4]

Jarvis and Wood's business endeavors thrived and prospered while the proprietors amassed a small fortune. But the two men lived lavishly and foolishly, squandering and depleting their earnings.[5] By the end of the decade, personal disagreements and growing financial problems led to a bitter dissolution of their once flourishing partnership. Wood abandoned New York for Philadelphia in 1813. After three years, he moved to the nation's capital, which was still in the process of rebuilding after having been burnt by the British during the War of 1812. It was in Washington, D.C. that Wood discovered a lucrative market for producing portraits of the new generation of American heroes and patriots from the recently concluded war. His subjects included such notables as Navy Commodore Oliver Hazard

Perry and General Andrew Jackson, as well as Henry Clay, Daniel Webster and John Marshall.[6] His most significant commission, though, came in 1817 when he was hired to paint President James Madison and his wife, Dolley.

Madison at 66 was now elderly and was preparing to retire from decades of public service. Dolley, though, was just 49 years old and still very much in her prime. She retained much of her youthful beauty as well as her elegant sense of style. For her portrait, the First Lady chose to wear a fashionable high-collared yellow dress along with her signature turban. Wood's completed

Dolley Madison portrait painted by Joseph Wood, 1817. Dolley was 49 years old when Wood painted her likeness. He also painted the President and John Payne Todd during the same time period.
(Virginia Historical Society)

paintings of the couple so pleased the Madison's that they soon gave the portraits as gifts to their close friends, Richard and Elizabeth Bland.[7] It was during this period that Wood was also able to arrange to paint a miniature of the 26 year old, John Payne Todd. HIs oval watercolor on ivory measures just 2 5/8" x 2 1/16 inches and remains the only known likeness of the Madison's son.[8]

The Joseph Wood portrait of James Madison is now on public display at the Virginia Historical Society museum in Richmond, Virginia. Madison gave the paintings of himself and Dolley as a gift to their close friends, Richard and Eliabeth Bland in 1817. The paintings remained in private hands until they were donated to the Virginia Historical Society by Katherine Davidge in 1962. (Philip Bigler)

After completing his Madison portraits, Wood once again relocated, this
time to Baltimore, Maryland. There, he
succumbed to alcoholism and his persistent drinking ravaged his health and
contributed to a precipitous decline in
his talent. He eventually moved back
to Washington where he still attempted to paint from a studio in his home
located on Pennsylvania Avenue near
9th Street. His constant drinking inter-
fered with his productivity and Wood
died on June 15, 1830 from "Dropsy
in the Chest."[9] An obituary for Wood
appeared in the *National Intelligencer,*
which reported a "Death of a Man of
Genius" but other journalists were not
so kind.[10] The *Washington Daily Journal* countered that Wood's had been
betrayed by his supposed friends who

Joseph Wood's grave at Congressional Cemetery in Washington, D.C. The artist suffered from alcoholism and died in 1830. His grave is a short distance away from that of John Payne Todd. (Philip Bigler)

"soothed his follies, palliated his errors and encouraged him to excess…[they] courted his company in prosperity…[and] deserted
him in the dark hours of adversity."[11]

Joseph Wood was buried at Congressional Cemetery (R27/120).
A few years later, a temperance pamphlet used the artist's life as a
parable against the evils of alcohol. It noted that Wood's excessive
drinking had led him to a tragic fate where he was "to expire, neglected and forgotten." [12]

ENDNOTES

1 Anson Dickinson, "Portrait Miniatures in the New Republic," available at http://www.themagazine-antiques.com/articles/portrait-miniatures-in-the-new-republic.

2 George C. Grace and J.T. Chase Willet, "Joseph Wood: A Brief Account of his Life and the Frist Catalogue of his Work. The Art Quarterly, Vol. III, #2, Spring 1940, p. 150.

3 *Ibid.*, p. 150.

4 James K. Paulding quoted in Grace, p. 151.

5 Grace, p. 152.

6 The two portraits are now on display at the Virginia Historical Society in Richmond, Virginia. See the "Story of Virginia, an American Experience" at the Virginia Historical Society: http://www.vahistorical.org/storyofvirginia.htm.

7 The John Payne Todd miniature is owned by the Metropolitan Museum of Art in New York City (Accession #36.73). See http://www.metmuseum.org/Collections/search-the-collections/20011102.

8 Grace, p. 154.

9 Dickinson.

10 Obituary from the *Washington Daily Journal* on June 16, 1830 quoted in Grace, p. 153.

11 S.A. Elliot Wood's "Latter Days, and his Death" published by the Temperance Association in 1834 quoted in Grace, p. 154.

Appendix E
The Dolley Madison
Daguerreotype

In the mid-1830's, Louis Jacques Mandel Daguerre began experimenting with a new process designed to produce photographic images on specially treated, light sensitive copper plates. By the end of the decade, he had perfected the technique well enough to announce his discovery to the prestigious French Academy of Sciences. Although Daguerre's early streetscape images of Paris were devoid of color, the pictures captured perfectly an instant in time with such a realism that no artist or painter could ever hope to duplicate such scenes on canvas.[1] Immediately, there was widespread public curiosity and excitement surrounding this new, revolutionary technology. Within months, American entrepreneurs started to duplicate Daguerre's photographic techniques and studios began to appear in numerous cities. Within ten years, there were over 900 registered deguerretypists operating within the United States.[2]

Mathew Brady was one of America's earliest photographers. He began his initial work in New York in 1843 and actively sought out the most well-known citizens in an effort to be first to capture their photographic likenesses. Brady realized that his unique daguerreotypes could be easily sold to the public or the images could be copied and etched onto plates by artists and massed produced profitably as lithographs.[3] Brady's New York studio became a popular attraction, where curious patrons paid to have their own photographic portraits done.[4]

John Plumbe was the first photographer to capture images of the nation's capital. Above is a remarkable daguerreotype of the south side of the White House, circa 1846. (Library of Congress)

The east front of the United States Capitol with the distinctive Bullfinch Dome. The photograph was one of five Washington scenes taken by John Plumbe for his Capital Views *series.* (Library of Congress)

In Washington, D.C., the city's most distinguished photographer was John Plumbe. His National Daguerrian Gallery & Photographic Depot was located on Pennsylvania Avenue. Plumbe's pioneering work includes the earliest known images of the city's major federal buildings including noteworthy pictures of the Capitol, the White House, and the U.S. Patent Office.[5] Plumbe also enjoyed an advantage of having easy access to members of Congress and other notable federal government employees. As such, he was able to produce numerous portraits of the country's leading politicians. This was a remarkable feat since the primitive cameras of the day required that a subject remain virtually motionless for at least 90 seconds to avoid blurring the final exposure.

In New York, the ambitious Brady realized the fiscal advantages of establishing a new satellite operation in the nation's capital to compete with Plumbe. Initially, he would take lodging at the National Hotel while he solicited various politicians for their business. In 1848, he successfully persuaded the incumbent president, James K. Polk, to have his picture taken.[6] The President recorded the auspicious event in his diary,

Photographer Mathew Brady. His daguerreotypes of Dolley Madison were taken on July 4, 1848, when the first lady was 80 years old. (Library of Congress)

writing: "I yielded to the request of an artist named Brady of New York by sitting for my Daguerreotype likeness today. I sat in the large dining room."[7] The overall quality of Brady's images received widespread acclaim and as one Washington newspaper noted: "The success of Mr. Mathew Brady in taking Daguerreotype portraits is truly remarkable."[8]

Brady was also successful in convincing Dolley Madison to pose for a series of photographs.[9] The former first lady was living full time in Washington after having been forced by debt to sell Montpelier four years earlier. Still, despite her personal hardships, she remained a beloved and revered figure, one of the last living icons of the nation's revolutionary beginnings. The daguerreotypes taken by Mathew Brady on that day in 1848 were truly historic, and Dolley Madison earned the distinction of being the earliest presidential spouse to have ever been photographed.

Some of Brady's distinctive images were given to Mrs. Madison and remained in her possession until her death the following year. Afterwards, in the quarrels surrounding Dolley's meager estate, the daguerreotypes were quickly forgotten. Payne Todd, always desperate for money, attempted to sell off many of his mother's personal belongings and prized artifacts. Due to Payne's own massive debt, these auctions necessarily continued even after his own death in 1852. Annie Payne, Dolley's niece and closest companion, was horrified by the entire spectacle and loathed the idea that her aunt's private possessions could be dis-

One of several images of Dolley Madison taken by Mathew Brady in Washington in 1848. The former first lady was 80 years old. The picture disappeared until 1956, when it was discovered in the Pennsylvania home of Neva Kunkel. (Greensboro Historical Museum)

persed and purchased by greedy collectors and mercenaries. She and her new husband, Dr. James Causten, were able to successfully buy back and preserve many of Dolley's most precious items, but Annie died prematurely on November 9, 1852.[10] Eventually, her "Dolley Madison collection" was inherited by the couple's only child, Mary Causten Kunkel, who in turn willed it on to her own son, John Baker Kunkel.[11]

The daguerreotypes and other Madison treasures disappeared from public view for decades. John Kunkel died in 1944. His wife, Neva's, mental health deteriorated, as soon she became an eccentric recluse. Neva was rarely seen by her neighbors, but out of a sense of charity, they often left small caches of food for the widow. There were, however, persistent rumors throughout the Lehigh community that the shuttered Kunkel home contained priceless artifacts from the 19th century.[12]

In 1956, Neva Kunkel died and a local court ordered a complete inventory of her estate. A second year law student from Dickinson College, Charles Hafner, was given the odious task of sorting through piles of clutter and filth. He was stunned to discover that Neva Kunkel had spent the last six years of her life living without electricity. She was totally dependent upon an old, dilapidated stove for warmth, using twigs and small branches for fuel.[13]

The carriage trunk discovered by Charles Hafner in 1957 currently on display at the Greensboro Historical Museum. It contained a wide array of priceless artifacts, gowns, and letters from Dolley Payne Madison. (Philip Bigler)

After several days of work, Hafner had found little of historical interest. Then, he discovered an attic storage area that contained several volumes of leather bound books as well as a few old trunks. Incredibly, the chests contained a priceless array of Madison-era artifacts, including Dolley Madison's Quaker marriage certificate to John Todd, the vest that James Madison had worn during his presidential inauguration, several of the first lady's signature turbans, numerous documents, as well as the Brady daguerreotypes.

As news of the astonishing discovery spread, Eleanor Fox Pearson formed the Dolley Madison Memorial Association and successfully raised ten thousand dollars to purchase the Kunkel artifacts. Her intent was to bring the items to Greensboro, North Carolina, the site of Dolley Payne's birth in 1768. On what would have been her 195th birthday, May 20, 1963, the Kunkel treasures were given to the Greensboro Historical Museum and the Madison material continues to constitute the foundation for their collections.

The Brady daguerreotype of Dolley Madison along with her fashionable turban she wore for the pho-tograph on display at the Greensboro Historical Museum. Mrs. Madison was 70 years old at the time she sat for her portrait. Another picture was taken at the time with her niece, Annie Payne. (Philip Bigler)

ENDNOTES

1 The advent of photography directly lead to the Impressionist movement in Europe. Artists such as Pierre-Auguste Renoir, Paul Cézanne, Edgar Degas and Claude Monet used quick brush strokes and vivid color to give their interpretations of the effect of light on a particular scene.

2 Peter T. White, "A Rare Look at an Early American Heroine: Dolley Madison." Available at http://www.cosmos-club.org/web/journals/1996/white.html.

3 A daguerreotype is actually an image on a specially treated copper plate. No negative is produced, hence all such photographs are unique. Likewise, all daguerreotype images are always reversed.

4 Mary Panzer (1997). *Mathew Brady and the Image of History*. Washington, D.C., The Smithsonian Institution Press, p. 10.

5 Floyd Rinhart and Marion Rinhart (1981). *The American Daguerreotype*. Athens: University of Georgia Press, p. 65 and Philip Bigler (1988). *Washington in Focus: The Photographic History of the Nation's Capital*. Arlington, VA., Vandamere Press.

6 Polk was the first incumbent president to be photographed. Brady, however, also did pictures of the surviving former chief executives, John Quincy Adams and Andrew Jackson.

7 James K. Polk quoted in Roy Meredith (1946). *Mr. Lincoln's Camera Man*. New York: Dover Publications, Inc, p. 34.

8 *Ibid.*, p. 38.

9 That same day, Dolley had attended the ceremonies for the laying of the cornerstone of the Washington Monument. See Peter White, "A Rare Look at an Early American Heroine: Dolley Madison."

10 Annie Payne Causten was just 33 years old at the time of her death. She was buried in the Causten family vault at Congressional Cemetery. Her aunt Dolley's remains were removed from the Public Vault and stored in the Causten mausoleum, awaiting eventual return to Montpelier for burial.

11 Frank Whelan. "Man Found Treasure Amidst Clutter of an Old Woman's Shattered Life." *The Morning Call*. (February 22, 1987), Available at http://articles.mcall.com/1987-02-22/news/2562717_1_james-madison-worth-charles-hafner.

12 *Ibid.*

13 Greensboro Historical Museum Archives. Dolley Madison Family Collection. MSS Collection Vol. V, #1.

Appendix F
Elizabeth "Betsy" Bonaparte
February 6, 1785 – April 4, 1879

By 1800, William Patterson was one of the port of Baltimore's most renowned citizens. Born in Ireland, he had immigrated to the Maryland colony before the American Revolution and became extremely wealthy through hard work, sheer determination, and shrewd investments—the epitome of the American dream. His many mercantile interests continued to provide him with his primary source of revenue but this income was supplemented by profits from his numerous buildings and real estate ventures that he owned throughout the city. Patterson had married Dorcas Spear in May 1779 and the couple was destined to have thirteen children.[1]

Elizabeth (Betsy) was born on February 6, 1785. She was the Patterson's fourth child and their first daughter. She proved to be a bright and beautiful child and as a young girl, she was educated at Madame Lacomb's boarding school, located on 36 South Street in Baltimore. It was there that she was first introduced to the refinement of French culture and soon she became completely fluent in the language. As an adolescent, Betsy matured into a beautiful, vivacious if somewhat willful teenager.[2]

It was in 1803 that the 18-year old Betsy Patterson was first introduced to Jerome Bonaparte, the handsome, debonair youngest brother of Napoleon. Bonaparte was a French naval officer ostensibly on leave in the United States while awaiting safe passage back to France. During this prolonged interlude, Jerome attended countless parties, social events and other celebrations which were regularly held in his honor. He also spent substantial sums of money and required repeated loans from the French attaché.. Upon meeting the vivacious Betsy Patterson, though, he was immediately smitten and mesmerized by her beauty. After a whirlwind romance, he proposed marriage.[3]

Betsy's father was alarmed by the young couple's seemingly impetuous actions. There were already ominous rumors circulating that Jerome was, in fact, underage and could not marry without parental consent. The Frenchman consistently denied such accusations, but he was, in reality, just 19 years old. Even more ominous, though, were the anonymous written warnings that William Patterson regularly received about Jerome's questionable character and loose morals. One unknown author claimed that: "If you knew him, you never would [allow your daughter to marry], as misery must be her portion—he who but a

Napoleon Bonaparte. The French Emperor objected to the marriage between his youngest brother, Jerome, and Betsy Patterson. (Library of Congress)

few months ago destroyed the peace and happiness of a respectable family in Nantz by promising marriage, then ruined, leaving her to misery and shame…Nothing can be done will be binding on him; if you knew his moral character of disspation, you would never! No never! Even with the approbation of his family, trust your daughter to him…he is the most profligate young man of the age."[4]

Betsy Patterson, though, was determined to do whatever she pleased regardless of the potential consequences. She was unwavering in her desire to marry Jerome Bonaparte, move with him to France, and there become a celebrated member of the titled nobility. Their marriage ceremony took place on December 24, 1803, and was conducted by the Catholic bishop, Rt. Rev. John Carroll.[5] For the next several months, the newlyweds enjoyed travelling around the east coast attending various parties and fetes held in their honor. While en route to Boston, they even made the arduous trip to the New York frontier to see the wonders of Niagara Falls.[6]

When news of his youngest brother's marriage reached Napoleon, the French First Counsel exploded in rage. He anticipated using the marriage of his various siblings for political gain and strategic territorial acquisition.[7] Napoleon angrily declared that under French law, the marriage between Jerome and Betsy was illegal and void since Jerome was, in fact, not old enough to marry without his parents' permission. Napoleon also ordered his brother to return to France immediately and added that he should do so alone, unaccompanied by his new bride.

Betsy Patterson Bonaparte was supremely confident that she could quell Napoleon's ire by using a combination of her charm and beauty. As part of her plan, she and Jerome contracted with the renowned American painter, Gilbert Stuart, to paint her portrait as a gift to Napoleon. They were convinced that the French First Counsel would be so impressed with her magnificence that he would gladly accept the validity of their marriage. Stuart did, indeed, paint Betsy and did so using three different profiles on a single canvas. But after an argument with Jerome, he refused to give the couple the painting.[8]

Over the next several months Jerome, ignoring Napoleon's explicit orders, attempted to arrange transatlantic passage for both himself and his wife. After several aborted attempts, William Patterson finally provided the couple passage on one of his merchant schooners, the *Erin*. The swift ship successfully made the crossing in just three weeks, arriving in Lisbon, Portugal in late March, 1805. Betsy, who was now several months pregnant, stoically endured the rough seas.[9] Jerome wrote: "My dear wife has fortunately supported the fatigues of our voyage perfectly well. She has been very sick, but you know as well as anybody that sea-sick never killed no body."[10]

Gilbert Stuart's painting of Betsy Patterson Bonaparte. The artist was so impressed with her beauty, that he could not decide which pose to use. (© The Metropolitan Museum of Art. Image source: Art Resource, NY)

Upon their arrival, Jerome discovered that he had been summoned to Milan to meet with his still enraged brother. Betsy, however, was denied permission to accompany him and was forbidden even to stay on the European continent. Abandoned and alone, Betsy sailed on her father's vessel to Amsterdam, but there she was refused landing rights and was forced to seek sanctuary in England where the Emperor Napoleon had no authority.[11] It was there that Jerome Napoleon "Bo" Bonaparte was born on July 7, 1805.

Before meeting with Jerome in Milan, Napoleon had written to his mother that: "I shall treat this young man severely if, in the one interview I will give him, he shows himself unworthy of the name he bears and if he persists in wishing to continue this liaison. If he is not disposed to wash away the dishonor with which he has soiled my name in abandoning his colors and his ship for a miserable woman, I shall give him up forever and perhaps I shall make an example of him which will teach young officers how sacred are their duties and the enormity of the crime thy commit in deserting their flag for a woman."[12] Jerome, in fact, quickly capitulated to his brother's will and returned to the Navy, effectively choosing title, fame and France over beauty and love. Betsy had little recourse but to return to America accompanied by her newborn son.

Napoleon petitioned Pope Pius VII for an annulment of Jerome and Betsy's brief marriage but the pontiff refused the request. Napoleon then had the union declared invalid under the jurisdiction of a French ecclesiastical court in October 1806. Just ten months later, Jerome married Catharina of Württemberg and eventually became the king of the newly created province of Westphalia.[13] Betsy was humiliated and embarrassed by the whole affair. She sought and was granted a divorce by the state of Maryland in 1812, although she would continue to use the Bonaparte name for the remainder of her life.

During this difficult time, Betsy remained a close friend of the Madison's and frequently stayed with them while in Washington, D.C. Still, she preferred European culture to that of the infant American republic. She found her home country to be provincial and backward and once wrote that she was "miserable in a country where I never was appreciated and where I can never be contented."[14] In another letter she confided: "I was born in a country which was not congenial to my desires."[15]

Over the ensuing years and after Napoleon's abdication, exile, and eventual death, Betsy chose to spend much of her time in Switzerland, Italy, and France. Her son, Bo, was educated in Switzerland before attending Harvard. He eventually was able to meet his estranged father in 1826 after Jerome had been forced to abdicate his throne after his kingdom was dissolved. Bo visited Jerome and his current wife, Catharina, in Luciano, Italy and was shocked by their idleness and ennui. He wrote: "Nobody in this house is doing anything, and as far as I am concerned, I can neither read nor study."[16] He elaborated in a subsequent letter that "during the greater part of the twenty-four hours the whole family is assembled together in the parlor, principally for the purpose of killing time."[17]

Betsy remained bitter and never forgave her former husband for his cowardly behavior. She once wrote: "The sentiment of contempt to old Jerome is in my heart, & circulates with every drop of blood in my body. I look upon him as belonging to the lowest type of humanity."[18] When she learned that he was living in France, she penned: "This means that I can no longer go to Paris for I would choke if I knew that I was living under the same sky as my ex-husband."[19]

Her father, William Patterson, died in February 1835. In his public will, he added to Betsy's humiliation writing, "The conduct of my daughter Betsy has through life been so disobedient, that in no instance has she ever consulted my opinion or feelings; indeed she has caused me more anxiety and trouble than all my other children put together, and her folly and misconduct has occasioned me a train of expense that, first and last, has cost me much money."[20] He then

Charles Joseph Bonaparte, Betsy's grandson. He would be appointed Attorney General by President Theodore Roosevelt. (Library of Congress)

proceeded to leave the vast majority of his considerable estate to his five surviving sons, while Betsy was left only some Baltimore real estate. In bitterness, Betsy would compose a private manuscript entitled, "Dialogues between Jerome and My Father in Hell."[21]

After Bo return to the United States, he married the wealthy Susan May Williams on November 3, 1829. Her fortune enabled him to live a life of privilege, and Bo devoted much of his time to tending to his beloved horses. The couple had two sons, Jerome Napoleon and Charles Joseph. The eldest son attended West Point and graduated in 1852. He later accepted a commission in the French army and served with distinction during the Franco-Prussian War, rising to the rank of colonel. Brother Charles attended Harvard and became a lawyer. He served as a Secretary of the Navy and would eventually be appointed Attorney General of the United States in 1906 by President Theodore Roosevelt. [22]

Throughout his later years, Bo suffered from bouts of alcoholism. During one recovery, he wrote that "My health is better than it has been for the last twenty years, when unfortunately, it was always under the influence of monkey [whiskey]. I breakfast and dine very heartily, sleep well, take a great deal of outdoor exercise, drink nothing but ale, very rarely taste wine, and have not tasted monkey, in any shape for months."[23] On June 17, 1870, Jerome Napoleon Bonaparte, Betsy's only child, died from throat cancer at age 65. His estranged father had preceded him in death by a decade.[24]

The Green Mount Cemetery in Baltimore, Maryland. Betsy Bonaparte died on April 4, 1879 at the age of 94 and was buried here. (Library of Congress)

Betsy, spent her final years living in solitude in a Baltimore boarding house. She never lost her illusions of grandeur but had lived a frugal life and had proven to be an astute business woman. Her numerous real estate holdings as well as her shrewd investments in railroads and public utilities had made her one of the nation's most wealthy women.[25] She would write scornfully that "I have been alone in life and I wish to be alone in death."[26] Betsy Patterson Bonaparte died on April 4, 1879 at the age of 94 and was buried at Baltimore's Green Mount Cemetery.

Betsy Patterson Bonaparte's grave at the Green Mount Cemetery. The inscription on the tomb reads: "After life's fitful fever she sleeps well." (Philip Bigler)

ENDNOTES

1 Helen Jean Burn (2010). *Betsy Bonaparte.* Baltimore, Maryland Historical Society, p 13.

2 *Ibid., p. 30.*

3 Charlene M. Boyer Lewis (2012). *Elizabeth Patterson Bonaparte: An American Aristocrat in the Early Republic.* Philadelphia, University of Pennsylvania Press, 16.

4 Quoted in Burn, p. 51.

5 *Green Mount Cemetery: One Hundredth Anniversary 1838-1938.* Baltimore, Green Mount Cemetery.

6 Burn, p. 75.

7 Lewis, p. 28-29.

8 The portrait was never sent to Napoleon. It was eventually obtained by William Patterson and left to Betsy in his will. Burn, pp. 63-64.

9 Burn, pp. 78-79.

10 Jerome Bonaparte quoted Burn p. 80.

11 Burn, pp. 86-89.

12 Napoleon Bonaparte quoted in Burn, p. 92.

13 Lewis, pp. 40-41.

14 Betsy Bonaparte quoted in Burn, p. 169.

15 Betsy Bonaparte quoted in Lewis, p. 56.

16 Jerome Napoleon Bonaparte quoted in Claude Bourguignon-Frasseto (2003). *Betsy Bonaparte: The Belle of Baltimore.* Baltimore, The Maryland Historical Society, p. 221.

17 Jerome Napoleon Bonaparte quoted in Burn, p. 197.

18 *Ibid., p. 2.*

19 Betsy Bonaparte quoted in Bourguignon-Frasseto, p. 268.

20 William Patterson quoted in Burn, p. 211.

21 Unfortunately, this fascinating manuscript has disappeared. Burns, p. 245. The Maryland Historical Society is the repository for most of Betsy Bonaparte's papers and possessions. See http://www.mdhs.org./

22 Jerome Bonaparte II lived the later years of his life in Washington, D.C. and died in 1893. His younger brother, Charley, took care of his grandmother, Betsy, during her final years. Charley died without heir in 1921. See Burns, pp. 250, 252.

23 Jerome Napoleon "Bo" Bonaparte quoted in Burn, p. 244.

24 Jerome Bonaparte died on June 24, 1860.

25 Deutsch, Alexandra. Elizabeth Patterson Bonaparte Manuscript Collection. Available at http://mdhs.org/betsy-bonaparte.

26 Betsy Bonaparte quoted in Bourgugnon-Frasseto, p. 289.

Appendix G

Selected Excerpts from Payne Todd's Memorandum Book

1844

"Sick and unhappy" July

"…Had a high fever which has gone off by it…Chewed tobacco a little which after this seemed to taste well…I wish now endeavor to attend directly to business quickly with a change of character if it can be effected." Sunday Evening about 4 1/2 o'clock in the afternoon. August

"Sent Ellick with 50 cts to Orange CH to buy 1 Quart of Spanish brandy and rum mixed to give a little to James Chapman who paid a visit yesterday & seems sick for the want of it. I gave some whiskey to Mr. Hen…On Saturday last I lost or misplaced or was robbed of my watch & very improperly getting inebriated…" November

1845

"This morning it snowed & I took a dose of [illegible] powders feeling extremely unwell from the state of the stomach." March

"I am obliged to yield to circumstances felt & was obliged to drink beer to considerable extent which cured [illegible] under the circumstances of the teeth of the upper jaw." April

"Sat up during the night writing to France and my mother…and despatched Matthew who gave the letter to Capn. Chancellory. Went to bed at 4 ½ o'clock and rose at 9 felt pretty well, breakfasted on Mackerel fish, coffee, corn bread, butter and walked out over the premises to order cutting and the beginning of hauling dirt again and returned to eat some eggs having been drinking ice water during the morning—Yesterday otherwise Porter Brandy & Whiskey by tasting."

"Broke [appointments] for the 1st time…had a high fever which has gone off by it—probably should have not—more frequently as subject to excitement and violent feelings for conception of injuries. Sunday Evening about 4 ½ oclock in the afternoon. August

"Great pain in the back." November

"*Non Tali auxilio egemus, nec defensoribus istis.*" December 1845

1846

"Eat Breakfast of Ham & drank two tumblers of milk & 7 or 8 of pure water. Tea & Coffee at night & no tobacco but a smoke. I drank nothing spirituous which however was followed by a heart burn during the night & rather a nausea arising the following day. February 9

"I have a thought of building the chimney in the…room forward with a strong flue so as to divert the smoke downwards in the other chimney& false back so as to [c]atch the Sparks in a deposit as they fall to avoid chances of fire…at 4 ½ some t[ur]key soup & beans." Feb. 18

"I drank with Brown sugar some whiskey & either that or an undue quantity of pepper (black) the day before seem to give a kind of gouty Rheumatism which has continued for a day or more…I went to bed at 12 & sleep around 2 having choked in my legs which was somewhat Rheumatic pains before and by scratching they got easier. I drank several tumblers of brown sugar & water previously."

"I owe you an explanation & apology...Some short time since, I was at Orange C. House in this state and to favor an individual I drew upon your bank a check for 150$...payable on 10th of Feb'y expecting to be there about 5th; but having accidently undertaken some business which in traversing this country through bad roads accidently has delayed the trip beyond calculation & has placed me in the situation of endangering important interests."

"Went to bed at 4 o'clock rather a nausea without appetite rose in the same way without appetite...Rec'd a letter from my mother." Friday 13th March

"Spent the day thinking after...Mrs. M's affairs." Saturday 14th March

The unhappy effect of hot water of the summer since May it is hoped or preferred & that the lethargy & quiescent disease may be ended." Friday the 11th Sepr. About 20 Minutes past 11 o'clock

"Had a fever and strong diarrhea," October 22

"Felt better drank sweet cider...which gave me an appetite." October 24

1847

"I felt very much inflamed by excessive coffing, a pain in the side which abated with the coff & inflammation by taking bark sugar & 12 ½ ch of Paregoric sent for. Better to day..." March 15

"I sent to day to Mr. Wright for a half gallon of Maderia for Mrs. Madsion." Monday March 29

Todd, P. (1844-1847). Journal and Letters of Payne Todd. Peter Force Collection. Washington, D.C., Library of Congress. Reel 68 of 112. (LCCN mm 80020990).

Following Page: *An example from Payne Todd's Memorandum Book, October 1845. This material is available on microfilm at the Library of Congress. Todd's handwriting could be difficult to read and often deteriorated into illegibility.* (Library of Congress)

Orange Oct. 1845

Received through the medium of D. Hume Sixty six dollars & twenty six cents in part payment of Blacksmith's accounts.

     John P. Todd.

Rec'd through the payment to David Hume Sixty six dollars & twenty six cents from Mr Allen cure being in part of the acknowledged _____ _____ of _____ according of Dr. Allen Manager who had of work done at the Blacksmiths & furnished at request at _____

Received of Mr Wm Moncure Sixty six dollars a Twenty Six Cents by a payment to D Hume Esqre through a check to D Hume being in part of the acknowledged _____ of accts by his Manager sending work requested to be done by my Blacksmith.

Rec'd _____ for Blacksmiths work $66.26 in a check (by Wm W W Moncure) directed to D Hume Esqre _____ being a payment in part of acknowledged _____ of acc bill by his Manager _____ disinterested parties.

     Orange Oct 10/45

Rec'd for B: work $6.36 in a check directed to D Hume Esqre the transferee, by Wm W W Moncure, being part of acct whose _____ of work done was acknowledged by his Manager & otherwise testified to by disinterested parties

     John P Todd

Bibliography

(1790). *Pennsylvania Mercury*. Philadelphia: 4.

(1830). *Daily National Intelligencer*.

(1837). Mrs. James Madison. *The Madisonian*. Washington, DC I.

(1849). *The Weekly Herald*, New York. XV.

(1937). *The Free Lance-Star*, Fredericksburg, VA.: p. 6

Adams, Charles Frances, Ed. (1970). *Memoirs of John Quincy Adams, Comprising Portions of his Diary from 1795 to 1848*. New York, Ams Press.

Adams, Henry (1986). *History of the United States of America during the First Administration of James Madison 1809-1813*. New York, Literary Classics of the United States.

Ahlstrom, T. Robinson, Headmaster of the Alexandria Academy, interview by Philip Bigler, July 30, 2010, Alexandria, VA.

Allgor, Catherine (2006). *A Perfect Union: Dolley Madison and the Creation of the American Nation*. New York, Henry Holt and Company.

_____, Ed. (2012). *The Queen of America: Mary Cutts's Life of Dolley Madison*. Charlottesville, University of Virginia Press.

Amos, Mark and Dana, interview by Philip Bigler, January 16, 2015, Madison Run, Virginia.

Anthony, Katherine (1949). *Dolly Madison: Her Life and Times*. Garden City, N.Y., The Country Life Press.

Arnett, Ethel Stephens (1972). *Mrs. James Madison: The Incomparable Dolley.* Greensboro, Piedmont Press.

Bickham, Troy (2012). *The Weight of Vengeance: The United States, the British Empire, and the War of 1812.* New York: Oxford University Press.

Bigler, Philip (1988). *Washington in Focus: The Photographic History of the Nation's Capital.* Arlington, VA., Vandamere Press.

Bolton, Theodore, "The Life Portraits of James Madison," *The William and Mary Quarterly.* Vol. 8, #1, January, 1951, pp. 25-47.

Bourguignon-Frasseto, Claude (2003). *Betsy Bonaparte: The Belle of Baltimore.* Baltimore: The Maryland Historical Society.

Brands, H.W. (2012). *The Heartbreak of Aaron Burr.* New York, Anchor Books.

Brandt, Irving (1950). *James Madison: Father of the Constitution 1787-1800.* Indianapolis, The Bobs-Merrill Company, Inc.

Buchanan, Patrick J. "Democracy's Era is Over," *Daily News Record.* August 12, 2014, p. A6

Burn, Helen Jean (2010). *Betsy Bonaparte.* Baltimore, Maryland Historical Society.

Cappon, Lester J., ed. (1988). *The Adams-Jefferson Letters: The Complete Correspondence between Thomas Jefferson and John Adams.* Williamsburg, VA. The Institute of Early American History and Culture.

Chadwick, Bruce (2014). *James & Dolley Madison: America's First Power Couple.* New York: Prometheus Books.

Chambers, Douglas B. (2005). *Murder at Montpelier: Igbo Africans in Virginia.* Jackson, MI., University Press of Mississippi.

Chamberlayne, C.G. ed. (1992). *Ham Chamberlayne—Virginian: Letters and Papers of an Artillery Officer in the War for Southern Independence 1861-1865.* Wilmington, NC, Broadfoot Publishing Company.

Chapman, John Jay (1921). *William Lloyd Garrison.* Boston, The Atlantic Monthly Press.

Chapman, Thomas. "Who was Buried in the Madison Family Cemetery? A Study in Contextual Analysis." Master's Thesis, College of William and Mary, 2005.

Clark, Allan (1914). *The Life and Letters of Dolly Madison*. Washington, DC, W.F. Roberts Company.

Coles, William B. (1931). *The Coles Family of Virginia: Its Numerous Connections, from the Emigration to America to the year 1915*. New York, William Coles.

Congressional Cemetery. The Association for the Preservation of Congressional Cemetery from http://www.congressionalcemetery.org.

Cote, Richard N. (2005). *Strength and Honor: The Life of Dolley Madison*. Mount Pleasant, SC, Corinthian Books.

Crawford, Alan Pell (2008). *Twilight at Monticello: The Final Years of Thomas Jefferson*. New York, Random House.

Croce, George C., Jr. and J.T. Chase Willet (1940). "Joseph Wood: A Brief Account of his Life and the First Catalogue of his Work." *The Art Quarterly* III (2): 148-161.

Cutts Family Collection of James and Dolley Madison, 1794-1845. Library of Congress Archival Manuscript Material, Microfilm 14,326-1P.

Cutts, Lucie (1887). *Memoirs and Letters of Dolly Madison: Wife of James Madison, President of the United States*. Boston, Houghton, Mifflin and Company.

Dean, Elizabeth Lippincott (1928). *Dolly Madison: The Nation's Hostess*. Boston, Lothrop, Lee & Shepard Co.

Desmond, Alice Curtis (1950). *Glamorous Dolly Madison*. New York, Dodd, Mead & Company.

Deutsch, Alexandra. Elizabeth Patterson Bonaparte Manuscript Collection. Available at http://mdhs.org/betsy-bonaparte.

Dickinson, Anson, "Portrait Miniatures in the New Republic," available at http://www.themagazineantiques.com/articles/portrait-miniatures-in-the-new-republic.

"Dolley Madison," available at the White House Historical Association http://www.whitehousehistory.org/whha_about/whitehouse_collection

Finkelman, Paul (2011). *Millard Fillmore*. New York, Time Books.

Foster, Kenneth R., Mary F. Jenkins and Anna Coxe Toogood (1998). "The Philadelphia Yellow Fever Epidemic of 1793." *Scientific American*: 88-93.

Fox, Early Lee. *The American Colonization Society 1817-1840*. Baltimore, the Johns Hopkins Press, 1919.

Goodwin, Maud Wilder (1897). *Dolly Madison: Women of Colonial and Revolutionary Times*. New York, Charles Scribner's Sons.

Grace, George C. and J.T. Chase Willet, "Joseph Wood: A Brief Account of his Life and the Frist Catalogue of his Work. *The Art Quarterly*, Vol. III, #2, Spring 1940, pp. 140-161.

Green, Bryan Clark, Ann L. Miller, and Conover Hunt (2007). *Building a President's House: The Construction of Montpelier*. Orange, Virginia, The Montpelier Foundation.

Green, Constance McLaughlin (1962). *Washington: Village and Capital, 1800-1878*. Princeton, Princeton University Press.

Green Mount Cemetery: One Hundredth Anniversary 1838-1938 (1939). Baltimore, Green Mount Cemetery.

Greenberg, Kenneth S. ed., *The Confessions of Nat Turner and Related Documents*. Boston, Bedford Books of St. Martin's Press.

Hackett, Mary, ed. (2002). *The Papers of James Madison: Secretary of State Series 1 November 1803--31 March 1804*, Vol. 6. Charlottesville, University Press of Virginia.

Hamilton, Alexander, James Madison, and John Jay (1979). *The Federalist or the New Constitution*. Norwalk, CT., Easton Press.

Harlow, Mary Agnes Gipson, interview by Philip Bigler, December 22, 2014, Orange, Virginia.

"Heads of Families at the First Census of the United States in the Year 1790," available at http://www.census.gov/prod/www/abs/decennial/1790.html.

Hickey, Donald R. (2012). *The War of 1812: A Forgotten Conflict.* Chicago, University of Illinois Press.

History of the Congressional Cemetery (1923). Washington, DC, Senate Committee on the District of Columbia.

Hogan, Pendleton (1996). *The Lawn: A Guide to Jefferson's University.* Charlottesville, VA., the University of Virginia Press.

Houpt, David W. (2010). "Securing a Legacy: The Publication of James Madison's Notes from the Constitutional Convention." *Virginia Magazine of History and Biography* 118 (1): 4-39.

Hopkins, James F. and Mary W.M. Hargreaves, Ed. (1959). *The Papers of Henry Clay: The Rising Statesman 1797-1814.* Lexington, University of Kentucky Press.

Hopkins, James F. and Mary W.M. Hargreaves, Ed. (1961). *The Papers of Henry Clay: Rising Statesman 1815-1820.* Lexington, University of Kentucky Press.

Hunt, Gary, Ed. (1906). *The First Forty Years of Washington Society Portrayed by the Family of Letters by Mrs. Samuel (Margaret Bayard) Harrison Smith.* New York, Charles Scribner & Sons.

Hutchinson, William, Ed. (1962). *The Papers of James Madison 1751 March 16—16 December 1779* Vol. I. Chicago, University of Chicago Press.

Hyland, Matthew G. (2007). *Montpelier and the Madisons: House, Home and American Heritage.* Charleston, SC, History Press.

_____ (1969). *The Papers of James Madison 1783 January 1—30 April 1783,* Vol. VI. Chicago, University of Chicago Press.

Inaugural Addresses of the Presidents of the United States from George Washington 1780 to George Bush 1989 (1989). Washington, D.C., Government Printing Office.

Jennings, Paul (1865). *A Colored Man's Reminiscences of James Madison.* Brooklyn, George C. Beadle.

Johnson, Abby Arthur and Ronald Maberry Johnson (2012). *In the Shadow of the United States Capitol: Congressional Cemetery and the Memory of the Nation.* Washington, DC, New Academia Publishing.

Johnson, David (2012). *John Randolph of Roanoke*. Baton Rouge, Louisiana State University Press.

Kaplan, Fred (2014). John Quincy Adams: American Visionary. New York, HarperCollins Publishers.

Ketcham, Ralph (1990). *James Madison: A Biography*. Charlottesville, University of Virginia Press.

_____ (2009). *The Madisons at Montpelier: Reflections on the Founding Couple*. Charlottesville, University of Virginia Press.

Kortendick, Rev. James Joseph (1942). *The History of St. Mary's College: Baltimore 1799-1852*. Unpublished Master's Thesis in History, Catholic University.

Kranish, Michael. *Flight from Monticello: Thomas Jefferson at War* (2010). New York, Oxford University Press.

Kreider, Angela, J.C.A. Stagg et al., Eds. (2008). *The Papers of James Madison: Presidential Series 8 February-24 October 1813*. Charlottesville, University Press of Virginia.

Levasseur, A. (1829). *Lafayette in America in 1824 and 1825; or, Journal of a Voyage to the United States*, Philadelphia, Cary and Lea.

Lewis, Charlene M. Boyer (2012). *Elizabeth Patterson Bonaparte: An American Aristocrat in the Early Republic*. Philadelphia, University of Pennsylvania Press.

Looney, J. Jefferson Ed. (2004). *The Papers of Thomas Jefferson: Retirement Series March 1809-November 1809*. Princeton, Princeton University Press.

Lowery, Charles D. (1984) *James Barbour: A Jeffersonian Republican*. University of Alabama Press.

Madison, Dolley. The Papers of Dolley Madison (Microfilm). Washington, DC, Library of Congress.

Malone, Dumas (1974). *Jefferson the President: Second Term 1805-1809*. Boston, Little, Brown & Company.

_____ (1981). *Jefferson and His Time: The Sage of Monticello*. Boston, Little, Brown, & Company.

Mason, T., Richard Rutland, and Jeanne Sisson, Ed. (1985). *The Papers of James Madison: 24 March 1793-20 April 1795*. Charlottesville, University Press of Virginia.

Mattern, David, Ed. (1997). *James Madison's "Advice to My Country."* Charlottesville, University Press of Virginia.

_____ (1991). *The Papers of James Madison: 31 March 1797—3 March 1801*, Vol. 17. Charlottesville, University Press of Virginia.

_____ (2000). *The Papers of James Madison: Secretary of State Series 16 May--31 October 1803*, Vol. 5. Charlottesville, University Press of Virginia.

_____ (2009). *The Papers of James Madison: Retirement Series 4 March 1817--31 January 1820*, Vol. 1. Charlottesville, University Press of Virginia.

_____ (2003). *The Selected Letters of Dolley Payne Madison*. Charlottesville, University of Virginia Press.

McCoy, Drew R. (1989). *The Last of the Fathers: James Madison & the Republican Legacy*. New York, Cambridge University Press.

McCullough, David (2001). *John Adams*. New York, Simon & Schuster.

Meacham, Jon (2012). *Thomas Jefferson: The Art of Power*. New York, Random House.

"Memorandum Book of John Payne Todd, 1844-1848," *The Papers and Collection of Peter Force*. Library of Congress Archival Manuscript Material, Microfilm 17,137 (reel 68) mm 82043026.

Meredith, Roy (1946). *Mr. Lincoln's Camera Man*. New York: Dover Publications, Inc.

Miller, John Chester (1991). *The Wolf by the Ears: Thomas Jefferson and Slavery*. Charlottesville, The University of Virginia Press.

Moffatt, L.G. and J. M. Carrière. "A Frenchman Visits Norfolk, Fredericksburg and Orange County, 1816," *The Virginia Magazine of History and Biography*. Vol. 53, No. 3, July 1945, pp. 197-214.

Moore, Virginia (1979). *The Madison's: A Biography*. New York, McGraw-Hill Book Company.

Mount, Charles Merrill. "Gilbert Stuart in Washington: With a Catalogue of His Portraits Painted between December 1803 and July 1805," *Records of the Columbia Historical Society*. Vol. 71/72, pp. 81-127.

Nagel, Paul C. (1983). *Descent from Glory: Four Generations of the John Adams Family*. New York, Oxford University Press.

Nevins, Allan, ed. (1951). *The Diary of John Quincy Adams, 1794-1845: American Diplomacy, and Political, Social, and Intellectual Life, from Washington to Polk*. New York, Frederick Unger Publishing Company.

Panzer, Mary (1997). *Mathew Brady and the Image of History*. Washington, DC, The Smithsonian Institution Press.

Peter, Grace Dunlop (1944). "Unpublished Letters of Doll[e]y Madison to Anthony Morris Relating to the Nourse Family of the Highlands." *Records of the Columbia Historical Society* 44-45: pp. 215-232.

Pillsbury, Samuel H. "Understanding Penal Reform: The Dynamic of Change," *The Journal of Criminal Law and Criminology*. Vol. 80, No. 3, pp. 726-780.

Pitch, Anthony S. (1998). *The Burning of Washington: The British Invasion of 1814*. Annapolis, Md., Naval Institute Press.

Powell, J. H. (1993*). Bring Out Your Dead: The Great Plague of Yellow Fever in Philadelphia in 1793*. Philadelphia, University of Pennsylvania Press.

Presidential Elections 1789-2004 (2005). Norwalk, CT., Easton Press.

Preston, Paul (1914). "Some Incidents of the Yellow Fever Epidemic of 1793." *The Pennsylvania Magazine of History and Biography* 38 (2): 232-239.

Reeves, Matt, personal communication, November 17, 2014.

Rinhart, Floyd and Marion Rinhart (1981). *The American Daguerreotype*. Athens, University of Georgia Press.

Roberts, Rebecca Boggs and Sandra K. Schmidt (2012). *Historic Congressional Cemetery: Images of America.* Charleston, SC, Arcadia Publishing.

Rothery, Agnes (1954). *Houses Virginians Have Loved.* New York, Rinehart & Company, Inc.

Rush, Dr. Benjamin (1794). *An Account of the Bilious remitting Yellow Fever as it Appeared in the City of Philadelphia in the Year 1793.* Philadelphia, Thomas Dobson.

Rutland, Robert A., Ed. (1984). *The Papers of James Madison: Presidential Series 1 March--30 September 1809*, Vol. 1. Charlottesville, University Press of Virginia.

Seager, Robert (1963). *And Tyler, Too.* Norwalk, CT., Easton Press.

Seager, Robert, ed. (1984). *The Papers of Henry Clay*, Vol. 8, 5 March 1829 – 31 December 1836, Lexington, University Press of Kentucky.

Scharff, Virginia (2010). *The Women Jefferson Loved.* New York, Harper Collins Publisher.

Schulman, Holly. "The Dolley Madison Digital Archives" from http://rotunda.upress.virginia.edu/dmde/.

_____ (2011). "Madison v. Madison: Dolley Payne Madison and Her Inheritance of the Montpelier Estate 1836-1838." *Virginia Magazine of History and Biography* 119 (4): pp. 350-393.

_____ (2010). "A Constant Attention': Dolley Madison and the Publication of the Papers of James Madison, 1836-1837." *Virginia Magazine of History and Biography* 118 (1): pp. 40-70.

Scott, W. W. (1907). *A History of Orange County: From its Formation in 1734 (O.S.) to the end of Reconstruction 1870 compiled mainly from Original Records.* Richmond, Everett Waddey Company.

Seager, Robert (1963). *And Tyler, Too: A Biography of John and Julia Gardiner Tyler.* Norwalk, CT, Easton Press.

Shepherd, Jack (1975). *The Adams Chronicles: Four Generations of Greatness.* New York, Little, Brown & Company.

Smith, James Morton (1995). *The Republic of Letters: The Correspondence between Thomas Jefferson and James Madison 1776-1826*. New York, W.W. Norton & Company.

Smith, Mark A. (Oct. 1996). "Andrew Brown's 'Earnest Endeavor': The Federal Gazette's Role in Philadelphia's Yellow Fever Epidemic of 1793." *The Pennsylvania Magazine of History and Biography* 120 (4): 321-342.

Stagg, J.C.A., Ed. (1989). *The Papers of James Madison 27 April 1795—27 March 1797*, Vol 16. Charlottesville, University Press of Virginia.

_____ (1992). *The Papers of James Madison: Presidential Series 1 October 1809--2 November 1810*, Vol. 2. Charlottesville, University Press of Virginia.

_____ (1999). *The Papers of James Madison: Presidential Series 5 November 1811—9 July 1812*, Vol. 4. Charlottesville, University Press of Virginia.

_____ (2004). *The Papers of James Madison: Presidential Series 10 July 1812—7 February 1813*, Vol. 5. Charlottesville, University Press of Virginia.

_____ (2008). *The Papers of James Madison: Presidential Series 8 February—24 October 1813*, Vol. 6. Charlottesville, University Press of Virginia.

Stampp, Kenneth M. (1990). *America in 1857: A Nation on the Brink*. New York, Oxford University Press.

"Story of 'Todd's Berth' Recalled by Old Photo," *The Free Lance-Star*, 28 January 1837, p. 6.

Stowe, Harriet Beecher (1852). *Uncle Tom's Cabin or, Life Among the Lowly*. Boston, John P. Jewett and Company.

Strine, Gerald, ed. (1976). *Montpelier: The Recollections of Marion duPont Scott*. New York, Charles Scribner's Sons.

Taylor, Alan (2013). *The Internal Enemy: Slavery and War in Virginia 1772-1832*. New York, W.W. Norton and Company.

Taylor, Elizabeth Dowling (2012). *A Slave in the White House: Paul Jennings and the Madisons*. New York: Palgrave/McMillan Books.

Teeters, Megley K. (1955). *The Cradle of the Penitentiary: The Walnut Street Jail at Philadelphia, 1773-1835*. Philadelphia, Pennsylvania Prison Society.

Thurson, Mynna (1930). *The History of Doll[e]y Payne Madison: Wife of James Madison, Fourth President of the United States.* Washington, D.C., District of Columbia Society.

Todd, John, Dolley P. Todd, J. Madison Jr., Paul G. Sifton (April 1963). "'What a Dread Prospect...': Dolley Madison's Plague Year." *The Pennsylvania Magazine of History and Biography* 87 (2): 182-188.

Todd, Payne (1844-1847). "Journal and Letters of Payne Todd." *Peter Force Collection* (Microfilm). Washington, DC, Library of Congress. Reel 68 of 112.

Twohig, Dorothy, Ed. (1998). *The Papers of George Washington: Presidential Series December 1790-March 1791*. Charlottesville, University of Virginia Press.

_____ (1999).*The Papers of George Washington: Retirement Series April-December 1799*. Charlottesville, University of Virginia Press.

Unger, Harlow Giles (2012). *John Quincy Adams*. Philadelphia, Da Capo Press.

Walker, Frank S., Jr. (2004). *Remembering: A History of Orange County, Virginia*. Orange, Orange County Historical Society.

Wead, Douglas (2003). *All the President's Children: Triumph and Tragedy in the Lives of America's First Families*. New York, Atria Books.

Weintraub, Stanley and Rodelle Weintraub (2000). *Dear Young Friend: The Letters of American Presidents to Children*. Mechanicsburg, PA., Stackpole Books.

Wheelan, Joseph (2003). *Jefferson's War: America's First War on Terror 1801-1805*. New York, Carroll & Graf Publishers.

Whelan, Frank. "Man Found Treasure Amidst Clutter of an Old Woman's Shattered Life." *The Morning Call.* (February 22, 1987), Available at http://articles.mcall.com/1987-02-22/news/2562717_1_james-madison-worth-charles-hafner.

White, Peter T. "A Rare Look at an Early American Heroine: Dolley Madison." Available at http://www.cosmos-club.org/web/journals/1996/white.html.

Wills, Gary (2002). *Mr. Jefferson's University*. Washington, DC, National Geographic Society.

Wood, Gordon S. (2009). *Empire of Liberty: A History of the Early Republic, 1789-1815*. New York, Oxford University Press.

Woolfley, H.L. Dufour (2013). *A Quaker Goes to Spain: The Diplomatic Mission of Anthony Morris, 1813-1816*. Bethlehem, PA., Lehigh University Press.

315

B

D

G

H

I

N

O

R

S

X

Y

Z

AppleRidge
PUBLISHERS

About the Author

Philip Bigler is the author of nine books including *In Honored Glory: Arlington National Cemetery, the Final Post*; *Hostile Fire: The Life and Death of Lt. Sharon Ann Lane*; and *Teaching History in an Uncivilized World*. He holds a Bachelor's degree in history from James Madison University and advanced degrees in Secondary Education from JMU and in American Studies from the College of William and Mary. In 1998, Mr. Bigler was named the National Teacher of the Year during a Rose Garden ceremony hosted by then president, Bill Clinton. He has received numerous additional honors and recognition for his classroom instruction and innovative teaching methods. Mr. Bigler has been a featured guest on such programs as *Late Night with David Letterman*, *Nightline*, and *Good Morning! America*, and has been a consultant with the Discovery Channel, the National Geographic Society, and an on-air historian on the History Channel. From 1983 through 1985, Mr. Bigler also served as the historian at Arlington National Cemetery and worked on the interment of the Vietnam Unknown Soldier.

In 2001, Philip Bigler was appointed as the Director of the James Madison Center and he held this position until his retirement in 2010. He has taught numerous courses at the collegiate level in history, education, American Studies, and Political Science. He currently resides in the Shenandoah Valley with his wife, Linda.

For more information

www.scandalous-son.com

217 Bob White Lane
Quicksburg, Virginia 22847
info@appleridgepublishers.com

www.appleridgepublishers.com